## "Together"
## Black Women

# "Together" Black Women

### Inez Smith Reid

*Prepared for the Black Women's
Community Development Foundation*

New York: Emerson Hall Publishers, Inc.

"TOGETHER" BLACK WOMEN
Copyright © 1972 by Black Women's Community Development Foundation. All rights reserved. No part of this book may be reproduced or used in any manner, except for brief quotations in critical articles and reviews. For information write to Emerson Hall Publishers, Inc., 209 W. 97th Street, New York, N.Y. 10025.

First Edition

ISBN 0-87829-003-6

Library of Congress Catalog Card Number 73-188561

Distributed by Independent Publishers' Group
c/o David White, Inc.  60 E. 55th Street   New York 10022

*IN MEMORIAM*

BEATRICE VIRGINIA BUNDY SMITH
*The "together" Black mother
of Sidney, Inez, and George*

# Contents

| | |
|---|---|
| PREFACE | ix |
| INTRODUCTION | 1 |
| CHAPTER I | |
| Not Militancy But Togetherness | 13 |
| CHAPTER II | |
| Liberation Can Be A Trick Bag | 31 |
| CHAPTER III | |
| Traditional Political Animals? A Loud No | 123 |
| CHAPTER IV | |
| Of Marx, Mao and Uncle Sam | 185 |
| CHAPTER V | |
| Pan-Africanism? What's That? | 245 |
| CHAPTER VI | |
| Something's Got to Be Done—But What? | 285 |
| CHAPTER VII | |
| Thanks To Martin, Malcolm, Stokeley, Et Al. But The Rest Is Up To You and Me | 373 |

# Preface

In the Winter of 1970 I was approached by Jean Fairfax, President of the Black Women's Community Development Foundation, and asked to direct a study of the "militant Black woman." The idea was to engage women called "militant" in a taped in-depth interview designed to determine their thinking on a variety of matters as well as to gain some insight into their interests and activities as they relate to the current Black struggle. A probe questionnaire was developed which covered attitudes toward marriage and related issues, women's liberation, the role of the Black woman in the current "revolution," ideological and philosophical orientations, awareness of and feelings about events, personalities, programs, organizations, etc. on the international, national, and local scenes. The latter focused mainly on economic, political and social phenomena. Then, too, the probe questionnaire was concerned with views on Blacks and the communications media, particularly television, movies, theatre and magazines. The interviews took place in several geographical areas of the country; the West, South, Midwest, and East.

In a study of this nature random sampling techniques appeared clearly inapplicable since the intent was to focus upon a group of women who, loosely, could be called "militant." Therefore, instead of employing normal social science techniques of random sampling, we relied heavily upon a "reputation in the community for militancy" method for selection of those to be interviewed. Interviewers in the field made initial contacts with local persons who supplied leads as to who might possibly be considered good for the study. These leads were followed up and often resulted in interviews or other leads. The results of the study indicate that the method of selection, while not being the normal "scientific" one, proved effective in obtaining a good sample of women who might be called "militant." Utilization of this method also avoided a time consuming process of weeding out non-militants from a random sample and having to redo the sample in the event that a sufficient number of "militant" women did not appear in the first one.

Selection of interviewers represented an important but not difficult aspect of the study. Most of the interviewers were college students known to myself or to Rev. James Joseph, a member of the Board of Directors of the Black Women's Community Development Foundation. The students included: from Barnard College —Annette Adams, Marcia Anderson, Ruth Louie, Michelle Patrick, and Karla Spurlock; from the Claremont Colleges: Wendy Lowe, Robin deShields, Donna Wills, Brenda Williams; from Radcliffe College: Wanda Williams. The other interviewers were young professional or semi-professional women: Jean Billingslea, Lenore Jenkins, Patricia Roberts, and Meredith Wilson. These women turned out to be extremely effective and efficient despite the abuse, obstacles and headaches they encountered in the performance of their task.

The interviewers represented all geographical areas touched by the study—East (4), South (3), West (2), Midwest (5)—even though they did not necessarily work in the area of their origin. For example, two interviewers—one originally from the South and one the East—completed their work in the West. In fact, only five persons actually undertook their assignments in areas where they had spent most of their lives. Working in a relatively new area of course had its advantages and disadvantages—the disadvantage being almost total lack of familiarity with the sur-

# Preface

roundings and the need of an additional period of time to locate those who might fit within the framework of the study; the advantage being no tendency to seek out friends and acquaintances when others proved reluctant to participate in the study. Needless to say the advantages and disadvantages of operating on familiar ground would be just the reverse of those for virgin territory. The results of the interviewers' tasks demonstrate that the disadvantage of plowing new ground and retracing steps in old environs was overcome substantially as those in known territories did not content themselves with approaching friends and acquaintances, and those in strange places soon found the necessary contacts for interviews.

In terms of socio-economic background the interviewers, with one possible exception, fell within the Black middle class. All had had some exposure to college—ten then enrolled therein and four already graduates. The parent(s) of most could be classified as "professionals" in terms of the Black community; for example, at least two fathers of interviewers were medical doctors and one a high level administrator. One pertinent question to be posed is whether the socio-economic backgrounds of the interviewers produced attitudes which might have had a spill-over effect on the interviewees, that is, did the thinking of the interviewers influence the responses of the interviewees? This is of course a ticklish problem and one of perception. A close examination of the taped interviews, however, proves that virtually none of the personalities and thoughts of interviewers were injected into the conversations with interviewees. That is, interviewers maintained a neutral ground even when interviewees succumbed to requesting their opinion on certain matters. Moreover, it should be noted that the manner and bearing of almost all interviewers did not convey automatically what many Americans have come to describe as militancy or a militant attitude. In fact, at the time they were sent into the field the group might best have been characterized as "nice young Black women from good families."

In terms of an American conception of militancy only two interviewers might have been called militant. The application of one for a summer project in Africa had just been rejected on the ground that she would not have fit into an integrated setting because of her racial views. The decision, however, was not unanimous. Another might have been singled out for a verbal militancy because of her tendency to be quite vocal on specific issues.

Others could have been described as socially involved—that is, engaged in some kind of extracurricular activity designed to unite Black people and/or benefit the Black community in some fashion or another. To illustrate—the college students generally carried at least nominal membership in the campus Black student organization, and a couple actively worked in a freedom school designed to supplement the learning process of Black children.

With respect to the influencing of interviewee responses by interviewers one might add that at the time these young women were selected to work on the study, perceptively only four of the fourteen would have been chosen as actual participants. In other words, at the time they were chosen to be interviewers only four, perceptively again, would have been declared the prototype of the "together" Black woman, a concept which we explain later in our study. Interestingly, however—and there simply has not been time to test this hypothesis—the experience of working on this study might have transformed one or two of the interviewers into "together" Black women.

Special appreciation must be extended to: Marian Wright Edelman who suggested that I direct this study, to Jean Fairfax, President of the Board of the BWCDF whose conversations and encouragement always proved timely; to Dr. Joyce Ladner of Howard University who took time from her own enormously busy schedule to read and critique the manuscript; to Dr. Pauli Murray of Brandeis University whose extensive experience in women's rights and the civil rights movement made her comments on the manuscript most invaluable; to Frantz Louis-Charles whose mathematical skills were of great assistance in tabulating statistical data; to Patricia Murray for her valuable help during the final editing stages; to my twin brother George Bundy Smith who reviewed a portion of the manuscript with his usual meticulousness and concern—despite his own unbelievably heavy agenda; to my brother Sidney R. Smith who displayed a continuing and persistent interest in the work; to my husband Frantz F-J. Reid whose patience sometimes surpasses understanding and whose

# Preface

ideas are always helpful and brilliant; to the Educational Opportunity Program students and staff at Brooklyn College who understood that my resignation as their director was not a desertion, nor an abandonment of my responsibility to them but a continuation of my duty to the Black community at large; to the Afro-American Studies Department of Brooklyn College, Professor Daniel Mayers, chairman for their assistance and support; to Peter Felcher, Esq. of Paul, Weiss, Goldberg, Rifkind, Wharton and Garrison whose legal skills proved invaluable; to Alfred Prettyman, President of Emerson Hall Publishers, Inc. who helped us realize a desire to have the study published by a Black firm; and to members of the BWCDF Board of Directors (Marian Edelman, Jean Fairfax, James Hargett, James Joseph, and Unita Blackwell) and staff (Sarah Herbin and Betty Hawkins) whose continuing enthusiasm contributed enormously to the actual completion of the study.

It is my strong belief that the BWCDF should be commended for having commissioned a study of this nature. I say this not to express gratitude for having been asked to direct this study which incidentally was funded by the BWCDF. Rather, I say it to stress the need for more Black oriented organizations to begin to involve themselves—through funding, leadership, and direction—in the study of the Black community. This is a task left too often by default to scholars or laymen from the White community who almost invariably write and compile their results from a White perspective. Much truth rests with the assertion that Blacks must interpret their own experience if an accurate and meaningful work is to emerge.

Inez Smith Reid

*April 1971*

# "Together"
# Black Women

# Introduction

*Hurdling Mistrust*

Mistrust is deeply ingrained in the Black community. It is so pervasive that even one with all the outward insignia of a Black awareness (naturals, dashikis) may be viewed as a potential CIA undercover agent, or as a front for one. Even the assertion that the contact is simply for the purpose of completing a study may not diminish the suspicion; on the contrary, it may accelerate it rapidly and lead to all kinds of accusations and assertions. For example, one Black woman approached in the West launched into a tirade of charges suggesting that the interviewer and those involved in the study were doing the same thing as White people, that is, "pimping off" the Black community. She further asserted that Black women don't need to find out about other Black women because they already know about it. As a parting shot this woman, as did others, indicated that if a "barter" were set up she would be willing to participate in the study; if she were paid or if her own work (in the prisons) were financed in exchange, she would grant an interview.

Some interviewers were condemned for accepting pay for their work and for not having a clear idea of the source of funds for the study. One of the first questions hurled at some of them was: How much are you being paid?—followed by, Where did the organization get the money? One interviewer, invited to speak before a women's organization in California, was "torn to pieces" following her presentation as biting and cutting questions were thrown to her. "Why are you getting paid?" asked the women. "If you are getting paid, you must be pimping Black people. You should be doing it voluntarily." Where did the organization get the money for the study was a persistent question leveled by this group of women as well as others across the country.

Still a few others raised questions about the Board of Directors of BWCDF. The women's group in the West which raised the most cutting questions asserted that if anybody wanted to talk with them it should be someone from the Board of Directors like Marian Edelman. Another western woman stated: "To me the people on this Board are the bourgeois people. They don't know what's going on."

Questions were posed also about the director of the study. Who is she? Why didn't she come herself? How much will she obtain in royalties?

Many women questioned the value of a study, and even more important, asked to what use the results would be put. Said one woman: "The struggle is not in no survey but in the grass roots level." An interviewer in an eastern city indicated that Blacks were attempting to set up a review committee to "evaluate all survey and research proposals before they can be given in the Black community." She pointed out that scholars at a large nearby university "have continually gathered information from the Black residents in the community for individual gains and no gains for our own people." Therefore, many Black women in the area were deeply suspicious of the purpose of this particular study. The Panther women, particularly those in the West, were willing to talk provided they received assurances that the results would be published and not compiled for someone's private, personal use. Other women wondered aloud whether the study was being conducted for the FBI or the CIA. Even though some of those sus-

# Introduction

picious of intelligence agency connections agreed to be interviewed, they would not respond to any questions about the specific role they themselves would take in the Black struggle. In one eastern city women with a Pan-Africanist bent unanimously refused to be interviewed. These women, described by an interviewer as "an exclusive, elitist group" no doubt were representative of those highly cohesive, closed circles who would not tolerate outsider involvement.

A few women feared that our work would actually intensify a split between Black men and Black women. As one interviewer wrote: ". . . some women felt that a study of this sort might only widen the gap between Black females and Black males. In some cases, the idea of Black women's organizations and groups was not accepted. That is, these women felt that Black women's organizations were unnecessary and could only be a divisive force between Black men and women."

Suspicions increased with news of the deaths of some Black leaders. For example the interviews in the West were hampered and slowed up when the body of Melvin X, the leader of a western Black student alliance, was discovered. After attending a party he was found dead, mysteriously stabbed to death. As a result of his death, women in the local Black student alliance initially refused to cooperate with the study. The seizing of Judge Haley and others as hostages from a California courtroom and the subsequent deaths resulting in that seizure could well have had an impact on the study. A good stroke of luck befell us, however, since most of the interviews had been completed by the time of the court incident.

Many women would agree to interviews but would not show up at the appointed time and place. This phenomenon seemed to occur in most of the cities. One interviewer described a particularly vexing situation where she had to get up at 6 A.M. to arrive at a scheduled 8 A.M. interview only to have the woman not show. Another recalled that she had scheduled an interview with one woman on two different occasions and each time she failed to appear.

At the appointed time of one interview the subject, refusing then to be a part of the study, requested that only her reasons for not participating be recorded. In a sometimes hesitant manner she made the following statement:

> I'd like to talk to the whole research project. I think the first thing the Black Women's Community Development Foundation needs to do with this research project is first to evaluate whether or not the interests of the foundation in terms of gathering this kind of information outweighs the potential risk involved to Black women in the country. This kind of information could come very easily because of the trust a Black person or a Black woman would have in this kind of foundation. So therefore the person would be more apt to express themselves in a more real way, however at the same time creating the risk that they themselves could be seen as some potential threat to the status quo.
>
> I realize that here it states that there is an absolute need for confidentiality in terms of these kinds of things. These surveys are usually available on one level or another and can easily fall into the wrong kinds of hands. I realize that the survey asks more about the feelings of the individual and their whole psychological makeup rather than specific acts but this in itself indicates that this particular person has the mentality for creating some kind of revolutionary act either presently or in the future. And this in itself is a risk. The research material should be designed to talk to generalizations rather than specifics. What I mean by that is some of the material asks specifically the age, how many children in the family, where you were born (sic) and this kind of thing which doesn't seem important for a research analysis. Actually whether the person comes from a rural area or a highly populated area would be important. If the woman had men in her home at a young age or just all females would be important but these are statements that could be asked in a very general way and without being specific.

# Introduction

> And this is one part of the survey that bothers me. The questions about our feelings about the present administration I think is another question that doesn't tell me much in terms of what this could mean on the survey. I think you have the liberal point of view, and you may have a militant point of view or the conservative point of view but I don't think that says too much for what Black women feel in our present society. I don't think this administration really is necessarily the issue politically. And this again creates the risk of a highly paranoid political system or should I say an administrative or executive system in Washington that is prone to any verbalizations about what it does or how it carries out its functions. So therefore I don't feel this issue should even be dealt with.
>
> I realize that this project only represents the possibility of a couple hundred Black women in the country but your surveyor seeks out those women who are evidently involved in some kind of revolutionary movement and so therefore this could create a cadre of Black women with certain kinds of mentality that can in some way suffer by it. So I personally don't feel I want to be a part of the survey mainly because I don't see anything here that substantiates the reasons why you want it or why it's necessary, or that it's going to do anything in the future for Black women.

The interviewers are indeed to be praised for their persistent efforts to overcome mistrust, and their patience and tolerance in coping with the myriad questions of deeply suspicious Black women. Without these interviewer qualities the survey surely would have been a failure.

### *On Becoming Paranoid: A Personal Note*

Directing a study of this nature instills a particular alertness to danger and suspicion, suspicion (some might call it paranoia) especially conveyed by reactions responsive to people in the field. As the interview period drew to a close I faced the task of picking up interviews by hand since I did not trust the mails. My distrust of the mails increased as I received a feedback from those in the field concerning the difficulties involved in securing interviews and overcoming suspicions. I was armed with a realization of these difficulties and suspicions as pick up time drew near.

On a train trip to an eastern city I noticed a man who sat directly in front of me. My sole purpose in going to this city was to pick up the interviews so even though the train had just deposited me in the city at 12:30, I was back on it by 2:45 P.M. the same day. As I settled in my seat I noticed a man who bore a remarkable similarity to one who had caught my interest on the morning trip. This time he sat directly behind me. The only way I could be absolutely positive that the man was indeed the same one who had sat in front of me that same morning was by looking at his hair which was speckled with gray. For some reason I dared not turn around to look directly at him to confirm my conviction that this was the same man from the morning train. As the man got off the train about an hour and a half before I was scheduled to do so I glimpsed his head which truly was speckled with gray. To this day I don't know if I imagined the faintest of smiles as he stood outside the train and cast a glance toward my window. Even though the man got off before I did a nagging doubt lingered as to whether he was just another passenger.

On another train trip, this time to the West, my suitcase was searched while I was in the dining car. I have a special way of leaving the suitcase so that I can tell in a second if it has been opened. Upon my return from the dining car I discovered the suitcase did not pass the test. Now the suitcase may have been opened by a curious porter but the opening recalled to mind the incident on the eastern train trip and I began to wonder whether I was being followed.

I had decided to remain in the West for about a month, after securing the western tapes, to escape a busy life in the East which interfered with giving maximum attention to the study. After being admitted to my hotel room I made a careful examination

# Introduction

of it and to my horror discovered that I was in a room which not only looked directly across at two other rooms, (one of which was designed as a locker and supply room for hotel personnel), but was also connected to those other rooms by a little rock garden which could easily be traversed. I did not want to call attention to myself by requesting another room. So, although the room was overheated, I tended to make certain that both windows were locked when I went out and while I slept at night. I could not escape visions of someone stealing across that rock garden, stealthily entering my room, and walking off with the tapes and my notes.

Two events which took place at the hotel did not help ease my developing paranoia. One day someone knocked on the door while I was typing and transcribing tapes. When I asked who was there a male voice replied, "I have another radio for you; somebody reported your radio out of order." Well I had been a guest in the hotel for six days and each day had played the radio without any difficulty. Moreover, I had not reported it out of order. I had, by that time, developed a truly suspicious mind, so I informed the voice on the other side of the door that my radio was functioning perfectly and I had no need for another. The instant thought which crossed my mind as I sent the "radioman" away was: He's been sent to see what I'm doing. The next episode instilled paranoia to an even greater degree. Not long after I arrived the woman who normally cleaned my room became curious as to why I spent so much time in the room and did not act like a normal vacationing tourist. Since I was typing so much of the time I told her I was a writer. Subsequently a Black male worker in the hotel came and asked me to look over some chapters of a book that he was writing so that he could get some idea of the good or bad nature of his work. I said I would. One day upon returning to my hotel room my heart stopped beating as I discovered a man sitting on the bed writing something. I had run down only to get a sandwich to bring back to the room and thus had left a few papers out of interviews which I was in the process of transcribing. Normally I placed all papers under lock and key whenever I left the room and made certain both windows were locked. Only one thought crossed my mind as I spied the man whom I soon discovered was the same one who had asked me to read his chapters: He's been reading those papers. Even though I had talked with him a few days earlier when he asked me to look over and evaluate his written work my imagination, running wild, led me to believe that he had been sent to spy. Learning that he was a former prison inmate on death row did not ease my mind as my training made me recall the numerous times former inmates are used as informants in exchange for dropping charges, lighter sentences, or parole. Only during a couple of subsequent conversations was my mind teased into thinking that he could not possibly be a police informant or undercover agent. As I look back on the incident the whole thing seems strange in that I did not experience the normal female concern that the man was trying to make a pass (which he even hastened to assure me he was not); the only thing I was concerned about was that he might have looked at my interview transcriptions, some of which contained pretty strong language. Thus functions the mind of a researcher involved in a study of Black women described as "militant."

The task of listening to and transcribing tapes presented was a very sensitive issue: Who could be trusted with such a delicate chore? A professional transcriber was deemed to be out of the question because that person might prove unsympathetic to a study of this nature, and even worse, prone to make premature revelations to third parties. Interviewers were pressed already by the herculean task of overcoming suspicions and conducting several interviews, each between one and two hours in duration. Therefore they simply did not have the time to conduct the interviews and transcribe them too. Finally, a former student of mine and a recent graduate of Brooklyn College, Ruby Birt, was tapped for service and managed to complete about 15 tapes prior to entering law school. This left approximately 180 tapes. Although it proved to be a time consuming process, I decided to assume the burden of transcription myself. Perhaps this was yet another reflection of paranoia but it seemed only just to assume this task personally since so many women had placed their faith and con-

# Introduction

fidence in the BWCDF—particularly with respect to protecting their anonymity and making a discrete use of the tapes.

At one point my paranoia was developing to such an extent that I found it necessary to "leave" the study for about ten days. This ten day "leave of absence" enabled me to try to restore some order to the thinking process and to emotional reaction. Yet, for me, working on this study proved to be just about the most engrossing project of my life—almost reaching the level of intensity which my life sustained as I spent the year 1963–1964 in Congo-Kinshasa during the emerging stages of the Muleleist and CNL (Committee of National Liberation) rebellion. Completing this study evoked reminiscences of the sense of adventure and total involvement experienced during my Congo episode.

*Some Preliminary Notes*

Although it is quite difficult to put together a book which is readily usable and of interest to a wide variety of audiences, "Together" Black Women was designed to appeal to diverse parts of the population. For this reason some may find certain sections tedious and overly intellectual; others may become annoyed at the failure both to employ "social scientist" terminology and concepts, and to draw upon an existing body of "scholarly" literature in analyzing certain findings of this study. For example, certain audiences may find that chapters entitled: "Of Marx, Mao and Uncle Sam," and "Pan-Africanism: What's That?" do not constitute in depth analyses of economic philosophies and the concept Pan-Africanism. Other audiences may be "turned off" totally by the historical and descriptive material in the same chapters and find themselves anxious and impatient to move on to discover what "together" Black women themselves think about economic doctrines and Pan-Africanism.

While there is always the danger that a book designed to be read by diverse segments of the population ends up being unsatisfactory to all, we felt that the material gained from this study was of such importance that it had to be shared with as many people as possible. For this reason we were quite willing to assume the risk of pleasing no one in the hopes that we would not alienate everyone.

Intentionally, we have given the reader only a glimpse into the specific backgrounds of the women whose thoughts represent the major part of our study. In some instances we followed certain direct quotes with background data to afford some insight into what age or educational group, for example, would take what position on a given issue. Yet, in some of the more sensitive chapters this type of information was withheld altogether. Then too, while it would have been much more enlightening and quite exciting to draw many more specific profiles of the women interviewed, we limited the number of case histories and character types in the interest of safeguarding identities as much as possible.

If someone were to request that the fundamental findings of the study be identified, it would be quite difficult to single these out since virtually all the information gathered seemed to be so significant. However, in the interests of complying with the request the following findings might be cited:

1. The adoption of the concept "together" as a substitute for militant;
2. The feeling of "together" Black women that their interests are almost diametrically opposed to those of the women's liberation movement;
3. The gross disenchantment of "together" Black women with national and local political and social conditions in the United States;
4. The willingness of "together" Black women to embrace violence as the only viable solution to Black oppression;
5. The "state of limbo" in which many "together" Black women find themselves while awaiting the next stage of the Black struggle.

It is hoped that these fundamental findings, as well as the others, will serve not only to spark serious debate about the future and direction of Black people, but also to afford a basis for that kind of Black social activism which can have an imaginative, lasting, and deep impact in terms of erasing the oppression which still is all too familiar to Black people throughout the United States. If these results occur, then the study will have served its purpose well.

# CHAPTER I
# Not Militancy But Togetherness

*When the study* was first commissioned several of us spent hours trying to define "militant" so that we could get a better idea of the kind of woman for whom we were searching. As the study unfolded, and after listening to numerous tapes, my thinking began to swing away from a conception of "militancy" towards a perception of "togetherness." What began to emerge, in the language of the Black community, was a picture of a "together" group of Black women. What follows is an attempt to relate the shift from "militancy" to "togetherness."

### *Blackness Equals Militancy*

We approached our task of defining militancy with the full knowledge that the American society often equated Blackness with militancy or radicalism. One has only to pick up a newspaper to see repeated references to Black militants. It is ironical that even the most bourgeois Negro or a strong believer in the non-violent method may not escape the label "Black militant." Or, someone who dresses in a dashiki and accidentally brushes past a little old

White lady may even be called "militant" or "damn Black militant" as he hurries to his $25,000 a year job in a White public relations firm. Or a young Negro elementary school teacher who timidly and hesitantly suggests that her fifth grade class might read three paragraphs about the life of Booker T. Washington might be ostracized as a Black militant, or as a radical ill-suited for the task of shaping the minds of young children.

To illustrate the point further, the Internal Security Committee of the U.S. House of Representatives compiled a list of "radical" campus speakers, a list which allegedly contained a number of "black militants." Included in the list were Rev. James Bevel and Wyatt Tee Walker. Among the White "radicals" initially were Rev. John C. Bennett, former President of Union Theological Seminary, John Ciardi, poet and writer, Jessica Mitford, an author who wrote a book on the trial of Dr. Benjamin Spock, and Jerome Skolnick, sociologist and criminologist whose work we quote later in the study. (*New York Times*, October 15, 1970).

To avoid this simplistic approach to militancy our first inclination, in true scholarly fashion, was to search the literature for definitions of militancy. We confronted an almost total vacuum, emerging with only two relatively current, concrete pieces of scholarship which had hazarded a treatment of "militancy." One was the work by Guy T. Marx on *Protest and Prejudice* (New York: Harper Torchbooks, 1967, 1969). The work, sponsored by the Anti-Defamation League of B'Nai B'Rith and directed by the Survey Research Center of the University of California at Berkeley, was conducted during late 1964, prior to the emergence of the Black Power movement.

Marx' study attempted to form an "Index of Conventional Militancy." This index was derived as a result of positive responses to eight statements:

> In your opinion, is the government in Washington pushing integration too slow, too fast, or about right? (*Too slow.*)
> Negroes who want to work hard can get ahead just as easily as anyone else. (*Disagree.*)

## Not Militancy But Togetherness

> Negroes should spend more time praying and less time demonstrating. (*Disagree.*)
> To tell the truth I would be afraid to take part in civil rights demonstrations. (*Disagree.*)
> Would you like to see more demonstrations or less demonstrations? (*More.*)
> A restaurant owner should not have to serve Negroes if he doesn't want to. (*Disagree.*)
> Before Negroes are given equal rights, they have to show that they deserve them. (*Disagree.*)
> An owner of property should not have to sell to Negroes if he doesn't want to. (*Disagree.*)
> (*Marx*, 1969, p. 41.)

If an individual scored at least 6 points he was considered militant; if his score was between 3 and 5 he was labeled moderate; and those with scores between 0 and 2 were called conservative. Marx described the "militant Negro" in these terms:

> The militant Negro is one who actively opposes discrimination and segregation. He feels barriers now exist which keep Negroes from getting ahead, and is impatient with the speed of social change. He demands his rights *now* and is likely to agree with Martin Luther King that "the oft-repeated cliches, 'the time is not ripe,' 'Negroes are not culturally ready,' are a stench in the nostrils of God." The militant Negro encourages civil rights demonstrations and his concern with the here and now leads him to think that Negroes should spend more time in the secular activity of demonstrating than in the otherworldly one of praying. He also would, or already has, taken part in such demonstrations and is likely to agree with St. Augustine that "those that sit at rest while others take pains (to act) are tender turtles and buy their quiet with disgrace."
> (*Marx*, 1969, p. 42.)

Thus Marx seemed to equate participation in a nonviolent demonstration such as a sit-in with militancy. In light of the Black Power movement, the Panthers, the Republic of New Africa, the Revolutionary Action Movement, and a host of other phenomena relating to the Black community, it seemed highly incongruous to define Black militant women in the decade of the seventies as those who would participate in a nonviolent demonstration.

The other piece of scholarship discovered was one study resulting from the work of The National Commission on the Causes and Prevention of Violence. The Commission entered into a contract for an analytical study of protest with Professor Jerome Skolnick of the Center for the Study of Law and Society at Berkeley. The study was completed in the Spring of 1969 and appeared under the title *The Politics of Protest* (New York: Ballantine Books, 1969). Chapter 4 of the book is titled "Black Militancy" and although there is no apparent effort to define the phrase explicitly, the author seems to conclude that Black militancy is Black nonviolent or violent protest, with the current emphasis being on the former since: "There has so far been relatively little violence by militant blacks in this country—as compared to nonviolent black protest—despite the popular impression conveyed by the emphasis of the news media on episodes of spectacular violence (or threats of violence)." (Skolnick, 1969, p. 127) Skolnick felt, however, that the content of contemporary militancy had begun to change with three themes now being predominate: "self-defense and the rejection of non-violence; cultural autonomy and the rejection of white values; and political autonomy and community control." (Skolnick, 1969, p. 150) While Skolnick's analysis of militancy was much more usable in the decade of the seventies, still he did not seem to have enunciated a neat, clear, wholly applicable definition for our purposes.

We therefore formulated and posited the following suggested working definition of Black militant women, even though imbued with a belief in the impossibility of effectively defining militancy:

> Those women who believe that American subsystems (political, economic, social, educational) are so ineffectual in coping with the demands of the Black commu-

# Not Militancy But Togetherness

nity that radical changes in the functioning of these subsystems must be made; or in the alternative, total destruction of these subsystems must occur if there is to be an amelioration in the situation of American Blacks.

To obtain some idea of what Black women themselves thought about the question of militancy we asked the women interviewed to define militancy. Included below is a sampling of their responses:

> To be militant you have to be aware and on the front of whatever is going on.... There are many people who are fighting in the background with bills to Congress and this and that and the other, but the militant ones are the ones who will get out and pound the pavement, go from door to door, join the marches and whatever they feel or whatever the consensus of opinion tells them this is what you must do, then the militant ones do this, at risk to life and limb.

> People can be militant about anything I think. It's just an aggressive stand that you take with respect to your views on something.

> Militancy is when you can actually analyze, make an analysis of a particular situation that you want to change or affect change in and you have a plan for how you're going to carry it out and then you begin to proceed in stages without backing down or backing out of the stages unless it's going to jeopardize the long range goals that you set in the beginning. I don't think militancy is where people just refuse to change their position for no reason at all; they're just going to be militant and for no reason because they really don't have a plan and it's not intended to be a step or a stage in a long range plan.

> Doing whatever you do in a zealous fashion. That's all being militant is. You can be militant if you're green— if you do it like you mean it.

> At this point that doesn't mean a lot to me. I've seen a lot of phony militants and that has a bad connotation.

To me a militant person is one who is not afraid to speak out, who is not afraid to go forward with things and he feels that he is fighting for the right.

I think a militant person is, for Black people, anybody who decides that it's time for White folks to stop kicking my ass. It's just anybody who's tired of being messed over.

I don't know what people call a militant cause some people have called me a militant. The origin of militant means one who carries a gun. I never thought I was very much like that but I've been called that. I don't know that I know anybody who is a militant in the terms that people like to cast aspersion on. Any Black person is militant who publicly takes a stand against racism and against discrimination. Now they'll call that person militant. Well to me that's not a militant person. That's only a person who's doing what he should do. So really to me even a Black Panther is not militant because a Black Panther sees that this is the thing he has to do in order to make the public aware of the very lowly position of Black people in this society. So actually I think the whole term militant has been misconstrued. Definition? I have no definition. If people want to say a person is militant who takes a stand against racism and discrimination, they're welcome to their term.

So many are hollering that they are militant and they don't want the White man to do this and the White man to do that but they still want the White woman. And the same goes for the women: they want the White men and go on and marry them. So I really can't say what a militant person is.

Right now anytime I disagree with the administration's idea then I'm a militant woman, that is, disagreeing with the entire system that I feel is doing a rotten job of bringing up a younger generation that has to be tomorrow's society.

# Not Militancy But Togetherness

I was kind of leery about even talking with you under the heading of militant because of how it's misused. But anytime you live in a dictatorial system that tells you what to think and how to think and then, whenever you rebel from this dictatorial situation, when you see the truth and make it be known and stand for what you believe in, then this is termed militant but the aspect of survival itself is militant because it means that you have to oppose all forces that tend to take or destroy your right to be, but survival mainly against opposing forces —then we'll call it militant.

It is becoming a dirty word too. I feel strongly about Black people and the Black community. I feel that by any means necessary we're going to have to arrive at our goal. I feel that if we don't get it nobody will have it. That's what I call militancy. I feel we don't say we'll fight up to a point. I say all the way. Count up the costs. Whatever it takes, if it takes your life, that's what I call militancy.

A militant person is a very violent person.

When they say Black militant I automatically think a Black fighter, a man who wants something and the only way he knows how to get it is to fight for it. Come hell or high water he'll fight for it and he's ready to lay down his life for this particular cause.

It's like this guy came into the library where I work and he read Dubois' *The Souls of Black Folks*. He was a Black guy and I thought I knew what militancy meant. He threw the book down on the floor and he told me he didn't like that book because it wasn't militant enough. And then he said, "Come on sweet, let's go." The book wasn't militant enough for him and the sweet he was calling which was his wife was White. So like I thought militant pertained to a person who was really extreme in a goal—could only see it one way. It has to be my way, or forget it. But I don't think it's that. I don't

> really know what it is any more. The technique can be
> used to I guess get your goals or whatever you want but
> I don't really know what it means because I've heard it
> and I just thought it was a one way street. But it isn't
> undoubtedly. A Black militant is a guy who speaks up
> for Blacks, all Black. He talks about Whitey but Whitey
> is always the man because he has high regard for the
> White woman.
>
> I sort of define militancy not just sort of a physical kind
> of militancy but just a Black person no matter where he
> is and no matter what capacity he's working in or finds
> himself, can stand up against racism and institutional-
> ized racism and individual racism without turning about.
> It doesn't necessarily mean a person who's using cliches,
> cursing, who wears naturals or boubas or anything. But
> as long as he aggressively stands firm in terms of his
> goals of pointing out racist institutions, and racist be-
> havior, and racist decisions and not turning around on
> them.

Perhaps the one woman in the study who led us, more than any other, to abandon the term "militant" and to adopt instead the word "together," was a 26-year-old southern woman with a tenth grade education who used to work in the cotton fields prior to assuming her present job. When asked to define militant she responded:

> I really feel it's just a name that the White people gave
> the Black people. They call them that name because
> they speak the right things for the race. . . . I don't think
> there's such a word as that.

Or, as a young Black medical student and teacher of mentally disturbed Black children said about militancy:

> (It's a) label that has been attached to Black people
> who are considered militant, have been labeled (so) by
> the White press. So I don't think we can deal with that.

*Blackness Equals Togetherness*

The more the backgrounds of the women involved in the study were examined, the more the tapes were analyzed and reanalyzed, the more ridiculous it seemed to apply to them a badly used, overworked and misconstrued concept like "militant." Upon reflection it dawned on me that we are dealing with, not a group of Black militant women, but a group of "together" Black women, women involved in all sorts of activities and groups including Black student unions, the Black Panther Party, neo-Panther groups, local Black women's groups, Black study groups, traditional civil rights groups, day care centers, Black high school organizations, domestic workers unions, urban renewal, welfare rights, revolutionary Black workers organizations, and Black professional groups.

We managed to interview (most of the interviews lasted between one and two hours) 202 women: 66 from the East, 83 from the West, 33 from the South, and 20 from the Midwest. Of these women most had received some college instruction. (See Table 1.) A large number of women professed or gave no religious affiliation while several adhered to religious doctrines which are not widespread

TABLE 1
Educational Background*

|  | *Number* | *Percent* |
|---|---|---|
| Less Than High School | 10 | 5 |
| High School Graduate | 41 | 21 |
| Some College But No College Degree | 67 | 35 |
| College Degree | 32 | 17 |
| Some Graduate Study But No Graduate Degree | 18 | 9 |
| Masters Degree | 17 | 9 |
| Law Degree | 4 | 2 |
| Doctor of Philosophy | 3 | 2 |
| Total | 192 | 100 |

* Note: Categories are mutually exclusive and represent the highest grade completed at the time of the interview. Ten persons did not reveal their educational backgrounds.

in American society. (See Tables 2, 3 and 4.) Most of the women in the study may be described as apolitical in terms of traditional politics as most did not identify with any political party. (See

TABLE 2
Religious Affiliation

|  | Number | Percent |
|---|---|---|
| None Given | 90 | 45 |
| *Catholic | 13 | 6 |
| **Protestant | 77 | 38 |
| Other | 22 | 11 |
| Total | 202 | 100 |

* Three stated they were inactive Catholics.
**One stated she was a non-practising Episcopalian.

TABLE 3
Religious Affiliation: Protestant

|  | Number | Percent |
|---|---|---|
| Baptist | 33 | 44 |
| Methodist | 13 | 17 |
| **Congregational | 6 | 8 |
| *Episcopal | 5 | 7 |
| AME | 4 | 5 |
| Lutheran | 2 | 3 |
| Church of God in Christ | 2 | 3 |
| Disciples of Christ | 1 | 1 |
| **United Church of Christ | 1 | 1 |
| Presbyterian | 1 | 1 |
| Unitarian | 1 | 1 |
| Protestant (No particular denomination identified) | 7 | 9 |
| Total | 76 | 100 |

**Congregational and United Church of Christ are now one and the same as a result of Congregational Churches having merged with Evangelical Churches to form the United Church of Christ. However some people still persist in calling themselves Congregationalists.
* One Episcopalian stated she no longer practices the religion but still calls herself an Episcopalian.

Table 5.) The ages of the women studied ranged from 16 to over 50, with most being in the 20 to 30 age bracket. (See Table 6.) Finally, in terms of occupations, many of the women could be placed in the professional, semi-professional or student category although a number of jobs were not easily classifiable (e.g., social health technician, assistant in urban technology) and therefore were lumped under an "Other" category. (See Table 7.)

TABLE 4
Religious Affiliation: Other

|  | Number |
|---|---|
| Black Christian Nationalist | 4 |
| Pentecostal | 3 |
| *Kawaida | 5 |
| Personal Belief | 2 |
| Black Humanist | 1 |
| Independent Black Church | 1 |
| Astrology | 1 |
| Spiritualist | 1 |
| Sunni Muslim | 1 |
| Jehovah's Witness | 1 |
| **Muslim | 1 |
| Pantheist | 1 |

* Kawaida is the religion associated with the US movement.
** One subject identified herself only as Muslim, i.e. not Black Muslim, or Sunni Muslim, or Sufi Muslim.

TABLE 5
Political Affiliation

|  | Number | Percent |
|---|---|---|
| None Given | 104 | 51 |
| Democratic Party | 66 | 33 |
| Republican Party | 2 | 1 |
| Black Panther Party | 13 | 6 |
| Peace and Freedom Party | 4 | 2 |
| Independent | 6 | 3 |
| US | 4 | 2 |
| Communist Party | 2 | 1 |
| Sunni Muslim | 1 | 5 |
| Total | 202 | 100 |

TABLE 6
Age

|  | Number | Percent |
|---|---|---|
| 16–19 | 28 | 14 |
| 20–25 | 62 | 31 |
| 26–30 | 29 | 14 |
| 31–35 | 26 | 13 |
| 36–40 | 18 | 9 |
| 41–45 | 15 | 7 |
| 46–50 | 7 | 4 |
| 51 and over | 11 | 5 |
| None Given | 6 | 3 |
| Total | 202 | 100 |

TABLE 7
Occupations

|  | Number | Percent |
|---|---|---|
| Professional, Semi-Professional and Business | 61 | 31 |
| Student | 39 | 19 |
| Community Organizer and Community Worker | 20 | 10 |
| Clerical | 10 | 5 |
| Housewife | 4 | 2 |
| Other | 37 | 18 |
| None Given | 14 | 6 |
| Unemployed | 17 | 9 |
| Total | 202 | 100 |

Other characteristics of the women and their families were notable. Although several women were extremely reluctant to talk about their family background, the greater part of them eagerly responded to these questions. Indeed many seemed to welcome the opportunity to reminisce about childhood experiences and, speaking with animation, reflected a deep interest in their families while recounting fond youthful memories. The parents of several women died early—leaving their siblings to be raised by a grandparent or another relative. In a few cases the early deaths of parents meant

# Not Militancy But Togetherness

independence at a rather tender age. For example, one woman reported that she was on her own by age 15. Family size ranged from an only child to one of 16 children. Occupations of parents varied from domestics and laborers to self-employed businessmen and teachers. More females than males were present in the overwhelming majority of families. This was the impression gained when women were asked to estimate whether or not more males or females were in their total family. Responses to the more specific question of how many brothers and sisters interviewees had provided hard data to support the initial impression. The data produced the following statistical breakdown:

|  | Number | Percent |
| --- | --- | --- |
| Equal Number of Brothers and Sisters | 35 | 19 |
| More Brothers Than Sisters | 27 | 14 |
| More Sisters Than Brothers | 102 | 57 |
| No Brothers Or Sisters | 18 | 10 |

Of the 182 women willing to relate the number of brothers and sisters in their families, a sound majority—57%—asserted that there were more sisters than brothers in their families while only 14% indicated that they had more brothers than sisters. One woman recalled, for example, that her father's mother had 15 girls and 1 boy. Preferential treatment, especially in terms of a greater degree of freedom, was given to male children as a rule. A young woman from the West reflected the sentiments of many respondents when she stated:

> I was treated like a traditional thing; dudes are going to get it better because of the whole thing that guys have to be raised in a different way. They are more permissive to men when you are growing up because you have to be nice young ladies. There had to be a division as far as mother was concerned. The men got away with everything. The women did all the work for them. The guys could run the streets all the time. Mother would take up for my brothers because she was preparing the girls for our later life.

Another young woman remembered her father favoring the male child simply because he believed males ought to play the dominant role in the family. As she put it:

> I come from a very male chauvinistic family. My father was one who favored the son over the daughter mainly because he was a strong believer in male dominance. My mother, from a southern background, had the role of the female as being very submissive, very passive, very feminine in terms of these two descriptions, just passive-subservient to cater to the male but also just to be sort of the clinging type of individual.

While many women reported that greater freedom was given to the male child, some also indicated that females tended to receive a higher level of education than the males. In the South, in particular, females seemed more likely to attend college. And even though several respondents revealed that brothers had begun college, they were also likely to point out that the brother did not complete the four-year program. One woman asserted that her older brother had already spent time in three or four universities but had yet to complete his BA even though he was 26 years of age. She felt this state of affairs may have been traceable to an over-protective mother.

Still other women recalled that males had been singled out for favored treatment with respect to education. As one young woman said:

> Education was highly stressed in my family for both male and female but the thing about it, mine was secondary to my brother's because it was more important for him to choose some kind of profession and be "successful" in the society that we know. I was supposed to get married and have babies.

Despite a brother's college education and college degree, a few women mentioned the really difficult time male siblings had in securing decent employment in their respective fields. One woman stated that her brother was forced to complete two tours of duty in the army before he could get a job in his chosen field of computer science. One brother was forced to leave the United States and travel to Africa to find employment in his field of architecture. But regardless of the hardships involved in securing a college education, and despite the favorable or unfavorable job market awaiting the Black college graduate, the great majority of women reported that every child—whether male or female—was encouraged to obtain a college education.

Another characteristic of the women in our sample was that of the southern origins of their families. Most women stated that their parents, and in some cases they themselves, had been born in a southern community. Subsequently, in many cases, a family decision was made to migrate to a more northerly area of the country. Even after having made an initial geographical change with their families many women did not remain stationary. On the contrary, one definite characteristic of the Black women interviewed was their mobility. That is, they seem to move with ease and frequency from one geographical location to another—whether for education, or employment, or just to attend conferences and meetings. To illustrate, one woman moved from a job in the New York City anti-poverty program to a position where she could serve a southern community. Another whose home base is the midwest traveled often to the East. Still another who resided in the South spoke of frequent trips to the West coast, the East, and the Midwest. Then, too, there was a good deal of migration from the South to the West, and from the Midwest to the West. This mobility may indeed have served to make the women of our study much more aware of various events touching Black people in different communities across the country.

It is not surprising, perhaps, to discover that many of those Black women interviewed did not belong to a poverty category. In fact of those interviewed who could be designated as poverty-stricken—for example the welfare mothers—many reflected an inculcation of, or at least an aspiration to, many predominate American middle class values. In her analysis of "The Black Revolution in America," Grace Lee Boggs writes:

> At the present time there are three distinct social classes represented inside the Black power movement. These are (1) the Black middle classes; (2) the Black student youth in the universities; and (3) the Black city youth on the streets.
> (P. 214 in Toni Cade, *The Black Woman*, New York: Signet Books, 1970)

In her estimation "the Black middle-class elements are the ones now being celebrated as 'Black militant leaders' by the mass media. . . ." (Boggs, 1970, p. 214) Thus Boggs recognizes the middle class origins of many who are aware of and actively involved in the Black struggle. In his book *Protest and Prejudice* Gary Marx posits as one of his working propositions that "high social status produces militancy." (Marx, 1969, p. 49) Applying this proposition to our study it is possible to conclude that Black women who are relatively comfortable in economic terms would be more likely to be aware of and actively involved in the Black struggle. The emphasis is on "relatively comfortable"—that is to say "comfortable" using as a reference group the entire Black population. This would mean, then, that those Black women who are aware and actively involved may not have the same "high social status" as a White "militant" woman. Many of the younger Panther women for instance do not come from poverty stricken families but neither do they stem from the kind of affluent families from which an SDS weatherwoman may come. A case in point is Angela Davis, whose father described her upbringing as being in "comfortable" circumstances. (San Francisco Examiner, August 17, 1970) Yet the Davis family's socio-economic status could in no way be compared with the affluence of the families of Kathy Boudin or Cathy Wilkerson, two women who allegedly are part of an SDS faction which has resorted to tactics deemed terroristic by a segment of the American society.

Just as it is impossible to view Black people on a comparable socio-economic level with Whites, so too we believe it impossible to describe Black women in terms of a White establishment term such as "militant." As we have said, more appropriate to the Black woman is the concept "together."

As the study unfolds a deeper insight into the "together" Black woman will emerge. Suffice it to say at this point that we are burying the term "militant" as an alien phenomenon imposed on the Black community, and adopting "together," a concept whose origins are deeply rooted in the Black community and readily understandable to Black people. For those who are not familiar with the term "together" a further explanation is in order. According to the *Dictionary of Afro-American Slang* (compiled by Clarence Major, 1970) "together" means "to have one's mind free of confusion; to be positive, functional; to emerge as a whole person." Furthermore, "together", in our more collective connotation, is characterized by a spiritual closeness in a common endeavor—that of a singular or peculiar commitment to erase oppression. Finally, for our purposes, the term denotes a refusal to take on, uncritically, the total value structure of the White community.

The profile which emerges of the "together" Black woman, then, is one who is relatively young, apolitical in traditional terms, semireligious, working (at a variety of jobs), and exposed to some college education. More important, the "together" Black woman is typified by a high degree of consciousness (Black or social), commitment (especially to the Black struggle), involvement (in the Black struggle), selflessness (i.e., the primary goal in life is not a new car or a new home but a dedication to a larger community), fearlessness (i.e., a refusal to cower to the wishes of a wider, White society and a willingness to employ non-traditional or commonly unacceptable methods for change), conviction and confidence (i.e., a strong belief that commitment and involvement will produce change).

# CHAPTER II
# Liberation Can Be a Trick Bag

*When this study* concerning Black women was first commissioned, a quick search of the library was made for existing materials. Surprisingly, little of consequence turned up, with the possible exception of Chapters in various sociological texts. Thinking that perhaps something had been overlooked I sought the assistance of Pauli Murray, a Black woman who for years has held an intense interest in events concerning Black women. She confirmed the sad state of affairs concerning literature on the Black female and revealed that a work by her would appear in the next several months. Subsequently I also discovered that Joyce Ladner, attached to the Institute of the Black World, had completed a work on the Black female published in 1971 under the title: *Tomorrow's Tomorrow: The Black Woman*, *The Black Scholar* devoted half of one of its early issues to the Black woman. And *Ebony* magazine periodically has devoted attention to the Black female. As the study was being put together *The Black Woman* also appeared. An interesting and, for the most part, compelling anthology edited by Toni Cade and published by Signet Books (1970), *The Black Woman* contains a variety of materials by Black women—poems, essays, and short stories. But it does not purport to represent the views of Black women in general since each contribution seems to stem from an individual effort and an individual thought process. Also discovered under the same title, *The Black Woman,* was a rather fascinating photographic endeavor by Chester Higgins with words by Harold McDougall, an excellent work but one not meant to be a serious analytical study of Black women.

Even with the appearance of these works, however, a literature gap on the Black woman still exists. This is indeed surprising given the tendency of many to profess a deep and sound verbal knowledge of the Black woman, especially her role in the Black family. How often one hears comments about the matriarchal structure of the Black family, or the strength of the Black woman, or the tendency of Black women to have more children in order to increase welfare funds available to them.

We felt that given the lack of literature on the subject and given the existence of certain unproved assumptions about the Black woman, our study should seek to gain some insight into the Black woman's thoughts about certain feminine issues: women's liberation, Black male/Black female roles in the liberation struggle, and marital liberation.

### *Black Women and Women's Liberation*

> Is there any logical comparison between the oppression of the black woman on welfare who has difficulty feeding her children and the discontent of the suburban mother who has the luxury to protest the washing of the dishes on which the family's full meal was consumed? (Linda LaRue, "The Black Movement and Women's Liberation," in *The Black Scholar,* vol. 1, No. 7, May 1970, pp. 36–42.

On the heels of the civil rights movement emerged a full scale drive for women's liberation. American women suddenly realized their disenchantment with the daily routine of housekeeping and the normal female functions of giving birth and taking care of children. Viewing themselves as degraded beings, exploited fully by the American male, these women mounted a campaign for liberation—or at least for cooperation from their spouses, who were urged to share the burden of the housekeeping chores. Husbands and wives began to work out arrangements under which each could spend a half day at some gainful employment and the other portion caring for the home.

Fed up with discrimination in employment these women also began to make attacks on a persistent American attitude: women are not capable or strong enough to hold jobs, or if they are permitted into the job market, it must be at a rung considerably below that of the male. Moreover, certain professions were believed unsuitable for women. Thus women began to press the issue: Why can't we be welders? Why can't more of us become doctors and lawyers? Why can't we receive tenure and promotions in higher education? Why do graduate and professional schools make it so difficult for us to complete our studies? Why shouldn't we have a share of editorial positions on popular magazines?

Not satisfied with the push for emancipation from routine housewifely chores, nor the drive to end discrimination in employment, women began to seize certain kinds of personal freedoms. Assaults on all-male bars and eating places became popular. Disdain for bras surfaced—to the delight of some male egos. Long hours of "beautifying" also were abandoned.

Although women bore the brunt of many jokes, they pressed on in their surge for total freedom. Perhaps ignoring the amusement with which a rider to prevent sex discrimination was attached to the 1964 Civil Rights Act, women began to utilize this and other laws to circumvent American tendencies either to ban them from the job market or to allow them an insignificant crumb—usually of the secretarial cake. Soon an implicit question posed by the women's liberation movement was: Would women's liberation and the Black movement—or at least its Black female segment—join forces?

Perhaps Pauli Murray, more than any other Black woman, has seen a clear relationship between the liberation of females and the cessation of racial discrimination. Long before women's liberation became popular Professor Murray's exhortations to terminate Jane Crow along with Jim Crow were well known. In a 1964 article entitled "The Negro Woman In the Quest For Equality" Professor Murray, now at Brandeis University, wrote:

> In the larger society, Negro and white women share a common burden because of traditional discriminations based upon sex. . . . Despite the common interests of Negro and white women, however, the dichotomy of the segregated society has prevented them from cementing a natural alliance.
> (*Address delivered to the Leadership Conference of the National Council of Negro Women, November 14, 1963 in Washington, D.C.*)

In an effort to "cement the natural alliance," no doubt, Professor Murray and another Black woman, Aileen Hernandez, joined forces with several White women including Betty Friedan, one of the leading proponents of the women's liberation movement, to form NOW (National Organization of Women) in the Summer of 1966. Eventually, in early 1970, Aileen Hernandez was elevated to the presidency of NOW.

With this brief background in mind we were curious to know whether Black women had any real knowledge of and interest in women's liberation. The fact that one of the feminist movements had recently elected a Black female to head it might have led to an increasing interest and involvement in women's liberation. Moreover, we wanted to determine the extent to which Black women saw a connection between the Black struggle and the fight for female freedoms. In other words, we wanted to test their acceptance or rejection of the proposition that the elimination of racism in this country is dependent upon the abolition of sexism. That is, is it necessary for women to gain their freedom before Black people can be liberated? Or, is the women's liberation only using the Black struggle as a means of highlighting their own, without any serious intent to pave the way for the demise of racial discrimination. Linda LaRue, convinced that women's liberation has no serious interest in the Black struggle, wrote:

> It is entirely possible that women's liberation has developed a sudden attachment to the black liberation

movement as a ploy to share the attention that it has taken blacks 400 years to generate.
(LaRue, 1970, p. 37)

Despite the popularity of the movement several of the women in our study had very little if any knowledge of feminist movements or women's liberation. This was particularly true of the southern region where many women tended to confuse the work of a traditional Black women's organization with that of the women's liberation. When the subject of feminist movements and women's liberation was mentioned, quite a few women in the South began to talk about the work of the National Council of Negro Women. Still other women outside the South seemed surprised to hear a question on women's liberation and offered only a few, skimpy comments.

For the majority of the women, however, women's liberation was a subject which evoked much response. Few women attempted to be objective analysts of the movement by examining its virtues and its liabilities. Most had definite views which they related. At least two women, however, did try to be completely neutral by pinpointing those aspects of the movement which had merit while decrying those believed to be silly or of little value. As one westerner in her twenties pointed out:

> I think there's different aspects to the women's liberation movement. You have the feminists: the ones that blame women's oppression on the men in society and go around not wearing bras and doing all kinds of silly irrelevant things as far as I'm concerned. Then you have other women's liberation groups who are seriously trying to deal with the question of women's oppression, the question of child care centers and on the job child care centers, the problems of working women with children, and the problems of male supremacy in the society, which is a big danger. I think it's something that has to be attacked, but saying that, I don't think men are the enemy. I think men have been the victims of capitalist morals and lifestyles just like women have. Men have

to be made aware that they cannot oppress women and that that's not going to help them. So generally I think the women's liberation movement has raised some very valid questions, and has at least got people to begin thinking about the oppression of women. I don't think the women's liberation has as yet related to Black women. It's sort of paradoxical because Black women are the most exploited women . . . people *period* in this society because they are not only exploited as women but as workers and as being Black. It's three levels of oppression that they face in society.

I think Black women have been very turned off—I know I have—by the kinds of activities that the more vocal, prominent women's liberation groups have involved themselves in. Black women don't want to be associated with that kind of irrelevancy. The women's liberation movement has been made up of White middle class women, very tired of something but they aren't seriously dealing with what the problems are.

Another woman in her twenties, whose education had been received in the North, broke into a relatively long dissertation on women's liberation:

I think the whole movement is a revolt against the fact that there is an unnatural distinction in society between the male role and the female role. The male role is the achiever and breadwinner, the doer. The woman's role is the housewife, the mother, the passive role. There's no reason, there's no logical reason for making that distinction. Things should not be labeled masculine or feminine, or if a man does a dish in the house he compromises his masculinity. Masculinity should not be that easily compromised. Nor should femininity be compromised because a woman wants to have a Ph.D. I don't think the feminists really object to marriage. They say they do but I don't think that's where they're coming from. I think they're revolting against the distinction that is made between the male and female role, and the fact that a woman cannot fulfill herself or be a creative person in this society unless she's construed as masculine. I think their objections to marriage are that if a woman is not married by the time she is 25 there's a stigma attached to her. A man can go until he's 45 or however long he wants to and nobody questions him. There's no stigma attached to him. There's no reason why the marriage should be younger for women than men. There's just no reason why men should have that advantage over women. I think some Black women agree with a lot that's being done in that, but I don't think that Black women know why they are not participating in it. I don't think they realize why they can't get up enough emotion to participate in something like this. I think the reason is that there is a very big distinction between White women and Black women. White women are definitely cast in the role of homemaker, housewife, and mother. It's traditional for them not to do anything else; whereas, because of historical conditions, Black women have been favored economically and have been forced to get out and earn a living because society discriminated against their men so that they have a long history of careers, jobs, getting degrees and being professionals. It's much easier for a Black woman to get a job than a White woman. People going into big professions won't hire White women but they say they tell these White women, if you were Black or a Black woman we'd give you the job. As a White woman we just can't do that. So therefore this has created a situation where a very large majority of Black women have held jobs and have been allowed to be in a career. Therefore they are, in terms of the cultural ideal of the achievers, they are the freest women in western society. There's no other group of women in western society that has had the same economic opportunities to express themselves as Black women have. Therefore they don't need women's liberation. They have all those freedoms. They have economic freedom; they have intellectual freedom and most Black women grow up, if they are bright enough, expecting to get degrees, to go to college, to do creative things. If they're not doing it, it's because they've been influenced by the White middle class. They're trying to adopt the values of the White middle class. I think if they thought about it long enough they'd realize that they should keep their own values and they'd do a whole lot better. Black women are past that stage. They have achieved emancipation already. The only problem that they are facing now is that now that their Black men are coming into their own, Black men want their women to stay back and assume the position that the White woman has traditionally assumed. Black men want their women to be just like White women, the homemakers and the mothers. And Black women ain't going to do it because once you got freedom you do not give it up without a fight.

It was extremely interesting to see the extent to which Black women incorporated some of society's negative reactions to the feminist movement. Several themes emerged from the responses which not only are indicative of a generalized American reaction but also of a particularistic reply stemming from the Black community. One theme stressed the need for Blacks to examine their priorities. Examination, they felt, would then reveal little or no time for women's liberation since the priority item is Black liberation. As some women stated:

1. I think it could be relevant to the Black woman. I'm really not sure that's the way they're going to go. I'm in strict sympathy with it but I don't see if White women get their rights it's really going to have any real relevance to us. They've made some comments about Blackness in passing but it doesn't seem to be central to their movement. What we've

# Liberation Can Be a Trick Bag

seen before in movements, for instance, is that you could have a fine movement on but when it's translated into reality Black people are damned like hell. So they have my full blessings but it's not a priority item in my life.

*(From the Mid-west, a woman just turned 40)*

2. I think it's a twofold kind of thing. It's being pushed out there for Black women to get into and that is not our priority. Our priority is not women's lib. Black women will be liberated when all Black people are liberated. . . . That's really what it is: it's shit; some chicks that are really uptight and I really strongly believe that these are the women that can't get Black cats any more. They've been rejected by Black cats. . . . They are the reject. Because of their association with Black cats, they can't go into the White community and get no White cats, so they're all around, from what I've seen, screwing each other; and then they are going to try to get Black chicks to turn around and do the same thing. . . . For Black chicks to get hung up talking about I want equality means for us to go back and to begin to run after a Freedom Now phrase. . . . I can't be a liberated woman without a liberated man.

*(From the Mid-west, a woman in her thirties)*

3. I don't think we can afford to dissipate our energies in that direction. I recognize certainly that there is sex discrimination, nevertheless I don't think it affects Black women nearly as much as racism. I see the liberation movement as a real fun thing—you hear about them throwing their bras around and things like that. I get very tickled sometimes with some of the things they are doing.

*(From the East, a well-educated woman in her forties)*

4. I'm not interested in being involved. I have other concerns. I believe that sex discrimination exists. I

think it should be eliminated but I'm more concerned about racial discrimination.
(*From the West, a social worker in her mid twenties*)

Another theme stressed the frivolous nature of the movement, its tendency to draw attention from the real struggle of the day, and its orientation towards a White thing—even perhaps a Negro female thing. This theme, as did others, also tended to imply the superiority of Black females to White females.

1. I can only speak from my own experience but where they're coming from is where we've been—maybe two hundred years ago. In fact they enjoy the luxury of pining how bad off they have it; when the chips are down with the Betty Friedans and the Pat Burnetts they can go back to their diamonds. They can go back and play at being whatever they are. I don't think any of them are real people, involved in anything real. There are other things that deserve priority over the fact of womanliness. I think if you are a woman you have your liberation at least in your own sphere and you have the strength to etch it out for your own level of involvement. But I think the leadership of whatever this is called is so bad. God only knows what their goals are. To me, maybe a lot of publicity for White women to say aren't we great. Now we are equal to whoever they want to be equal to but there's no concern for the working woman who has to work every day, who has always worked, almost the matriarch of today. And how to be equal may also be to enjoy the privileges of a woman in terms of its comfort. These things are never approached. The people who are leading it now have never had to do anything so they're kind of thinking it's a game to get out there in the hard world. And they're still going about it with may I please

## Liberation Can Be a Trick Bag

do this rather than a strong approach in what they are attempting.

*(From the Mid-west, a writer)*

2. Well, the little bit I know about women's liberation is from White folks going out talking about they want to be equal with the man. Black women just don't do that kind of stuff. A lot of time Black women are equal with the man because they are the head of the household. So it's no big thing for a Black woman. White women, that's the time they have to waste 'cause they don't have to get out scrubbing floors and they ain't got no maid jobs, and they can get out and discuss stuff like that. The Black women can't do that.

*(A community worker from the South)*

3. I'm not really anti women's lib. I find it hard to relate to White organized, led movements. They tend to be faddish. They fade out once they get a little bit of what they want and many times they don't deal with Black needs. I agree with women being allowed to work where they want to. . . . The goals of Black women are different from White women because our experiences have been different. As a matter of fact there's nothing I dig more than a liberated Black man and I want to be submissive, go along with programs, and cook and have his kids and all the other kinds of things that make a woman a woman. And I think whenever Black men are liberated Black women will be fulfilled. The lib movement doesn't deal with this.

*(From the East, a civil servant)*

4. As it's being presented now, it doesn't relate to Black women, although Black women have a movement going on that I couldn't very well call liberation because the average Black woman is trying to get back to her rightful position with her man. We have been liberated by slavery already so we are un-

doing it and in that way it's basically a movement for White women and Negro women who have become overly involved in this system's thing. . . . It's not necessarily middle class. It's the average Negro woman who has had to take on responsibility for her family and has had very bad experiences with her men and in not understanding why they are all open to this movement because once a woman takes on the bread winning capacity and gets on the jobs and all of this which has turned her role entirely around; it's only natural that the next thing would be this type of competition. Realistically it's entirely out of focus; it's taking the woman out of her true domaine as mother. It's putting her on a competitive basis with men, Black or White, which is unrealistic to me. Women have a role. Men have a role and I think we need to go back and interpret these roles again and then start out again; but Black women of the Black movement do not adhere to the feminist movement.

(*From the Mid-west, a believer in astrology*)

5. I think it's awful. Most of the people who take part in that come from middle class White America. Those are the ones whose husbands fly here, to Atlanta for this, fly to Los Angeles for that. And women remain at home by themselves. They watch tv and most of the women are against marriage because their husbands are not there. They wake up, send the kid off to school and there's nothing else to do the whole day but to shop or look at tv. I don't believe 1% of the people in there are Black women. . . . All I see them going on about because men whistle at you, they don't like that. Now you have to go and whistle back at them. I think that's off. I don't like that, the women's liberation movement. I don't think women in this country are really the underdogs. They say that they are oppressed and suppressed. They want to be as equal

# Liberation Can Be a Trick Bag    43

as men but you can't have that, not in the same sense as the word equality. You can have equality on the racial level, where a whole race of people should be equal. But the women's liberation seems to be a different kind of equality. They deal mostly with two different behaviors for men and women. They claim the only honest woman is a prostitute. That's an insult 'cause then they're saying I'm not honest; other people are not honest. If Black women fall in that trap of the women's liberation movement, you going to mess up the family structure more than ever.
*(From the East, a student)*

6. I am for women's liberation; however, I find it very difficult and I turned the White gals down who head the women's liberation movement because they are on such a low level that what they're talking about is something I've never experienced. Back in (a month) when X attacked me and—we were all invited to the White House on national goals and he attacked me (on the basis that) I could certainly not represent anyone at the White House level because . . . I was seen in Y consorting with our enemies from Hanoi. That was his statement. At that time I was co-chairman of the Z. I helped organize that. My co-chairman was a man and he stood up and said that every woman needs to stand up. This is the first Black woman in P that X has attacked and men are going to do it and women you had better take a look at what's happening and what X said about this woman because you'll be next and you'll need to speak out. It was great. I got a standing ovation and two or three hundred people (were) there. They all agreed they were proud and all this shit. And then women's liberation came to me and said boy, you know we're for you but we will not write a letter to X at this time simply because a man said do it. See,

they're on that level. That's why when you talk about women's liberation I cannot deal with them on that level. And that's where they still are. They have a thing because they're the ones who have always been raised as a sex symbol. That's what they tell me, and they're the ones who always had to look pretty for the man and have the house clean for the man, not us, not Blacks. So the level women's liberation is on is just so far below me that I cannot join them. (*From the East, a 45 year old woman*) Note: The letters X, Y, Z, and P are used so that places and persons referred to may remain anonymous.

7. I don't think Black women have any role in the feminist movement. In fact I think the feminist movement is co-optation of the Black movement because I place it in the category of the population explosion, and the ecological environmental pollution movement. To me the battle of the sexes among middle class White women goes into the same category. What will be taken as the issue for the seventies? The seventies will be concerned with legalized abortion legislation, about curbing the population. They, the White middle class, will be concerned about cleaning up the streams and rivers and the land in the suburbs and they've never been concerned about pollution by rats running and biting babies, about plaster falling off the walls and babies eating it and getting lead poisoning. (*From the South, an educator*)

8. As far as I can read it, I read it in the context of White women because I don't see the relation to Black women. It's loose-ended White chicks doing all kinds of funny things trying to get somebody to acknowledge the fact that they are females. (*A college administrator from the East*)

9. Nobody has to tell a woman she's liberated. A woman is liberated if she wants to be. You don't

have to have posters to tell you that you are free. You are free anytime you want to be free. The whole thing is a farce. I think it's the most ridiculous thing I've ever heard. I can't imagine being— I mean how can men be our enemies? They're a natural component. They are the natural opposite. I have very little sympathy. I just can't understand what they're yelling about. Obviously the liberation of my people is far more important than the liberation of myself as a sex. As a woman, outside of being Black, looking at the women's liberation movement I see it as kind of a farce. It's just absurd. I can't understand what all the bitching is about. The whole thing to me is terribly blown out of proportion. I wouldn't run around in a horrible race—600 miles in the rain to prove that a woman can do it. Who really cares? Black women have never been discriminated as far as jobs. I think Black women are women for the most part. I've met some very shallow White women who have no sense of themselves as women, as sexual beings. I think Black women are much stronger than they are as human beings. I've never been discriminated against as a woman but I have as a Black person. (*An instructor from the East*)

10. I view White women and Black women as totally different. It's nothing alike between them except that they are the female sex. They are completely different. Their culture even from the beginning of time has been different. In their culture the man has been superior back as long as they can remember, even back in Europe long before they came to these lily White shores. They have been inferior. Back in our cultural background it tells us that it was a complementary system, that it was no superior or inferior; people worked together. It was a circle. Consequently women's liberation is not anything we can want together because we are

not alike. I think for them it's just their thing. Let
them do it. We got other things to do. We don't
have no time for women's liberation. (*From the
East, a recent high school graduate*)

Yet another theme emphasized the confusion in male/female roles accentuated by women's liberation. That is, several women viewed the movement as a divisive force between Black men and Black women, as an anti-female drive leading to the abandonment of certain essentially female roles in a quest to be like males, and as a force increasing the degree of male "homosexuality" and female "lesbianism." Some typical comments follow.

1. Most of my information has come from newspapers and talking to a few folk that have been in the movement and most of these women are White women. I can understand their viewpoint as far as equality of jobs, salaries, etc. But on the social aspect of it I think the Black woman's aims, as far as the struggle is concerned, should be a more unified type of fight, a more unified type of struggle with her Black man. The Black woman has always been at the head of the family, has always taken on a responsibility of support and I believe as far as Black people are concerned there is as far as women's liberation no place for it, to the point of putting the Black women in front of her man. (*A college student from the South*)
2. I think they want to create a definite identity for themselves as women and on an equal basis with men. They feel that they have been put in a subordinate role just because of their sex and ideally I can agree with them but only up to a certain point. As far as Black women are concerned I don't think we can afford at this point such luxuries as being able to come into conflict with our men. We need complete unity even if we have to sacrifice our

own identities as women at this point. (*From the East, a recent college graduate*)

3. I still feel that women have a place. I'm not saying that they should be under a man or a step lower, or second class citizens to a man. But for women to be yelling for equal rights, equal standards or equal something with the man, I think she's taking away something from being a woman. White women can do that. They can say their garbage all they want because they have been put up on a pedestal. They've been worshipped. They've been adored and they can afford to stand up and yell equal rights. But I think the Black woman ought to shut her mouth about equal rights until her man is placed where he should be. Let the White woman holler about equal rights.

( *A community worker from the East*)

4. I haven't followed it that closely. Some of the women I think have valid gripes but some of the women are fanatics. I don't think you should want to be equal to a man. A woman isn't physically constructed so that she's equal to a man. When she has a child, that takes really 18 years that it takes to help bring up that child out of her life. I just don't see the point of women's liberation. I really don't understand what it's all about. Maybe they feel suppressed and all like that but the Black woman I don't think has any cause to be in it because they have been with the jobs and working with the men. The White woman's been the one sitting home and taking care of her family. If she doesn't dig that, then that's her problem.

(*From the East, a recent high school graduate*)

5. I don't relate to that at all. I think that's (i.e. the sexual aspect of the feminist movement) all a part of the sick society, which White people have continued to live in, swallow in, wallow in, whatever; be-

cause as it is they have a growing amount of homosexuals and it's because of the bitch that the White woman is literally. She emasculates her man and the whole thing now is like the woman, she's so fully independent between the pill, being able to have sex whenever she feels like it, a man doesn't even have to go so far as to court anymore because if she wants to have sex with him she can. And if she wants to, she will and he has no role anymore. That's why you find so many White men, although I think it's inherent in them anyway, homosexuals more so now than ever; because you pick up a magazine and between the White men designers designing clothes so that when you walk behind someone on the street—because men and women now wear bell bottoms, because women now wear belts around their sweaters, because men now wear stringy vests —you don't know who's in front of you, besides the fact that the man's hair is now down to his shoulder. Don't believe this hasn't been planned. If you were a faggot and you were a designer, you could see the power, just the free hand you would have in determining exactly what kind of clothes women would wear and how they could begin to look just like you, also saying that you can look just like them and be accepted.

*(From the East, a college student)*

6. Everything I read about lesbianism (and the women's liberation movement) I definitely agree. I don't think that I agree with the women's liberation movement that women got to be free of all restraints and oppressions. They seem to forget you can't carry on a society loving other women. I'm looking at the point that if all women got together and decided to become lovers and all men got together and decided to become lovers, well the society would end right there.

*(A college student from the South)*

7. I'm afraid it's being taken over by some people who believe in a trend I don't like. Now I don't care what anyone does. That's their business whether they want to be homosexuals or whatever but I don't think they should inflict it upon the entire populace. I honestly believe men and women were created differently for a specific purpose. That is to replenish the earth and I certainly believe in that and I would not go along with anything that would change that type of set up. I think White people are sick. I really do. I think a woman can serve as an executive just as a man can and not relinquish her role as a woman. I think she should emphasize her feminity just as I want to emphasize my blackness regardless of wherever I go.
(*A writer from the Mid-west*)

Not every single comment about women's liberation was negative or derogatory. Even most of the women who levelled criticism at the movement recognized the value of the drive to end discrimination in employment. That is, efforts of organizations like WEAL (Women's Equity Action League) that are striving through arbitration, pressure and litigation to eliminate prejudice against female workers are constantly praised. A few purely laudatory comments were proffered about women's liberation. Samples of these are from a college junior in the West, a Southern community worker, and a Mid-western community worker:

1. There are different groups from one extreme to another but I think they serve a purpose of letting the world know that what they want is a little more recognition as far as jobs are concerned and positions. It's just like any other organization, there are some people who are trying to see how much awareness can be stirred up and then there are some who are genuinely concerned about the different positions that women hold and the different positions that men hold and the amount of money they are

paid for these positions to show that there is a bit of discrimination as far as women are concerned.

2. I think that liberation of women is just as important as liberation of Black people or any other minority group. Women, according to statistics, would not comprise a minority. Yet, we have been given inevitably this subordinate role in life, not only Black women but White women as such too. . . . I think that the time has been far spent for women to come out of this role they have been placed in, and to be treated as equals. Inevitably women are put into a position where they are always discriminated upon.

3. I don't think it's anything new. I recall according to history that women tried to do some liberating way back yonder when they waged a fight for women to vote. Is that not true? All right, so what's new? I'm for it. Yes, in every way I'm for it. I want the women to be liberated not only to vote but also to liberate their bodies.

It was thought that some of the complementary remarks would have been made as a result of Aileen Hernandez' Presidency of NOW. The fact that Aileen Hernandez headed NOW, however, did not seem to have penetrated far into the Black female community. Few women were able to identify any leaders of women's liberation let alone Aileen Hernandez. Of the few women who did connect Aileen Hernandez to women's liberation, most live in the West. This was not surprising since Aileen Hernandez also resided in the West at the time interviews were conducted. No unanimity of opinion could be detected among those few women who were cognizant of her work in women's liberation. In fact the women tended to be either solidly in favor of Aileen Hernandez or solidly opposed to her position. A couple of women felt she was rendering a valuable service to the female and the Black female community. Two or three others, feeling she was totally on the wrong track, suggested that she ought to abandon her work with women's liberation. Instead of continuing with women's lib, they contended, she

# Liberation Can Be a Trick Bag

should take on a project which would allow her talents to be used solely for the Black community.

Despite a generalized praise for women's liberation efforts in the employment field, few women saw a valid connection between the elimination of sexism and the cessation of racism. Several women found the idea so alien that they simply could not grasp the intent of the question at all and hence refused to deal with it. Of those women who did tackle the issue, the overwhelming majority saw absolutely no connection between sexism and racism. One who felt that there might be a connection (although she also rejected an alliance between White women and Black women as invalid) recalled the comments of a classmate during a discussion in one of the Black Studies courses organized in a western college:

> I had a class and we had a long discussion about that. And a brother felt if we break up everyone of the links in the chain they have created, then you would upset the entire system. So he said by just having the White woman in the women's liberation movement, by having her to change her role, that would be a change disrupting the system. . . . To me the women's movement wouldn't be our strongest ally, but it would be the one that would change the basic underlying ideas of this society, the western man, if we could change the western people. If that concept could go over it might help.

Nevertheless, even if sex discrimination were eliminated, most of the women concluded, the demise of race discrimination would not necessarily follow. A sampling of comments follows:

> 1. I don't agree with that theory. I don't see any relationship of a White female's position in society and that of Black people.
> (*From the East, a lawyer*)
> 2. It really wouldn't matter because if you take sex away you will still have the problem of racism.
> (*A teacher from the South*)

3. No, I don't think they go together. In fact, that's one of the things that peeves me so much. Any kind of talk about Black folks in this country always follows the woman in the country. You know they talk about discrimination against women and Blacks. . . . It just seems like the whole Black race, male and female, are linked up in a classification that's behind the White woman. I don't think they have anything to do with each other, only in so far as it affects the Black female. Where I really get upset is to see the Black male linked up in that thing too.
*(A housing investigator from the East)*

4. I think the psychic of human nature is that there always has to be someone or something that is looked down upon or discriminated against. I'm not saying that to say that I'd like Black people to always be in that position where they are discriminated against. But I don't think that the elimination of sexism will in any way hamper or help progress made by Black people. I think it must be a unified struggle and I think Black people will get their freedom and should get their freedom before any elimination of sexism.
*(A southern college student)*

5. Some say that but I can't see it. I can't see any connection between the two really because there are a lot of women who complain a lot about discrimination in employment and jobs that have absolutely nothing to do with racial discrimination. I can't see how that will alleviate the racial discrimination at all.
*(From the West, a poverty program worker)*

6. I think that the elimination of racism will foster the elimination of sexism. I think it's the other way around. I don't think women's lib can achieve their goals without getting rid of racism. I think that racism is so entrenched in our society it will take a major, major upheaval to change that. And along

with that upheaval then the other will probably follow in its track.
*(A scientist from the West)*

7. I feel that it may cause more racism in that people always have to have a scapegoat. Right now I feel racism is at a minimum because they can be prejudiced against women. When you remove the prejudice against women and they become on the same level as men, then it seems like the alternative would be to seek some other kind of scapegoat and racism would be ideal.
*(A social worker from the West)*

8. I think it's just another thing to cloud the issue of racism. If people get concerned about sex, ecology, and all these kinds of things, it's intended to make people forget about the real issue of racism.
*(From the West, a civil servant)*

Three recurring themes or issues run through our respondents' discussion of the women's liberation movement. One is the fear of cooptation or subordination of Black liberation goals through a merger of interests with women's liberation. That is, Black women perceive some of the short range and even long term objectives of women's liberation as diametrically opposed to those of the Black struggle. Therefore, to join women's liberation movements is tantamount to abandoning, at least temporarily, intensive efforts in behalf of Black liberation and becoming immersed instead both in frivolous activities such as liberation from bras, and more solid but lower priority matters such as ecological concerns. A second and related issue is the fear of undermining relationships between Black men and Black women. Given the history of Black people in an oppressive and racist society many Black women now insist on the need for Black men and women to rebuild the kind of strong interpersonal links which would permit Black male and Black female to engage in a concerted thrust for Black liberation. Can Black women realistically add their strength to women's lib and still hope to unite with Black men in a constant and persistent struggle for Black liberation? This is the question which many

Black women are posing as they formulate a stance towards women's liberation. The third theme is that of empathy for certain specific goals of women's liberation which touch on the functioning of the total American system. Some Black women regard with approval that segment of women's liberation which concentrates on economic concerns—particularly discrimination in employment. This is true, no doubt, because Black women too are fed up with discriminatory practices which relegate them to secretarial positions, or saddle them with salaries not commensurate with their educational backgrounds and total experiences, or lock them into low levels of rank with little hope for the kinds of promotion rates to which men are accustomed. It is this third theme which reveals Black women analyzing their positions in terms of the wider society, not solely as Black women but as women who are Black. It is this type of wider society analysis which may have led some women who are Black to work within certain women's liberation-type organizations. For example, at least nine of the conveners of the National Women's Political Caucus held in July 1971 were Black women. No doubt these Black conveners felt that part of their oppression in society could be terminated only if wider American societal attitudes toward women were radically reversed to facilitate access by women to political and economic positions in various American institutions. It may be that those Black women who are extremely mobile in terms of employment and political action will be most likely to ponder a link with women's liberation. These extremely mobile Black women may well have experienced barriers to advancement in the wider society, not primarily because of skin pigmentation, but mainly because of their sex.

Currently the first two themes seem to hold more significance for the overwhelming majority of women in our study. Few as yet tend to analyze their positions, as women who are Black, in terms of a wider American society. Thus one is forced to conclude that if women's liberation aims to be an umbrella group for all American women, it has failed in its protective cover as far as the Black female community is concerned. The Black women of our study view liberation of the women's variety, as they understand it, as simply another trick bag designed at the least to detract attention from the Black struggle, and at the most to hamper seriously efforts to make the Black struggle a truly meaningful one in the sense of Black male and female united and pushing towards the common goal of Black liberation.

### *Black Men and Black Women*

For many White Americans analysis of the Black family begins with an assertion that a matriarchal structure characterizes the Black male/Black female relationship. By that they mean to say that Black males play no significant role in the Black family, that indeed the Black male may walk away after having fathered "umpteen" children—leaving a suffering Black female to cope with an odious burden of raising and feeding the family. Through the postulation of a matriarchy in the Black family, Whites (including White sociologists) mean to imply that the Black male may be found on the street corner sipping wine with his fellow family deserters, or gambling away his last fifty cents, or hustling in the Black community, or wandering around aimlessly and hopelessly, a completely defeated man. On the other hand, the Black woman may struggle up each morning, travel to her place of employment, put in long working hours, return home to cook and feed her children, help them with their school lessons, wash clothes, and clean the living quarters.

Perhaps the one person who popularized the "plight" of the Black family with its matriarchal structure more than anyone else was Daniel Moynihan. In the mid–sixties he released his now famous and controversial report on *The Negro Family: The Case for National Action* (Washington, D.C.: U.S. Government Printing Office, 1965). The report was compiled during his tenure as Assistant Secretary of Labor. (See also: Lee Rainwater and William L. Yancey, *The Moynihan Report and the Politics of Controversy* Cambridge: M.I.T. Press, 1967).

What incensed many Blacks about the Moynihan report and the subsequent generalization about Black families and their matriarchal structure, was that its interpretation represented a gross exaggeration. As of March 1965, according to Alphonso Pinkney and the United States Bureau of Census, "72 percent of all black families were composed of both husband and wife. . . ." (Alphonso Pinkney, Black Americans, Englewood Cliffs: Prentice-Hall, 1969, p. 93). Or, stated in different terms, "In 1965 . . . one-fourth of all black families were headed by women. . . ." (Pinkney, 1969, p. 96). Admittedly these statistics are higher for the Black population than for the Whites where 87% of their families found husband and wife together, and 9% of them were headed by White females. (Pinkney, 1969, pp. 93, 96). The 1970 census figures revealed a slight increase in the number of Black families headed by women. "In 1971, 29 percent of families of Negro and other races, compared with about 9 percent of white families, were headed by a woman." This represented an increase from .9 million in 1960 to 1.6 million in 1971 for "Negro and other races" and from 3.3 million in 1960 to 4.4 million in 1971 for Whites. (U.S. Department of Commerce/Bureau of the Census, "The Social and Economic Status of Negroes in the United States, 1970," 1971, p. 4). Parenthetically one should note that the phrase "Negro and other races" "describes persons of all races other than white" but "about 90 percent" of this category represents Blacks. (See "Notes" to "The Social and Economic Status of Negroes in the United States, 1970"). But, as Professor Pinkney points out: "Although there is widespread family disorganization frequently manifested in matriarchal family patterns, in a vast majority of black families, as in white families, dominance is shared between the mother and father (egalitarian pattern) or vested in the father (patriarchal pattern)." (Pinkney, 1969, p. 97). Moreover, the socio-economic source of much of the Black family instability must be placed clearly in focus. The higher the family income for both Blacks and Whites the less likely are parents to be divorced or separated. "At family income levels of $10,000 to $14,999 for both races, nearly all children live with both their parents. However the proportion drops sharply for families with incomes under $3,000—about 24 percent of Negro and 44 percent of white children in families in this income group lived with their parents in 1969. A very large share, about two-thirds, of the children in families headed by Negro women were in low income families in 1969." (The Social and Economic Status of Negroes in the United States, 1970, p. 4).

Assertions of a Black matriarchy also imply not only the ease with which Black women allegedly may secure employment but also a superior income, at least to that of Black males if not also that of White females. Yet as Professor Robert Staples reminds us: "It is a rather curious use of logic to assume that black females, who in 1960 earned an annual wage of $2,372 a year as compared to the annual wage of $3,410 for White women and $3,789 for black men, have an economic advantage over any group in this society." (Robert Staples, "The Myth of the Black Matriarchy," *The Black Scholar*, Vol. 1, No. 3–4, January–February, 1970, p. 11). Although the 1970 census figures revealed an increase in median income for both White and Black women, the median income still is extremely low. "In 1969, Negro women working 50 weeks or more had a median income level of $4,126, about 80 percent of the $5,182 for white women who worked the same length of time." (The Social and Economic Status of Negroes in the United States, 1970, p. 124). Furthermore, according to 1969 statistics the Black male median income stood at $5,130 compared to $2,808 for Black females. (The Social and Economic Status of Negroes in the United States, 1970, p. 33).

Is it any wonder, then, that generalizations about a Black matriarchy have been denounced so vehemently by various quarters of the Black community? In an interesting article entitled, "Is the Black Male Castrated?" Jean Carey Bond and Patricia Peery write:

> Moynihan and his gang postulate that Black society is matriarchal, and that Black women have been the primary castrating force in the demise of Black manhood. The casting of this image of the Black female in sociological bold relief is both consistent and logical in racist terms, for the so-called Black matriarch is a kind of folk character largely fashioned by whites, out of half-truths and lies about the involuntary condition of Black women. . . . A matriarchal system is one in which power rests firmly in the hands of women. We suggest that whatever economic power may accrue to Black women by way of the few employment escape valves permitted

them by the oppressing group for their own insidious reasons, this power is really illusory and should not be taken at face value.
(Toni Cade, *The Black Woman*, 1970, pp. 116–117).

Robert Staples states simply: "The myth of a black matriarchy is a cruel hoax." (Staples, 1970, p. 8). He continues, exploring his reasons for describing the black matriarchy as a cruel hoax:

It is adding insult to injury to black liberation. For the black female, her objective reality is a society where she is economically exploited because she is both female and black; she must face the inevitable situation of a shortage of black males because they have been taken out of circulation by America's neo-colonialist wars, railroaded into prisons, or killed off early by the effects of ghetto living conditions. To label her a matriarch is a classical example of what Malcolm X called making the victim the criminal. . . . Any profound analysis of the black matriarchy proposition should reveal its fallacious underpinnings. Recognition of this fact raises the crucial question as to why white society continues to impose this myth on the consciousness of black people. This writer submits that it has been functional for the white ruling class, through its ideological apparatus, to create internal antagonisms in the black community between black men and black women to divide them and ward off effective attacks on the external system of white racism. It is a mere manifestation of the divide-and-conquer strategy, used by most ruling classes through the annals

of man, to continue the exploitation of an oppressed group.
(Staples, 1970, pp. 8, 15)

In a most informative paper read before the July 1971 annual meeting of the National Urban League, Robert Hill stressed the need to retreat from a "pathological" perspective of the black

# Liberation Can Be a Trick Bag

family which emphasizes "instability, disintegration, weakness" and to readopt instead an approach, reflected in the writings of W. E. B. DuBois, Charles Johnson, St. Clair Drake, Horace Cayton, Andrew Billingsley, Elizabeth Herzog, Hylan Lewis, Charles Valentine, and Joyce Ladner, which highlights the "strengths of Black families." These strengths are identified as: "strong kinship bonds, strong work orientation, adaptability of family roles, strong achievement orientation, strong religious orientation." Careful examination of "adaptability of family roles" points toward a rejection of a matriarchal syndrome as typical of most Black families. As Hill states, "Although the literature is replete with references to a 'matriarchal tradition' among black families, most empirical data suggest that an 'equalitarian' pattern is characteristic of most black families." "Moreover," according to Hill, "the husbands in most black families are actively involved in decision-making and performance of household tasks that are expected of them. And most wives, while strong are not dominant matriarchs, but share with their husbands the making of family decisions—even in low-income black families." (Hill, *The Strengths of Black Families*, New York, Emerson Hall Publishers, Inc. 1972).

Most women in our study refused, or did not, discuss Black males and Black females in terms of a matriarchy. In fact, those who employed the term did so only to castigate its use. As some women said:

1. I think it's bullshit. I think it's coming from their point of view which is totally irrelevant in terms of ourselves. What they see as weaknesses are in fact strengths.
  (*A 35 year old woman from the West*)

2. I think the matriarchy is a White man's dream and a racist nightmare to begin with. As a matter of fact I really don't accept too much of the sociological jargon that an oppressor puts on you in terms of definition. I don't see where a poor old Black widowed mother is a matriarch because she doesn't vamp on her young or eat them, turn cannibalistic or

kill them. Certainly if Queen Elizabeth of England isn't a matriarch, or the rulers of India and Israel are not matriarchs, and Lurleen Wallace when she took over from George wasn't a matriarch, then I really can't understand how some Black welfare mother who gets a measly check is a matriarch.
(*A 42 year old college teacher*)

3. This matriarchy thing bugs me. Like I read this long report this guy made up about the psychological effects of the females being stronger than the males in past roles and all that crap.
(*A 24 year old library clerk from the West*)

4. I think the Black woman is powerful and always has been powerful and it's necessary to be powerful. We'll have to save ourselves and our men too because the system has crushed the men so bad. I don't think that the men should be listening to what Moynihan and others have to say because they're not in any position to have any discussion of any of us at any time.
(*A beautician from the East*)

On the other hand, three or four women recognized the matriarchy as a distinct problem in the Black community:

1. It's a problem in the Black community because there's been a matriarchal system and Black women are very much aware of the fact that Black women dominate Black men per se—in areas like jobs and their homes. And they're very conscious of it and they try to exert as much control of "manhood" as possible. It's very disturbing.
(*A 17 year old high school student from the Midwest*)

2. I feel that the Black woman in most of the families I know plays too strong a role, definitely too strong a role and sometimes I feel maybe the man wants her to. I think maybe to a large degree you can see

# Liberation Can Be a Trick Bag

situations like—where do you want to go? Well, anywhere you want to go. Now if he wanted to go he should have said I want to go so and so but a lot of times he waits for her to make a decision. It's not all her fault. Possibly it's just the way things are. I don't know why.
(*A 17 year old recent high school graduate from the East*)

3. Talk to the dudes and they'll tell you that Black women have been made into a matriarchal society. I would have to agree. This has been because of White men preying on Black women. My sister has 100 students to be tutored to get into college. Four out of five have no fathers. From just that I would have to say there has to be a matriarchy.
(*A 21 year old college student from the West*)

Some of those who admit to the existence of a matriarchy or a predominate female role in the Black family structure decry it, among other reasons, because of its tendency to smother male attempts at self-assertion and male manifestations of aggressiveness. Born and raised in a pervasively racist society with predilections for castration and violence toward Black males, Black females instinctively spreading their protective wings, urged—indeed insisted and compelled—their Black sons to hide anger behind a smile, to grit teeth instead of punching bellies, to employ pleasant diplomatic language rather than surly, blunt, and hostile tones, to change sides of the street to avoid walking past a group of whiskey drinking, giggling White men—all out of a deeprooted fear that this society would tear precious sons away from them before they could reach adulthood. Evidence of the matriarch's clipping the wings of incipient manhood was recorded by George Jackson, brother of Jonathan, in a brief autobiographical statement:

> It always starts with mama, mine loved me. As testimony of her love, and her fear for the fate of the manchild all slave mothers hold, she attempted to press, hide, push, capture me in the womb. The conflicts and

contradictions that will follow me to the tomb started right there in the womb. The feeling of being captured . . . this slave can never adjust to it, it's a thing that I just don't favor, then, now, never.
(George Jackson, Soledad Brother. *The Prison Letters of George Jackson*, New York: Bantam Books, 1970, pp. 9–10)

Even though George Jackson could assert, "It always starts with mama, mine loved me," we were curious to discover just what Black females were thinking about Black males: did they in reality reveal a love for Black males, or at least respect and confidence in their abilities to direct the Black struggle? In an effort to secure responses to these questions we asked the women of our study to discuss their perceptions of the role of Black women in the Black revolution and their interpretations of just what Black men were after and trying to accomplish against the background of revolution.

A few women did not even get to a discussion of roles. Instead they bemoaned—some quite extensively—what they considered very negative qualities of Black men, all the while implying an impossibility of seeing men in any kind of leadership role or working with them in any serious manner. These negative qualities included obnoxiousness, helplessness, weakness, and the development of a kind of closed Black male society bordering on, or at least reminiscent of, homosexuality. Said a 27 year old typist from the West:

> I find that with the Black man having the role now he has become so overbearing until actually it's hard to know what to do because I think in many ways he's lost. He's really never had this role to really play. Now this thing of "I am now the man" is like there's no sitting down and discussing anything. It's more or less, "I'm the man of this family. Now you got to do what I say do, not work."

# Liberation Can Be a Trick Bag

The alleged helplessness of Black males was underscored by a 22 year old college student from the East:

> People have to help themselves. It's condescending to go to a man and try to help him. The only thing you can do is within your womanhood help him find his manhood, because that's the opposite of you. There is a common misunderstanding between Black men and Black women. We just don't get along. It's very strange. We have to understand that to be a man is so much more different than to be a woman. There are so many demands put upon a man and a Black man especially, this generation especially. It is the redeeming of an entire history—we're Black men. What can you do in a helpless position? Men are probably more helpless than before because they are confronted with a situation: be a man, but at the same time what is a man? . . . I don't think you should condescend a man into saying I will bow. I'll just pretend that I'm not the woman I am so he'll think he's better than I am. It's like trying to lose a game of chess to a man. It's saying in a sense I know I can beat you if I really try, so I'll lose. That's bullshit. If you really, really believe in Black people and what they are, there's no need to bow for anyone. You can be your perfect old aggressive self and he will learn to deal with you. Or, he will learn not to deal, and he has to learn to deal. I've known some beautiful men and I've never had any problem with men who are men.

What this eastern college student seems to be saying, then, is yes, helplessness is characteristic of Black men in general but there are exceptions. Moreover a Black woman confronted with a "helpless" Black man should not conceal her own talents just to give the Black man a feeling of leadership and power because such a feeling will be illusory, clearly illusory. Two other women stressed the allegedly weak qualities of Black men, one a former nun from the South, the other a 45 year old woman from the East who seemed to see nothing positive in Black males during her lengthy dissertation on the subject. Their comments follow:

1. The Black men here, they simply don't give a darn. They don't want to get up and better themselves. Then if someone bring it up it's all talk talk and no action. Everybody's afraid to take action. Take for instance when they had this strong thing going about segregation of schools. It was a good opportunity for them to show themselves and to show that they are real men and stand up, but they hid behind the children. They want the school children to get out there and stand up but they don't want to stand up. That's what gets my goats. I get ready to shoot them when they do that. I can't stand them. That's why I feel that the Black woman have an important role to play because if she doesn't do anything all these men going to do—I'm going to tell you like it is— any time a man—I call him less than a man—when he stoop low enough to go down and grab these little girls out of the baby crib, 13 years old, to me this don't give me no type of respect, not anything for me to hold on to, to look up to a man and say he's going to be a good leader for me because he's not. He got to learn to control his ownself and then maybe he could get out there and really tell the White guy where he stands. You can't even force them to tell a White guy where he stands. Those that do have views and good points to say, they don't say it because those other guys that's hanging around with these young kids and drop them, pull them down; instead of men building up the society or community, they pulling it down. They're dragging it in the dirt. To me they just darn scared. If they not scared and if they can dip so low, look like to me at least you can take one out of ten to make him stand up but you can't. I don't know what the reason for it is. It's like this, a woman—I

# Liberation Can Be a Trick Bag

realize the garbage they say about a woman supposed to be under her man, but that doesn't hold true any more baby. These days are gone. In many cases the woman is the man of the house. Let's face it. And because of this I really think the world is not going to move until the women get in there and do something about it. The men are gone bye-bye. Ain't no more for him; messed up his good days.

2. It is Black men who have put their foot on a woman's neck, faster than a White man will because he has more respect for his strength. The whole struggle of Black men trying to find who they are and where they are causes them to push the Black woman farther back than he would ever attempt to push a White woman and certainly not be on a real par with her. I think today the power structure is trying to do its best to develop Black men.

There was a time when women were saying we've got to project Black men; we've got to do it. You work so hard trying to do that until you get nothing accomplished and then as soon as the Black man realizes where he is, who does he put his foot on? The woman who pushed him. You could find very few Black men on picket lines here, a very safe place to picket. Who did you see? You'd see a lot of Black women out there, a lot of Whites and children but few Black men. I think that they were saying I can't walk that picket line because there may come a time when I'll have to suffer some reprisal on my job. So you begin to produce Black men and you write speeches for him and you have them giving these speeches and by and large they'd finally say I'll take the lead. You go back in the house. This has happened. Many men said to me, 'You ought to be home taking care of your children.' I said, 'Look, I got my children right here and I'm taking care of them.' 'Your husband ought to be ashamed of yourself letting you out here;' when all I was saying was,

'Well I shouldn't be out here either: you ought to be out here. Take my place on this line.' And he would say, 'No, I'm not going to take your place. I got a job.'

Even as we talk about public assistance to families the government came up with a law that (said) if a man is in the house the family cannot get any public assistance. So this helped to deteriate the manpower simply because I think women are a stronger people and can endure more. But you do have many many families where the system has aided the man in really leaving the family so it could get some help. Men did not have that umph that you need to stand up and say I'm not leaving my family. You got to help me. When that law was changed who had a lot to do with changing it? Women, not men. I don't know why the weakness in men, except the history today. But even today you find men selling out much faster than women, getting tired, giving up, saying what's the use, much faster than women. It's very hard for a woman to be pushed when she has for a hundred years been the strong moving force in the family. And suddenly you try to project Black men. This is the Black woman trying to project him into a leadership role and you find that he is not standing up to it, that we move further behind than in front.

I believe in equality. I don't believe the woman should be super the man. I think they should be equal and I think the man needs to assume that role of being equal. And I think it's the only way it should be. Women are naturally something stronger than men and men are so tied up on this damn thing called projecting masculinity, that, 'I wear the pants in this house.' What does that mean? He's not working. The woman makes more money than he makes. He begins to feel inferior somewhat. Women too have to learn that control, that it does not neces-

# Liberation Can Be a Trick Bag

sarily make me superior because I have more income than you have.

But it's hard to control that when a man tries to push you back into washing the dishes, back into doing all the cleaning, and he doesn't help any and you are both working. It tells you right there who's the stronger. The man is not strong enough to decide that he's got to share in the whole upkeep of the family. Once you attempt to give them that feeling (of power over the family) most fathers are not capable of making decisions. They say, 'Go ask your mother.' It happened in my own family and my husband was good. I never wanted for anything like that but the kids would want to do something and I would say, 'Why don't you talk to your daddy about it?' And they'd go, 'Daddy. . . .' 'Go ask your mother.' I think they are fearful of making a mistake, fearful of making a wrong decision. It's a lot of fear that comes out of them that they won't be able to support it once they make it. I think it's very important that men take the role, but why do Black men beat their wives more on Saturday night? They hate everything and had a bad week and a bad job. Why do they beat their wives? That's that whole instinct that's been imbedded in them for a long time: you got to be brutal in order to be superior or unequal and I have so many difficulties with that. While I think it's important (to give men power) I think somebody has to develop how do we really do it? How do you do it? Can the man control the power that he gets? Is he willing to stop being fearful of making a mistake or a wrong decision and do something? I have real difficulties because I see men so weak, so weak.

And, a 23 year old mid-western graduate student related how she had drawn the conclusion that Black men were being transformed into a closed society seemingly patterned after that of homosexuals:

When I first came here there seemed more of a unity in the organizations—men and women working together; but then about the time the Black student organization started at (X) it was headed by two men. I was taking notes at the first meeting I think, then they asked me if I would be secretary. I remember the first committees that were formed. The committee I was on, there were 12 men and I was the only sister on it. Other committees were about the same. They had men chairmen and women working as secretaries or recorders. Other political organizations are organized along those lines. The difference there, and the thing I have seen change over now, then there was a big thing growing around the country through Project Woman Power and some of the other women's movements or groups of women that would come in and talk with sisters. They were going through this big thing that Black women had been leaders for a long time so you have to be quiet and you have to take this submissive role to men. This lends a lot of negative things I feel because it was really like saying in order for a man to be a man women have to sit in the back. Men that accepted this began to treat women in more of a subjective or removed type of position.

Over the past three year period it's changed into another thing where I see now a lot of just groups of men together and you don't see them in association with women at all. I see really developing just a strange kind of group of men that are treating Black women in kind of a way that you are not really there. It's almost like a glass pane. There are a lot of sisters I've talked to who are secretaries and they come to work and work for Black cats in some of the newer political offices, urban development offices and different businesses that have grown up since the riots. Like they say cats come in and they act like they don't even see them. They don't relate to them as women. They don't say, 'You look nice.' They don't say, 'How do you feel today?'

Or, 'Wow you're pretty today.' They don't make any of those type suggestions. They just spend the whole day in association with the men.

My husband and I have talked about it a lot and he said he's seen it. And brothers that he knew before didn't act this way and are going into really strange things so I don't know whether it's a result or a response to that or not. But I just feel a strange thing happening between Black men and Black women. And a lot of Black sisters are leaving the country or leaving the city, going to other cities looking for the men. It seems like the men have just moved from a position of saying we are going to take the leading role within organizations to saying we're going to assert ourselves as being totally independent of women which is something— well from the outside it looks like a form of homosexuality. On the other hand it's different from the old homosexualities of men which is obviously effeminate. It's like saying if we stay around women they're going to dominate us so we're just going to remove ourselves and then we're going to set up our own superior thing over here. We're not going to let women in so if they're not in they can't affect us. I don't know what it is but I see it. And it bothers me. I don't know whether it's a reaction to matriarchy or women going into this big thing three or four years ago of saying well we're going to be quiet and let men speak out, that concept we have to let them be men.

Although these few critical comments about Black men were forthcoming, most women tended to see specific roles for both men and women in the Black struggle. Yet there was little unanimity in what the nature of these roles ought to be. The debate centered around whether or not Black women ought to have a subordinate, supportive, non-leadership role; or whether there should be an egalitarian role for women and men; or whether a unique, civic-type role ought to be carved out for the Black woman. The two dominant opposing positions were highlighted in two articles appearing in *The Black Woman*. One relates the experience of a college student trying to function within a Black student organization:

> During the break before the workshops began, the chairman invited us all to the refreshment table and urged the Sisters to help out in the kitchen. This would not have been so bad except that during the formation of work committees, the sisters were arbitrarily assigned to man the phones and the typewriters and the coffeepots. And when a few toughminded, no-messin'-around politico Sisters began pushing for the right to participate in policy-making, the right to help compose position papers for the emerging organization, the group leader would drop his voice into that mellow register specially reserved for the retarded, the incompetent, the lunatic, and say something about the need to be feminine and supportive and blah, blah, blah.
> (Cade, 1970, pp. 162–163)

The other position was stated by Frances Beale in her article, "Double Jeopardy: To Be Black and Female":

> Old people, young people, men and women, must take part in the struggle. To relegate women to purely supportive roles or to purely cultural considerations is dangerous doctrine to project. Unless Black men who are preparing themselves for armed struggle understand that the society which we are trying to create is one in which the oppression of *all members* of that society is eliminated, then the revolution will have failed in its avowed purpose.
> (Cade, 1970, p. 100)

As a result of the history of America's treatment of Black males, many women in the study felt that the role of the female should be supportive and that the male ought to be the dominant force in the struggle. Evident in many of the statements was a belief that Black men needed help from women—especially of the moral nature which means that women would encourage the man, instill strength in him, demonstrate respect for him, and give him a needed push. Others stated the supportive role more in terms of activities in which Black women could become involved, activities which related not so much to giving males moral support, but to carving out specific tasks which women could perform.

1. I think the woman should be behind the man. The man should be up first before the woman because Black woman has been over Black man through time in this country. Through no fault of their own they acquired better jobs and better status. They weren't equal to the White men and women but they were above Black men. And now that the revolution is taking place socially I think Black women shouldn't be foremost in the life. I think it should be Black men 'cause men represent the symbol of the race.
2. We should stand by our men and try not to take the leading role, unless it's necessary. If a man is not present to take the role the woman must be ready to. In some ways (a woman should play a) subordinate (role) but not to an extreme; just enough to make Black men feel like White men have always felt: superior. You have to start from that. If it means sometimes catching yourself back a little bit, I think that's acceptable and necessary.
3. I feel that the Black woman today got to have a role simply because it appears to me that it's the woman's duty to sort of give the men the courage.
4. I think number one the Black woman should have more respect for her Black man, bolster his ego but not humble herself. She should make him feel like he is king or all important, that he is somebody.
5. Women take on the supportive roles which we have found here is very rewarding because it allows the woman just to be, to vibrate as she really is. The

woman's mind works fast but it is not as thorough as man and the woman don't stand up to pressure as well as men but in a supportive position she has a chance to react and to be emotional and whatever and to make her point; then the man takes it and in his cold calculated way deals with it and the decisions are made and everybody is happy.

6. I think in anything a man does, Black, White, red or yellow, it's got to be either a mother, sister, wife, something feminine behind him to keep him going. I can't help but feel that way. Take Eldridge Cleaver. I think he has gone forth more and he's more outspoken since he married than before. I think a woman will give a man just that feeling, just that edge, just enough to make him go farther than he's been going.

7. I think a Black female can be one of the greatest assets in the revolution or in the struggle. I think Black women have a history of perseverance and strength. I would not like to see that strength turn into domineering tendencies or bossism but I do think we can be that silent strength that the Black man needs to fight the battle for his wife or his woman and his family.

8. I think we should be willing to be isolated because it's so beautiful to have Black men doing their thing that I don't have any quarrel with them. I'm willing to make cookies, lemonade, and whatever. I was very upset about it. Almost all of our real radical movements heretofore had been led by Black women. And I think it's beautiful now that Black men are taking these places.

9. Our commitment to our brothers is to let the brothers understand 1) the whole question of liberation, that is, when we talk about liberation we're talking about land, that we have control of the land and it's resources. Our commitment to brothers is we will be behind them as long as their commitment

# Liberation Can Be a Trick Bag

> is that—no matter what that means. If that means that I go out and scrub floors for the brother to be able to carry out that particular thing, then that's what I do and I understand that. As sisters we have a responsibility to sisters and brothers who are in exile. We have the responsibility to those sisters, the responsibility to those brothers' children, to those families. . . . The Fred Hampton's shouldn't have to worry about a thing. Black people should be responsible for them.

In contrast to a supportive role for Black females, quite a few women interviewed stressed the necessity of egalitarian roles— that is that Black male and Black female must share equally in the duties and responsibilities of the Black struggle. Some welcomed the egalitarian pattern as a release from the tendency of women to assume a more dominant role in the movement. Moreover those who adhered to the egalitarian position emphasized that no specifically female or male tasks existed. A couple of these women deplored the fact that some Black men were trying to create male roles which epitomized leadership and female roles which consisted of menial or less important tasks as typing or cooking.

> 1. We are strong women. I personally feel that we are the only true model of what a woman is within this entire society because we've always been liberated. We always had to go it on our own. We've always been allowed to, within the constraints of society, to develop to some extent. But moreover, in terms of our relationship to the White world it was Black women who had to negotiate the White world and the Black world. She was the buffer between the White man and the Black man because the White community refused to deal with her man. He either eliminated him or dealt with his woman, but he wouldn't deal with him as a man. That's what Black men are saying now. You deal with me instead of

with my woman. So I think Black women have transmitted a very lively resourcefulness and a very healthy and stable model of womanhood to our young girls. It is a forthright determination to withstand all kinds of odds. That's necessary now. In order to continue to survive we need to capitalize on those strengths. The other part of it is that we must recognize that we are dealing with a different Black man today and that he must be given all the opportunity to assert himself. So I just simply take a position that it is not necessary for Black women to step into the background so that man can step forward. I think we all can move forward together.

2. Strangely enough in Black literature you'll find that women have been isolated to the point where if they are mentioned, which they're usually not, they're mentioned in a negative sense. They're always running to some White man or something—especially in Chester Himes where most of his books are about Black women that go for White men, and that kind of thing. In current movements you'll find that most women have to take a place subordinate to the men. They either have to be quiet and say nothing or their role is to build up the man by taking a step down in a sense. Most of the leaders of it (student movement in college) are men. There are very few women, none that I know who actually take a position of leadership when it comes to the activities out there. I don't think it's fair. I think we're going from one extreme to another. I think women are valuable to the men and that we must work together. We really can't go from the extreme of female dominance if you wish to male dominance. We're both needed. We can reach a point of unity where we can work together as a unit and not as one over the other, one dominating the other.

3. I do a lot of lecturing and when I lecture I tell people if you want to know what your role in the

revolution is, tell me what you do and I'll tell you what your role is. If you're a teacher, stop teaching this institutionalized racism which Black and White teachers promote. If you're a nurse, liberate enough stuff for a first aid station in your home. Put that up; you never know when it's going to be needed. Whatever you do, if you're only a day worker, in every home you work there's a gun there —under the head of that bed, in the table drawer beside the bed, in the top dresser drawer. Now if you're smart you can just liberate that weapon and take it on your way to the bus stop and drop it in the trash can and tell the brothers where it is. You don't even have to carry it home. It can never be traced to you. If you're a social worker, stop harassing people and acting like it's your money. You're there to serve people? O.K., serve people.

4. I think there just can't be any difference between the role that a Black woman plays and the role a Black man plays, absolutely none except in terms of physical limitations. That would be the only limitations I would place on the role of the Black woman and I don't place that, nature does. I think that Black women have to be able to shoot a gun. I think Black women have to be able to organize people. I think they have to be able to chair a meeting. I think they have to be able to do all the things that men are now looked to to do. I think on the other hand that men have to learn how to wash dishes, change diapers, sweep the floor and do all the things women have to do. I don't think there should be any kind of division of labor in that sense at all.

Still a few other members of the sample saw a unique role for Black females, a role which stressed social concern and personal, feminine qualities. Most often the social concerns involved supervising the education and rearing of children; encouraging the

husband to proceed with his education; training Black males so
that they may assume some positions held heretofore by Black
females, and becoming more aware and conscious of phenomena
taking place in the universe, particularly events having an impact
on Black people. A couple of women thought that Black females
should now seek to take on certain purely feminine traits and
just simply enjoy the role of being a woman.

1. Black women, in a special sense, are the mothers of Black children, or the women who have the children. They have to especially be ahead and a vanguard in a movement of trying to re-educate their children and at the same time negating the power which the White establishment has given them and refusing to become a part of it because it has been used against their men. So what has to happen is that the Black woman has to be very important in the education of her children.
2. I think that the Black woman has a specific role to play. First with her immediate family: to see that her family is educated, well fed and well trained in the home. And she has the responsibility of seeing that all those of voting age should be registered and able to vote. She has a role of seeing that her children be brought up in Sunday School and Church. The best thing is upgrading the community where they live. She has a duty to perform there to see that her children try to be a part of the best things—to be in the best schools.
3. She has a real role to play in the Black struggle. She should stay at home and raise her family and help the community and maybe she can help someone else—the Black people.
4. (The role of the woman should be) to use her intellect, her patience, her infinite understanding to perceive what is going on, what people are about, what's motivating them.
5. I really think the biggest thing Black women could

do would be to help Black men get an education, to be willing once Black men are prepared to give up some of the power they have. You'll talk to them and they'll say they don't have any power but Black women do have power. I'm not saying Black women ought all be demoted. I get very uptight about this Black man, Black woman thing where some Black man strolls in here with green on green, hippitty hopping, telling me "Get out from behind that desk. I want your job." I'm not talking about that. I'm talking about preparing Black men to take over when they (women) can no longer do their thing. Black women ought to be working. They ought to be doing things like working in the schools. They ought to be being sure that there's Black men prepared to take their place.

6. I believe the Black woman is definitely trying to become more of a woman because this is something that we always have wanted to be but because of conditions we just weren't able to be, but I believe now that the Black woman wants to become a woman.

7. The men take on the leadership position mostly because we just sit back and let them do it but I don't think I mind because I have played the role of being man and woman in my family for quite some time. I would give the world to just going back and being a woman again. That's the way I feel. I would like to wake up in the morning and say well there's a man there saying I'll take care of this and I wouldn't have to take care of it. I'd feel like if I was liberated if I says well I think you should take care of this this morning and he would say well, o.k.

Two or three women saw the ideal roles for Black males and Black females as a kind of paradoxical hybrid—that is, neither supportive nor egalitarian but a combination of the two.

1. I think the struggle of Black people is much too important to get into who should lead at this point. I think that when Black men really recapture their manhood then they should go out for one reason only and that is that the male has been emasculated. He has been stripped of his manhood by this White, racist society. For that reason I think we should project our men in the forefront really. But where women have abilities I think they should assume the roles. Where a man has reached his manhood, it doesn't make too much difference to him. Only a leader who feels secure can be a true leader because then he becomes self-effacing.
2. My feeling in terms of both Black men and Black women is that whatever we do has to be seen in terms of mutuality—that we can no longer define each other in terms of some artificial criteria, that is, you as a Black woman must do a, b, c and d. I think it has to be based on some kind of mutuality in terms of our own personal histories and, in addition, to the larger history of Black people in this country. My personal commitment is one of certainly support both mentally and morally, physically. I think it's very important that we understand where we're coming from and that we begin to deal with each other on a basis of respect. In terms of my own personal commitment particularly for those brothers who are beyond the stage of giving lip service and engaging in mere rhetoric of the revolution, it's certainly a very definite supportive and active participation in whatever projects, in whatever is going on. We can no longer really afford to adhere to some kind of artificial criteria or some sort of role definition. I think that whatever skills, whatever talents we as Black people have, whether it be a Black woman or a Black man, we have to utilize them to the fullest if we are going to have any kind of productivity in the revolution.

## *Black Men and White Women*

Although no specific question on relations between Black men and White women was posed, the issue invariably popped up and evoked many heated comments from Black women. A Black brother walking down the street arm in arm with a White woman —most of all a White hippie—can make a Black woman ready to spit fire. The fire surfaces more rapidly when an accusatory glance in the direction of the brother brings no response other than a stone, expressionless face, or a slight smile which reads, "Yeah, I got her; what you going to do about it?" The return glance, equally accusatory, reads: "I bet you rapped the loudest the other day about the honky, whitey, the white devil, and off the pig. Furthermore, she's ugly as sin."

Black women who sometimes wonder what goes through the mind of a White woman as Black men and women exchange these fleeting but meaningful glances, may well have the answer in a reflective statement from a White woman caught up in the silent battle between Black male and Black female. In explaining the psychological limitations of being in the company of a Black man one White woman said: "The only bad thing I remember about being with him was when we'd walk down the street and a black girl passed us. She'd look at me accusingly. At that moment I would have gladly traded my blonde hair and white skin for her dark looks. I felt ashamed and embarrassed." (Rosemary Santini, "Black Man: . . . as seen through white eyes," *Essence*, July 1970, p. 12).

Why do Black men, even in the day of Black liberation still date, have affairs with, and even marry White women? A common explanation is that Black men have had impressed upon them for so long the impossibility of approaching—even remotely—the prized possession of White society, the White woman. Emmett Till remains the clearest illustration of what happens to Black men, or can happen to those who allegedly act as if they have not understood the sanctity of White womanhood. Yet time and time again Black men will seek, almost obsessively, the White man's "symbol of beauty" and will not rest until he has her safely entwined in his arms even if it's only for a night, a week, a month or six months. Another common explanation of a Black man's attraction to White women—even Black men who are the most persistent advocates of Black power—is that White women have a positive effect in terms of making Black manhood a reality and easing the nervousness and anxiety of Black men. In her article entitled "Black Man Do You Love Me?" Louise Meriwether cites the case of Stan Barrows, a Black man married to a White woman. Stan commented, "Let's face it, the cats really didn't dig Black women. With a White chick there's less conflict, less tension." (*Essence*, May 1970, p. 62). Meriwether also points out: "The white man not only idolizes his woman and makes her a goddess, but she also thinks he's a god and says so in many ways. The Black man needs a woman who believes that he is king, who believes he can survive and win." Or, as Stan Barrows put it, "If your woman thinks you're not worth shit, that you can't function, then you're not going to function. But a cat also has to feel he is a king. Nobody can look up to a guy who thinks he's nothing." (Essence, May 1970, p. 62).

Perhaps the one person who has summarized neatly why the Black male has found the Black female so wanting and the White female so desirable is Eldridge Cleaver. In Chapter IV (White Woman, Black Man) of his book *Soul On Ice* (New York: Dell Publishing Co. Inc., 1968), he has a section labeled "The Allegory of the Black Eunuchs." In this section the "Accused" makes a somewhat lengthy analysis of the Black female/Black Male/White female situation:

> Black women take kindness for weakness. Leave them the least little opening and they will put you on the cross. I hate a black bitch. You can't trust them like white women, and if you try to, they won't appreciate it and they won't know how to act. It would be like trying to pamper a cobra. Anyway, every black woman secretly hates black men. Secretly, they all love White men—some of them will tell you so to your face, the others will tell you by their deeds and actions. Haven't you ever noticed that just as soon as a black woman

becomes successful she marries a white man? I'm going by what I know. I know one black bitch who always says there ain't nothing a black man can do for her except leave her alone or bring her a message from, or carry a message to, a white man.

There is no love left between a black man and a black woman. Take me, for instance. I love white women and hate black women. It's just in me, so deep that I don't even try to get it out of me any more. I'd jump over ten nigger bitches just to get to one white woman. Ain't no such thing as an ugly white woman. A white woman is beautiful even if she's baldheaded and has only one tooth. . . . It's not just the fact that she's a woman that I love; I love her skin, her soft, smooth, white skin. I like to just lick her white skin as if sweet, fresh honey flows from her pores, and just to touch her long, soft, silky hair. There's a softness about a white woman, something delicate and soft inside her. But a nigger bitch seems to be full of steel, granite-hard and resisting, not soft and submissive like a white woman.
(Cleaver, 1968, p. 159)

For the "Accused," then, White women represent a sign of freedom, Black women an assertion of slavery. As he states the case:

. . . I don't know just how it works, I mean I can't analyze it, but I know that the White man made the black woman the symbol of slavery and the white woman the symbol of freedom. Everytime I embrace a black woman I'm embracing slavery, and when I put my arms around a white woman, well, I'm hugging freedom.
(Cleaver, 1968, p. 160)

The majority of the women incorporated into our study share the sentiments of Black women everywhere who are angered by any display of affection between Black males and White females. Most felt that relationships were established with White women when Black men suffered from psychological problems such as the inferiority complex, or the "denial makes it look good" syndrome; when Black men realized that they could be "spoiled" by White women and got away with it; and when there existed a decided lack of communication between Black male and Black female. Some representative comments follow:

1. I feel the Black man himself right now is schizoid. Brothers who are educated or who have some essential talent which could be utilized in the Black race are mostly found with White women. This irks me to no end. Most educated girls that I know in their early twenties, late twenties, and early thirties are really uptight about the scene with the Black male and White woman. When you talk with the dudes, educationally he's fairly well abreast of what's going on but he seems to have some psychological hangups that he thinks the White female can solve. I don't understand this.
2. I know a Black man who's marrying a White woman. He's a lawyer and he claims that his political thing has nothing to do with the fact that he digs White women, the way they look. His standards of beauty are White. I guess there're other things involved. He's gone out with several Black women and he's rejected them. He finds this White woman satisfying to his ego and everything else. To me of course I just see that he has an inferiority complex.
3. I think unfortunately that it's just an unfortunate situation but it does exist and the people involved have accepted the American dream or are living a part of what America has propagandized itself as being. If we are all Americans, what difference does it make whether I'm Black and you're White or what, and they believe this I think, so it really doesn't make any difference to them and it's sad that a person in that kind of situation, specifically

the Black person, hasn't been able to realize either because of something he considers love, or either he's just or he or she is just out to prove a point to themselves. Or just to have some kind of a goal fulfilled. I mean there are all kinds of things people want out of life, and if you can get something forbidden to you, it may mean a lot. I think that's the sad case.

4. I think there are some stereotypes that men have about Black women that makes it difficult for them to be sensitive to the needs of Black women. I think that Black women have a lot of feelings that are built up over a long time and it's difficult for them to relate to the needs of their men. When the two get together there's a lot of very destructive conversation and communication that goes on both ways. More often the Black woman is left alone while the Black man goes off and finds a White woman.

5. Here (in the West) it appears that White women are far more forward than they are anywhere else. Like here there's absolutely nothing they won't do for a Black guy—sending him to school, washing his clothes, taking care of him, taking care of his family, letting him do nothing. It's just a whole new thing for our guys to be able to sit home and still eat and nobody bitch about it. Whereas before we were going up off the wall because when he wasn't working, with that little money we brought in our kids weren't eating, we couldn't pay the rent, and all those kinds of weird things. Now he has someone who will sit him down while he grows a beard for instance, or he finds out where his mind is, or while he takes a trip mentally. You really can't cope with it.

6. I think the Black woman has come a long way as far as appearance, skill, whatever. They've come a

long way. And yet the more a Black woman progresses the more the Black man turns to the White woman. That's just like when you're a child and you pick up a cigarette. You know you're not supposed to have it but you want it more. And then if you see something that's illegal or something that you're not supposed to do, you enjoy doing it more than you would if it was open to you, if you could really just go and do it without thinking about the looks you're going to get, or how society is going to look at it. Some Black men—it's just the only way they can get it out of their system—to get a White woman. And personally, the White women these Black men get I wouldn't have no way. And I'm sure White men wouldn't have them.

It is not erroneous to assert that most Black women eagerly look forward to the day when all ties and relationships between Black males and White females will be severed. This is true because most women view such relationships as being incorrect. Even one woman, herself born to a mixed couple, quietly stated on the subject of miscegenation: "I'm a product of one. I'm opposed to it." Yet, the feeling of opposition to racially mixed relations was not unanimous although it approached unanimity. One woman, not particularly bothered by the sight of Black males and White females moving through society in intimate relationship, stated:

I think a lot of Black males are really trying to come into their own. At least as far as I'm concerned that's what all this Black-White business is. I guess that's why I'm not too worried about it. I think a lot of girls get uptight about it. I'm not particularly uptight about it. I think maybe they're trying to achieve some sort of equality or equal standards with White men and that's why they are doing as they are doing.

The segment of the Black female population that seems most affected by the racial liaison of Black male, White woman is the

# Liberation Can Be a Trick Bag

college set. And this seems to be an age group reaction rather than a generational one. That is, all generations of Black women —at least since the thirties and forties—upon passing through the college years became deeply annoyed by the sight of Black males and White females walking hand in hand. Often the White woman is viewed as a threat to the Black female's chances for marriage. Leslie Lacy noted this reaction while teaching Black college females:

> However individually and collectively, the principal concern of these college women, their congenital preoccupation, is the desperate, expectant-anxious search for Black men with whom they can "communicate." Vigorously and without exception, they claim that they can no longer, in principle, believe in or want middle-class Negro husbands. But they are equally convinced, as a result of their newly-discovered values, that the ex-Negro males, the brothers, are sad examples of the new men they seek, because these brothers still, not withstanding verbal denials, want white female relationships and are therefore "still shaky." In the main, these sisters, who champion the cause of Black female liberation and security, see themselves as tragic figures, destined to repeat their mothers' histories—damned to inevitable frustration and loneliness because they are a new species without sane, responsive and relevant mates.
> (Leslie Alexander Lacy, "Men On Women," *Essence*, May 1970, p. 6)

In one class session Lacy set out, not so much to defend the Black male, as to explain the reason for the too often sad state of personal relations between Black men and Black women. His approach in that class session is spelled out in some detail:

> I told the group that I felt there was some truth in their characterizations and general level of grievances but that at the bottom of it all, there were more funda-

> mental questions I thought would relate to their experiences: What could the definition of Black manhood be in a white, male, racist chauvinistic society? Or was Black manhood another American myth? Was it possible to have a reasonably healthy and creative relationship in a society that programs you into neurosis? How could Black men and women function in a world of competitive and inhuman values, and then function sanely at home with a set of compassionate ones? What I could not explain was that inevitable bitterness and hostility among Afro-Americans was not substantially a result of personal inadequacies, but of their inability to create new norms consistent with their political and social experiences. What should the definition of "love" be for people who are oppressed? What is the *real* role of the Black female? And most important, since none of these questions can be answered in one generation, what kind of relationships can Black people reasonably expect in the interim?
> (Lacy, 1970, p. 6)

The result of his attempt seemed to have made little or no impression on the Black female college students. On the contrary it left them cold, very cold. As Lacy reveals:

> But ultimately I had talked to myself. For as I spoke, one by one the new breed left their seats, faces twisted, heads shaking in disgust. I felt a strange inadequacy, not because I had not raised the right issues; I had only recently started thinking about the problem seriously, and I knew that nothing I could say would be conclusive. But as I looked into their faces, I felt that they had not even listened. They wanted men *now*, not promises of tomorrow. I stood in the classroom—alone. Another Black man found wanting. And that was rather sad because I think they represent by far the best generation of Black women we have ever had.
> (Lacy, 1970, p. 6)

From the perspective of most Black women, then, it is "sad" to think that Black men who became so aware in the decades of the forties, fifties, and especially the sixties turned to White women for their personal and intimate relationships.* Though steeped in a Black consciousness which sometimes bordered on the fanatic, a Black man could leave a podium with his own words of "Black Power" and "Off the Pig" still ringing in his ears only to join his White mistress, fiance or wife. For many Black women this kind of liberation represents just another trick bag. For the Black man can chastize the female hours on end for not having the kind of Black awareness and Black consciousness that can lead to liberation and yet at the same time consort with that individual whom he has just labeled the enemy of his own liberation.

After listening to these mostly unsolicited comments about Black males and White females, one is struck by the failure of Black women to indict with equal vehemence any liaison between Black females and White males. Not one single woman who held forth against dates, affairs, and marriage between Black males and White females also condemned the same associations between Black females and White males. It would be interesting to speculate whether this failure to comment stems from a double standard: White sexual patterns are acceptable for Black females but not Black males, or from a state of ignorance about relations between Black females and White males, or from a conscious or unconscious unwillingness to recognize or concede that Black females may, for a variety of reasons, find White men attractive partners. Whatever the reason, certainly it is notable that the women involved did not tackle the issue of the Black female and the White male despite their eagerness to share remarks about and attitudes toward Black males and White females.

*Personal Relationships: Marriage, Etc.*

Since the American society seems to have travelled a long way from the puritan, religious perspective on personal relationships,

---

* See A. F. Poussaint, "Problems of White Civil Rights Workers in the South," *Psychiatric Opinion*, vol. 3, no. 6, December 1966, pp. 18–24.

and since Black revolutionary thought has encompassed fledgling projections of needed changes between Black men and Black women on the personal level, we sought to determine how the Black woman viewed such things as traditional marriage, children, abortions, pills and polygamy. Our particular interest lay in discovering whether the women studied reflected a definite shift away from or a noticeable break with the traditional, more puritanical view on personal relations between men and women. In other words, have Black women turned to a "new morality" however that may be defined?

TRADITIONAL MARRIAGE

The question of traditional marriage evoked no consensual response; in fact, several different approaches to the issue were reflected in the variety of comments offered during discussions of the subject. Moreover, on this segment of the interview perhaps more than any other, many women hesitated, unsure of themselves, and even seemed to be working out their own positions as they conversed with the interviewer. Four fairly distinct views seemed to emerge on the question of traditional marriage: 1) marriage is still a necessary institution; 2) marriage is not a necessary institution but it is practical; 3) marriage is not a necessary institution and sometimes it is not even practical; 4) the decision on traditional marriage or non-traditional marriage should be left up to the individual. Having noted these fairly distinct positions, we were then eager to determine whether the variables of age, education and regional residence had any impact upon the view taken. We might have prophesized, for example, that younger women would adhere more often to the third position, or that older women and those from the South would more readily adopt the first view. Interestingly, the positions on traditional marriage were not conditioned on the variables of age, education or regional residence. For example, for those who took the first view, ages ranged from 17–55, education from the ninth grade to graduate studies, and regions included the West, East, Midwest, and South. In terms of the third position, ages ranged from 20–31, education from 10th grade to graduate work, regions from the East to the West, and Midwest to South. Although the top age in the first position was 55 and that in the third 31, we are not prepared, without further statistical data, to recognize age as a significant variable in terms of views on traditional marriage.

Those who opted for the continuation and necessity of the marital institution tended to underline the importance of such factors as cohesiveness of the family unit, respect, companionship, morality, and protection of children. Some typical comments follow:

1. I'm all for marriage. The reason for this—my personal self yes but for Black people definitely because we need to build a family structure. We have to have that because this is where we are breaking down mainly, our family structure. If we get that together, that's one more step to the revolution. We've always believed in marriages. You can't be following behind these hippies talking about communal living when we invented it and we know the rules too. We made the rules. We don't follow their little shoddy rules. Marriage is for family structure and we definitely need that.
(*A 17 year old easterner*)
2. I think it's a necessary institution because if a man is going to have any respect for a woman he should have a certain wife that he himself should have only, not every man in that particular area.
(*A 19 year old from the South*)
3. I really would have to say that I'm still in the old school. I think matrimony is important. I think that you do in fact get married rather than live together, free community, communes and this kind of thing. However, I'm not in a position to say what's right or wrong. This was not how I was reared and what I firmly believe in. I believe we ought to get married,

for companionship if nothing more. It gives you more—maybe respect from others.
*(A 45 year old easterner with a high school education)*

4. I think it's against moral law to live together. I believe in the Bible. I couldn't believe otherwise. I think we should marry. I'll just let it go at that. I had relatives that lived together. It bothered me because it didn't seem right. I accepted them.
*(A 55 year old high school educated woman from the East)*

5. That's one question I had a great deal of trouble with. Personally I think it is a necessary institution and that is because I have a prejudiced attitude and I'm speaking specifically in terms of Black women and Black men. I think that their needs—how can I say this? I think that abandoning marriage takes a great deal of responsibility between two individuals who have committed themselves to each other for whatever length of time. I don't think we have that much responsibility and discipline at this point. That is why I say it should not be abandoned yet. But on the whole I think it should be. I think it shouldn't be necessary for two people to be sanctioned by society in terms that you live together and have children.
*(A 17 year old from the Midwest)*

6. You find people who are together, who aren't married legally. And they have a sense of responsibility to one another but then they still have foremost in their minds freedom to go when they want to. I think when a person enters some type of union they shouldn't think first of all how easy it is to get out of it. This is the only thing that concerns me about living together and not being married. Marriage kind of assures that you will stay a little while and you won't separate as readily as if you weren't married. Plus you still have the sociological impact on

children—one from a family where they are married and one from a family where they are unmarried. So I think mainly for the protection of children.
*(A 28 year old western graduate student)*

7. I think it's a necessary institution because it brings about a certain bond that extra-marital affairs don't have. So then I guess the question would be, why is the bond necessary? It's sort of a strengthening thing, sort of a little extra strength that a woman needs. I'm in the minority now as far as marriage is concerned. A lot of parents find that they are in the minority because young people feel that this isn't necessary.
*(A 39 year old westerner with 3 years of college)*

8. I think it's still a viable institution. I think a lot of Black women are being put on an incorrect line by a lot of Black pimps saying that whenever a Black man is in trouble a Black woman should come to his aid; Black women should be having babies for Black men anywhere and there are some women who are doing that in the wrong track.
*(From the South, a 20 year old college student)*

9. The only reason why it's necessary is if a man finds something a little bit better and he's got papers on him, he'll think twice. If he don't have papers on him he can walk out any time. It all depends on the woman. I think if a person wants to shack, they shack. Maybe they can get along better that way. But I'm old fashioned. I believe in having that little paper, that paper that's binding us.
*(From the West, a 37 year old woman with a 9th grade education)*

There were a few women who concluded that while marriage is not a necessary institution, still it is a practical one. As some of them said:

1. I've only been married two and a half months and before we got married we lived together about four

years. It's really a big, big question. I don't know. I grew up all my life just waiting to get married. Even though I lived with my husband still I always felt funny about it and you meet people and they say do you live by yourself or do you have a roommate? And you have that little twinge inside of you and then you say it and then everything's o.k. But I still never really accepted it. Now that I'm married there are some responsibilities that are a part of marriage that are different from just living with someone. So your role is different as a wife. It would really be much simpler. All we did was went to Nevada and paid some money and stood in front of a man and got a piece of paper that said we were married. Now all of a sudden the world is different. That's silly. That's really silly. If we could change our moral codes about all of it, I think it would be great. It doesn't make sense to go through that little ritual just to make yourself legal.

*(A 26 year old social worker from the West)*

2. As far as people following their marriage vows I feel it could be abandoned. But for me I'm an old fashioned girl and I do believe in marriage. Right now the only thing keeping marriage going are children. If there weren't any children I don't think there would be marriage any more.

*(From the South, a 20 year old college student)*

3. I think that many marriages are worse than non-marriages where you get a more humane relationship between non-married people. But I think our society in general should look towards improving the quality of life for everybody. And, I think marriage would improve. I think our particular culture among both Blacks and Whites would not be served by a non-legal relationship as the norm. I haven't had enough experience to know which might be better. I know of common law relationships where the peo-

ple live much more beautiful lives, in respect and appreciation of each other, and rearing their children and doing all the things that affirms their humanity—better than people who are married. Marriage by itself doesn't mean anything. But I think we're so much a part of a tradition that has put a higher value on the marriage, that it would probably really be traumatic to switch over. But I think marriage is being eroded. There are so many bad marriages.
(*A westerner with a Ph.D*)

Still other women believed that marriage is not a necessary institution and sometimes it is not even practical. Several pointed to the evils of marriage, viewing it variously as a headache, conflict–producing institution, a limitation on freedom, and a form of possessiveness, and even a defense against loneliness. A few representative comments were:

1. Within this system the man is really not allowed to be that which he originally was in previous Black civilizations, so it puts us of later generations at a disadvantage unless you have went to college or have the means of making money and taking care of the family, and all this, marriage in this system becomes a headache. It pits one against the other. All of the conflicts are built into the marriage situation. Basically I feel that my going to a minister and having him say a few words over me do not constitute marriage but in following through on it the couple who finds love before marriage loses it as they move into this restricted institution as it is related to in this system. So in that way I feel that marriage goes down without the reading of the words and in many instances more ghetto marriages have been successful because they didn't pin the person in. It's a psychological thing that if both

people know that they can pull up at any time, then the tendency is not to necessarily pull up.
*(A 31 year old high school graduate from the Midwest)*

2. I don't know. I've never been married. I may want to be married two or three years from now. I don't think marriage is good for me at this point because marriage to me as is currently done with the so-called loyalty—loyalty to one's self in terms of meeting people and loving different people and experiencing different things is far more important than marriage or rather loyalty to another individual. I would want someone whom I really loved. I'm not talking about any soapbox bullshit on television. I'm talking about a mature and understanding love which I feel I have felt sometimes for people. Sometimes I have mistaken other things for it. I don't recognize the term adultery. That's absurd. To me I can't see placing that kind of restriction on myself. Marriage is legalized prostitution. It's a form of buying sex. It's a form of making people dependent on you. It's a form of possessiveness. It's a form of saying the eternal we as opposed to you and me. It's a defense against loneliness. And when you cannot feel this loneliness you are not dealing with parts of life because life for the most part is loneliness. There are sad parts and beautiful parts. When you are not dealing with something like that, you are not dealing period. I don't know if I'll ever need marriage. The times I have really wanted to be married, the person was slipping away and I wanted to grab him and keep him in place. It's a form of saying I want to possess you. I hope I never in life do it again. I wanted to like get that person's soul in a sense, grab him, keep him, possess him. That's not love. That's a negation of love because it's selfish and it's anti-respect.
*(A 22 year old college student from the East)*

3. It hangs up a lot of men. It hangs up a lot of very productive Black men and they need to be free at this point. They don't need to be free of women. They don't need to be free of children but they need to be free to move at will when they want to. They need that kind of freedom. Marriage has the tendency to stabilize you to the point where you feel obligated to do the things that may not be to the best interest of what you want to do, of what you feel you could do, or the part you could play in the revolution. It has a tendency to slow you down because you always have to come back and deal with particular situations that may not in any way have anything to do with your total life. As for me marriage isn't necessary at all. The legal type situation always causes problems. It always has. I feel that it always will. It gets people hung up in having to deal with each other. I have to stay here. I have to do this. I have to do that and it hangs you up in a lot of ways.

*(A 24 year old southerner with one year of college)*

4. Being married doesn't bind two people together and usually this is such a fickle world that you become restless and you quarrel and soon everything is just over any way. I don't think mariage is necessary. I don't know who thought of it. I often wonder.

*(A 20 year old southerner with a high school education)*

5. I think people are going to get together but I don't necessarily feel legal marriage is necessary. It seems to me that legal marriage is just like social security. It's just a way of controlling and containing people and finding out what they are doing. And where they are. I wouldn't go to a judge. I would probably construct my own spiritual ceremony but I think I don't need a White man to tell me that I can begin to relate to a Black man, in a particular way. Legal

marriage is so artificial. Marriages should just happen. It's a spiritual thing.
*(A 26 year old graduate student from the Midwest)*

6. I think it's dying out. I used to think marriage was necessary. Since if a chick gets knocked up—a long time ago people felt that they just had to marry and a lot of times they marry and the marriage don't work out, so I think a chick can make it with her baby when she really tries. So I don't think it's necessary to marry in that instance. Like for me I'll probably never marry.
*(A 25 year old southerner)*

7. I don't think marriage is that much because nowdays the way things are—married or no married—if a man get a child by a woman, marriage or no marriage he can be made to support that child. I don't think it's necessary to get married any more.
*(A 26 year old southerner with a 10th grade education)*

8. I think that Black people have to re-evaluate marriage to fit their own thing. Right now when we look at marriage it's the whole western White man orientation in what we know. Generally the same institution as far as marriage for the Whites is the same institutions that Blacks live under. They relate the same way—the father being the breadwinner and stuff like that. But when and if I get married again my husband and I would both have to be involved in the movement and I think that both parties should play a major role in there because I do not see eliminating no one be they Black from the movement and just like we re-evaluate anything else, Blacks are going to have to re-evaluate their own rules and regulations as far as marriage is concerned, and not by the White man's rules.
*(A 26 year old midwesterner with 2½ years of college)*

# Liberation Can Be a Trick Bag 97

9. From the point of view of religion today it (marriage) might just as well be abandoned. Religion today isn't what it used to be. I've gone to a lot of churches and it seems more and more people are going to see how the next sister dresses rather than what the minister says. They have this big wedding in a church for publicity, or for fun. They want to get out there and show how much their daddy can pay for this dress and how many bottles of champagne they have carted in and this sort of thing but then you get married one day and your old man spends $2000 on a big wedding and then the next night you fall out. And nine times out of ten you've done everything you going to do anyway by the time you walk down the aisle. So why not keep doing it and save your old man a whole bunch of money. And when you get ready to split from the dude just take it. That's the way I look at it because I know my old man put out a bunch of money when I got married. If you go into this thing wholeheartedly, if you're going to respect your vows, go ahead and do it right. But if you're going in knowing in your heart you're not going to do right, you're doing wrong to do it.

*(A 28 year old westerner with 3 years of college)*

Women in the fourth category of views on marriage did not take a personal stand on the issue of traditional marriage. Almost as an escape mechanism, it seemed, they resorted to an "it's up to the individual's argument." That is, whatever the individual, or the two people involved concluded on this question, that's the way the personal relationship should be arranged. As some women put it:

1. It's up to the individual. Personally I want to get married. It's up to the person. Sometimes some people in marriages feel restricted. They feel it's an unnatural relationship between a man and a woman that restrains you too much. Sometimes I think peo-

ple just living together or just shacking up get along a lot better than the people who are married. There's not that total freedom, but there's that little something that's not there that makes you get along better when maybe you're not married but it's up to the individuals.
*(An 18 year old high school student from the East)*
2. I think it should be left up to the individual. If you want to marry a man or a man wants to marry you, that's cool. But if you don't and you still want to live together that's cool too.
*(A 24 year old college junior from the West)*
3. I don't think it (marriage) is necessary except maybe for the people who want it, the pomp and ceremony, the long white dress and all that. I'll have to qualify that. I think it should be left up to the individual, without ostracism. I think it should be left up to the individual. If he wants to go through the ceremony, go ahead, but if he doesn't I don't think it's anybody's business.
*(A midwesterner with a college background)*

Perhaps the most intriguing viewpoint on traditional marriage was expressed by a 21 year old Sunni Muslim who, when asked if marriage should be abolished as an archaic institution, said:

> That is a rather difficult question to answer and I might answer it a little differently than you asked. I think marriage is a very beautiful and wonderful institution. I no longer feel that a marriage license is a necessary requirement to say that two people are married. I think that the marriage license should be abolished but I don't think that marriage should ever be abolished.

This may well be the conclusion which many Black women will reach as the decade of the seventies unfolds.

# Liberation Can Be a Trick Bag

CHILDREN, ABORTIONS, PILLS

One often hears two opposing positions enunciated in the Black community on the subject of children. On the one hand some contend that Black people have too many children, that these children eventually become an unwanted burden and interfere with the emotional, spiritual, intellectual and revolutionary development of Black people. On the other hand many Blacks vehemently maintain that there can never be too many Black children. On the contrary, they insist, the birth rate of Blacks must increase drastically if an army of liberation is to be formed. To adherents of this position birth control is anathema; in fact, it represents nothing more than a clear form of genocide.

As for the women in our study, most took a non-political position on the question and concluded that Black women should have as many children as they wanted as long as they could take care of them. For example, some stated:

1. I would say that some people have too many children simply because they can't afford to take care of as many as they have. I don't think we can sit down and draw the line as to how many children a Black person should have because I feel they should have as many as they can take care of.
2. I don't think it's helpful to reproduce children unless you are prepared to take care of them. They have to be cared for. They need adequate clothing and food and shelter and love. If you can't give them all this, they are being cheated. I know we need to increase our Black population for the revolution but I don't see it as—that you should manufacture children toward that purpose.
3. To some extent I think they're having more than their financial means. I think if a woman is able and can take care of them or find a dude to help her take care of them, let her have them if she loves

kids that much and she want to watch her kid come up doing without because she's too trifling to take the pill or if she's too trifling to get up.
4. I think a lot of Black women have children that they don't want. To say it's too many children, I don't know. It seems to me to be part of our culture to have families, to have large families and to love them. But like Black women are under so much pressure and so much responsibility—Black women in the ghetto—and like another child is just so much. It's a burden.
5. At the moment, I would say generally, the more Black people we have the better. But I think to bring a child into the world that is going to have rickets and malnutrition constantly, and a lower I.Q. because he has never eaten enough is just a very terrible thing, and it gets back to the whole society.
6. I have a cousin that's 32 years old, and she is the mother of 11 children, 9 living. And they're doing fine now. Her husband is stepping forwards and all this stuff. But, I just can't see where these children are going. There's too many in the first place. You can lose sight of them. How in the devil can you do anything for them? And she's so arrogant. If you say anything about them, she's going to get mad. My main thing about Black people having too many children is that they don't stop and think: What will I be able to do for two? What will I be able to do for three? Can I afford to give two this or that? Or, can I afford to give three? If they could sit down and logically think about what they can afford to give them, x number of children, then there would be nothing wrong with having 10 if they had the means to give them a start in life. . . . I think we should reproduce but sanely. Don't get carried away —four, five, six, seven. I talked to a young girl the other day. She's 20 and she's having her third child. Well, it's her business but to me it's mad.

# Liberation Can Be a Trick Bag

Of those who took a political stand several felt that only White propaganda had convinced some Black people that they had too many children.

1. I think it's ridiculous to say we have too many children. That's just a part of white propaganda.
2. You know this book I was reading—a sociology book speaking that one of the major problems of Black people is that they are sex crazy and that they do have too many children. It was all statistics. It didn't come out and say well Black folk are crazy but the whole book was based on the fact that they had interviewed these women fortyish, thirtyish who were on welfare and had no husband. They all had so many children.
3. No, not too many children because it's the White man's concept of too many children. You do find a lot of Whites who have more children than Blacks but I guess because of the economic thing they say they're too many because it's harder to feed them but most of the time they manage to survive some way or another. I don't think there are too many because you have just as many who have no children or one child or two children as you do with families of 8 or more.

A few others saw procreation as an obligation for the Black woman. That is, they regarded it as a means of acquiring more bodies for the task of nation building; and as a mechanism for producing troops for the revolution.

1. They just don't have too many. A woman is supposed to have children from puberty to the change of life. They're supposed to have those children.
2. If we're talking about the revolution we've got to talk about more bodies which means that men have got to stop shucking and jiving and bring their money together with women and it's got to be an

> equal society where we can pool money to take care of children. This is the only way you get troops is by having Black children.
> 3. Being a Moslem woman we stress that Muslims have as many children as possible so that we can build a nation.

One woman felt, however, that Black women were already so involved in the Black struggle that they really might not have time to spend carrying and bearing children.

> I think that Black women, because of the role they have to play in some instances in nation building, in helping to bring about the progress of Black people, that they won't necessarily have time to have children but I think that in the majority of cases Black women should have children. It's important in the world today that Black women have children.

While most women readily indicated a willingness to have more children a few, again for seemingly non-political reasons, categorically stated they would not have any more.

> 1. No, (I wouldn't have more children) because the one I have is giving me plenty of trouble.
> 2. I plan to adopt some children but I don't plan on having any. I don't plan on getting married either.
> 3. No, even if I could afford them, I just wouldn't have them.

While it was clear that most women felt that Black people should have as many children as they wanted as long as they could afford them, their views on abortions and the pill seemed divided. Several women opposed abortions on the ground that they represented a tool for murder or that they would interfere with the survival of the race.

1. I think they (abortions) should be legalized so that women can have the opportunity to choose but I don't sanction abortions. Personally I don't think I would ever get one. I don't think I would want anyone else to get one for political reasons. I read just recently that they're going to institute a family planning program so that specifically welfare and low income moms will be able to limit the number of children. The government says this will not be mandatory and none will be penalized. You can't trust the government. I'm quite wary on that basis.
2. I think if people don't want to have children every necessary precaution that they can dream up should be taken. But I also think that as a Black woman, and for the sake of survival of this race that abortions are definitely out.
3. Usually when a Black woman finds out that she is pregnant she goes on and has the baby because she has never had any money for abortions and there is always a lot of loving for that child when the child comes. I do not believe in abortions. I feel that when she becomes pregnant she should go on and have that Black child because I believe in a lot of Black children, in building a Black nation.

On the other hand, other women obviously favored abortions on the grounds that unwanted children would not have to be born; the mother's health might have to be safeguarded (the concept of the therapeutic abortion); and children who could not be provided for would not have to enter the world.

1. I guess in social work you see too many people who have been forced to have children they didn't want and the laws just didn't reflect how a woman could really feel. I don't think they are sensitive to a woman's feelings. I think a woman should be able to make a choice of whether she wants the child or

not, instead of bringing it in the world and then seeing it neglected.
2. Yes definitely (I believe in abortions). I feel if a woman gets pregnant, not intentionally. It's just too bad that when I was coming up I couldn't get an abortion: six children at the age of 23. Every time my husband went to sea and came home again I was pregnant again.
3. I strongly believe in having abortions because I think the unwanted child is the worst thing somebody could have.
4. I think a woman has to have control of her own body and that it is much better to have an abortion than to bring a child in this world that's not wanted. Adoption agencies are just filled with unwanted children that can't be placed. These children are kept in homes until they are 18 years old and I think that's just a terrible situation. I'm absolutely in favor of abortions. I think they're necessary.
5. I believe in them if it's against the health of the mother to have it and for a woman that's raped.
6. If a person has been unrightfully molested or something I think she should have the right to get an abortion. But for people who are just going to play around with it and have kids and say I can always get an abortion—like everything else they got good points and bad points about abortions. If you rightfully deserve an abortion, you should have one. If you're going to play house every day and end up having abortions, it's a different case.

Then, there was a category of women who felt that the decision on abortions would have to be left up to the individual woman:

1. It's an individual thing as far as I'm concerned. If a woman does not want to bear a child she should not be forced to. She should not be forced to hazard her health in order to avoid it. I'm all in favor of

a liberalized abortion law. I have some feeling that there is probably some political impact. I do not accept the White man imposing upon Black people his standards of what a family should be, the size of families, and how it should be constructed. I think Black women will be less inclined to seek abortions in the way White women will. I want us to have the freedom to do it if we so desire.

2. The woman has a right if she's out on the town one night and gets knocked up by someone else's husband, and the very thought of his child growing inside of her is a horrible thought and makes her sick—what kind of love is that kid going to get? What kind of a chance does he have in the world? I think it's her choice. It's her decision because she's the mother.

3. I think when you get into that whole moral question of whether or not it's correct or incorrect to kill a child I think that it's up to the woman who's having the child. It's her body. She's the one who's going to have to function with the child all her days, or think about where the child is all her days. And if she makes up her mind that the coolest thing for her is not to have one then it's her business. If she makes up her mind that she wants to have the child then it's her business.

4. I don't believe in killing lives but like sometimes if you can't take care of it there's no point in having it. But I don't think anyone should make that decision for anyone else and I think that if the two people are in some kind of relationship they should both make the decision about what they're going to do. And if it's just like a happening—the chick gets knocked up—she should do what she wants to do.

Although responses to the question of abortions were pretty low key, those to the pill were precise and sometimes heated. That little cancer-producing, physically stifling pill is how numerous women viewed birth control pills. Many were the women who related personal histories or who cited cases of friends which were indicative of the evil side effects the pill can have upon the human body.

1. I'm developing all kinds of weird things about the pill. In terms of what the pill is supposed to do I think it's marvelous. But in terms of side effects on women I think it's horrendous.
2. No (I don't believe in the use of the pill) because they almost killed me.
3. I think anything that messes with the natural process of the body is harmful.
4. I wouldn't take a pill and I wouldn't even have one of my girls take a pill. I read too much where they are cancerous.
5. I don't like them at all. If I had a daughter and I had anything to do with what she is, it wouldn't be birth control pills because I don't think your cycle, or your system, or whatever should be disturbed. It has a certain way to go and I think that pill upsets it.
6. I used to take it. I stopped taking it because I think it really fucked up my system. I kept thinking here is a little pill that somebody made to put inside me. It's not right. I don't know what's in it. I'll be damned if I'm going to take it every day and I don't have the faintest idea of what's in it. That really bothered me. So I've really said in a way yes, yes to life. If I have a baby I have a baby. If I don't have a baby I don't have a baby.
7. I can't use it because I am subject to blood clot. I know this so I fear it. I may try it off and on ever so often and then I get a panic streak and I don't want to see it. I don't even want to talk about it.
8. The pill I think is physically a detriment. I have taken it. I don't want to take it any more. I have

seen the results of what it could do to me as well as what it could do to other women. I've also read some statistics on it. These statistics prove that it does not kill but at the same time it does deform. Any chemical that you take in your body will affect you in some way or other. I think that if I'm interested in being a woman then I'm interested in being productive as a woman.

Also, the pill was often viewed as playing a central role in a quiet campaign to practice genocide on the Black race.*

1. I don't believe in that (the pill). I think it's a form of genocide. I really do. I feel they should have as many as they can support really.
2. If we go for this (the pill), between Vietnam with all of our young men, the pill with all of our young women, within ten years—and that's not even counting the jails and the system right out here—within ten years we could easily just be carted off because we do not have the work force to protect and demand. The birth control pill was invented basically for us in order to cut down this thing of reproduction that we have going for us.
3. When you mention birth control I think about my situation. I don't want to get pregnant because I'm in school and I have some other plans. But as far as the man trying to control our race I don't go along with it. I guess with the new birth control laws and trying to pour these pills and things into the Black community, I guess this is a way of controlling.

* This view is in sharp contrast to a recent New England study of "159 black households" sponsored by the University of Massachusetts and printed by the Population Reference Bureau in 1971. That study concluded that "a majority of those in the reproductive age range do not accept the idea that birth control programs are an attempt to eliminate blacks from the population." (*New York Times*, July 27, 1971)

4. Up until three or four months ago (I believed) very strongly (in the use of the pill). But since I've been here and been around the people that are deeply into the revolution, and I have been in the thing that they are trying to wipe out the Black race, then I have my second questions about it but I'm still using it.
5. I'm against them, deadly against them. I think it's a quick way of committing genocide on the Black people. Old crackers are not taking all these birth control pills.

Interestingly enough, comments from some of the southern women in our study indicated that a strong effort was under way in certain communities in the South to launch and activate birth control and planned parenthood centers. These centers were being designed mainly to service areas where relatively large numbers of women were on welfare.

> I think that birth control should be available but I don't think it should be jammed down people's throats. It should be an optional thing. A lot of people tell women on welfare if you don't go down and get some type of birth control and we get a statement back saying you've been there and you've been fitted for IUD, you have pills or whatever they're going to give you, that you're going to be turned off welfare. I've had members to say this, that the threat has been put to them.

In one instance most of the individuals who were actively trying to make such centers effective, belonged to a traditional Negro woman's national organization. Some indication (but not enough to make a strong case for its prevalence) was evident of a deceptiveness being practiced by doctors to lure women into taking birth control measures. One 26 year old woman from the South who had only a 10th grade education and "quite a few children" revealed that her doctor had given her birth control pills, not to prevent birth but simply to regulate her system. Stating that she

# Liberation Can Be a Trick Bag

was generally opposed to the pill the woman implied that the only reason she had agreed to take it was so that a malfunctioning of her system could be corrected. As she put it:

> No, (I don't believe in the use of the pill) but the doctor put me on some in order to . . . to regulate me but in order for me to take some for a baby, I don't believe in it.

Some women, as on the abortion question, felt that use of the pill had to be an individual decision and could not be imposed upon any one.

1. I work in family planning so I think if a woman doesn't feel that she's ready to have a child she should be able to get the pill if she wants it. I think it should be her choice.
2. That's another one of those touchy questions about genocide and stuff but I believe again, freedom of choice. I don't think that people should be forced to take pills or sterilization to get their welfare checks as people are forced. I don't think people should come to your house if you are on the welfare rolls and you have a certain number of kids. The Planned Parenthood, they're referred to you. They come to your house. My mother works for Planned Parenthood. Maybe the people want birth control and they just don't know about it. And maybe they're not interested in it. But I think it should be made available to people who want it.
3. I believe in birth control for those women who want to control the birth. I think only the woman can say she has too many children. I've been running into other attitudes: that Black women should have as many children as they can. That to me is a personal decision. Although children are very beautiful you really don't know how much of them you can stand.

There were several women who did advocate and support the use of the pill. Most women reflecting a favorable attitude toward the pill saw it as a means of spacing children and therefore avoiding being placed in the tense and often depressing situation of not being able to give them proper care.

1. I think we can use that because it teaches them how to space their children and not have them too fast. That's what our clinic teaches, how many children the family is able to take care of.
2. I'm Catholic and I know the pope still hasn't come out for this. However I do feel that there are situations in which it should be. In our program we deal with women who have just had so many children and they are broken down and torn down with child birth and they can't feed the mouths that they have and they're having all sorts of trouble.
3. Yes (I'm in favor of the pill). I feel this is another means to help people that don't want children or can't afford to have them not to have them.

One woman took a rather novel stand by arguing that the original experiments with birth control pills had been conducted on the wrong sex, that in fact males and not females should have been subjected to the pill testing. Had this occurred the respondent undoubtedly would have given greater support for the pill.

I felt that birth control devices could have been developed for brothers. But politically that was wrong for Black people because a Black cat would really go into a psychological bag if you had something like that. I think that because of the situation of Black people in the United States it is a damaging thing to us. At the same time I'm puzzled and hurt about the treatment Black kids born in the United States are receiving: kind of neglect and general waste of our youth. I see sisters especially who sit home on welfare and talk all that shit about they ain't going out to get a job because they're staying home to take care of their kids and their kids ain't getting no taking care of. And they could probably do a much better thing for their kids. Don't take me wrong. I'm not eliminating birth control pills as a way in which people can control the population on this earth but I think that the experimental thing was never done properly so therefore you just get a whole lot of Black guinea pigs.

Thus, one can glimpse a wide ranging feeling on the pill with the most concentrated reaction stemming from a fear of the pill's side effects. This fear, even more so than that of genocide, has led many Black women to cast it aside. Yet, views on the birth of children and use of birth control devices are invariably linked. That is, those women who believe that no child should be born who cannot be given proper attention and care, must of necessity lean toward the utilization of some birth control measure—be it that of a simple abstention, or the pill, or a device such as the IUD, or abortions. What is not clear from this study is which of these measures are favored by women who reject the pill and yet believe that mass production of children is just not a wise idea because it can so easily result in neglect. It may be that women, unhappy with the pill, are experimenting with other devices and may end up leaning towards the IUD, or even abortions given the more liberal approach which many states are now taking towards that method of terminating an undesired pregnancy. In other words, in some areas like New York State it is no longer necessary to prove that the mother's health will be endangered by the birth of a child for the purpose of securing an abortion. One has only to request an abortion within a certain number of weeks after impregnation and may secure that abortion in a hospital and not in a grimy, unsanitary back room—all without having to go into a long dissertation concerning the reasons for the request. Given this degree of freedom, and given the notorious effects of the pill, more Black women may decide to seek abortions for unwanted children.

## POLYGAMY

While the idea of multiple spouses or polygamy may have been alien to Black people since the late 1800's and through the decade of the fifties, it began to seep into certain segments of the Black community most noticeably beginning in the middle to late sixties. Some nationalist, or nationalist oriented organizations claimed that polygamy most suited Black people since it is an obvious and important ingredient of the African heritage. That is, polygamy is a widespread custom among most African traditional societies, and polyandry is not unknown in areas such as the Congo. Therefore in an effort to reflect the true African family structure some nationalist groups began to practice polygamy. Then, too, as the influence of Elijah Muhammed's Nation of Islam grew, and after Malcolm X's pilgrimage to Mecca and his death, other Black people began to look to the Islamic religion as their true heritage. With the embracing of Islam and the Moslem way of life some communities of Blacks also began to adopt polygamy as their marital pattern. Finally, the idea of polygamy caught fire among some for neither historical-cultural, or religious reasons. Some men, noting the obvious excess of women to men, began to advocate the necessity of polygynous relationships if the existence of a frustrated band of Black women were to be avoided. In other words some Black men began to argue the necessity of several Black women sharing one Black man in the spirit of polygamy.

Given this new trend of cultural awareness, religious innovation, and social consciousness, we were anxious to see to what extent Black women were in agreement with polygamous relationships. Would they be willing to share one man with several other women? Would they be amenable to taking on more than one man?

The vast majority of respondents were opposed to the infiltration of polygamy into the Black American community. Many couched their opposition in an economic reasoning by contending that Black men today can't afford even one woman let alone two or three.

# Liberation Can Be a Trick Bag

1. I believe he ought to have just one 'cause he can't take care of the one he got. What the hell is he going to do with two or three wives?
2. I think one woman is all a man can handle. I think a man would not like to share his woman with another man. I think a woman is more capable of handling several men or husbands than one man is of handling a wife because he's the one who does the supporting and I don't think he can afford more than one woman. Even with one at a time, if you get a divorce you end up with alimony and child support so it's really hard on him, whereas the woman can go from husband to husband and really don't have any big responsibility.

Others raised a biological contention by insisting that Black men are incapable of satisfying more than one Black woman.

> One wife—that's right—one woman. I don't think a man can satisfy two women and still keep both of them happy. I just don't believe a man is that great.

Still others leaned toward a psychological dimension by revealing an inability to cope emotionally with a sharing concept; that is, sharing one's husband with another woman would represent too much of an emotional shock.

1. I think you have to know a historical backdrop on polygamy. Polygamy involved a system where there are more women than men. They're causing certain kinds of social problems like women that are free and unattended and yet needing the same kind of psychological and biological fulfillment as women who were lucky enough to have snared one. But when that situation doesn't exist then polygamy is superfluous. It exists in America today, but I doubt if it will ever flourish. There'll just always be

women who are loose and available, and unfulfilled or fulfilled in limited quantities and supply because we just aren't oriented toward having—men are oriented toward having a wife and girl friend maybe. But they are not even oriented toward having two wives. I don't think they would know how to function under that kind of system of having to divide between two women and keep it going and make it run smoothly. And women clearly, clearly don't know how to deal with it. Wives can't deal with girlfriends. Girl friends can't deal with wives. I don't believe in it. I'm greedy. I's a hog. I'm not married mostly because I haven't run up on the kind of fellow I want to marry. I've run up on some pretty hip fellows but some of them are already married. And then some others weren't to be married and some that were willing to get married I didn't want to marry them. So I guess I'm one of them women that are loose, available and free. But I don't see myself as being a second hand rose. It would be detrimental to my personality, to my self-confidence and to my inner concept of me to knowingly function in a polygamous system whether I was wife number 1, 2, or 3 because o.k. here I am. I'm his wife but he's got two other wives.

2. I know I couldn't cope with it. Though I don't like to admit it I think I'm kind of jealous. I would like to have my man to myself and not have to share him. I don't know how other women feel but if that's the kind of marriage they want—well do it. I'm basically jealous and selfish in some things. I want to have my man to myself.

3. I don't think I'm emotionally stable enough to compete with another full time woman. If I don't know about it that's one thing but if I knew about it I don't think I would be too wild about it.

4. I don't know whether I could be one of very many

wives—not unless I was the first wife. In that situation I think I could take it but as for someone telling me that he wants me to be his third or fourth wife, I couldn't. Maybe my daughter could but I couldn't.

5. I think if I got a horse I ride him by myself. I don't need no one else to jump up there and help me ride that one horse. I'm like a man about a car. If I got a car I'm the only one to drive it. I don't believe in sharing my man with nobody.

It is interesting to note that a few of the women who felt that men could not handle more than one spouse, did not assume the same attitude with respect to women. That is, a few women saw the female as perhaps being much more equipped to perform well in a polyandrous relationship than a man in a polygynous relationship.

Identifiable also was a category of women who were still thinking through the issue of polygamy and trying to react to those in the Black community who were certain of the need to substitute polygamous relationships for the monogamous pattern among Black people.

1. That's another issue of the day. I could only be happy with my husband having only one wife or one woman. If I knew about it I would be very unhappy. A lot of people I talk with nowadays are saying there are so many Black women, so few Black men. And there are a lot of men who could satisfy two or three women at a time. So then you have to deal with how much you feel for your sister that you want to share your man. It makes a whole lot of sense. I just don't know if I'm ready right now to deal with that. I think it's an interesting idea for women too. I'd probably, knowing me, it's so difficult to even say you believe in those kinds of things when you know the way people react to society but

I do think that it's more and more acceptable and it'll probably be more acceptable to consider having another man. I'm not that much against it.

2. In our society now we do have a shortage of men. We have many women, very few men basically because of Vietnam, the prisons, and all of this. With our young men being in Vietnam and getting killed, we have an oversupply of young women who are here frothing at the mouth because the society says we got to have a man. We got to go to bed. Now this gives a tendency for them to reach for the older men because all of the fine young men are gone. This means that the older woman who is usually the partner to this older man is in competition with the young women. Now however we are going to resolve this has to be looked at. We have always lived in a society where a man had more than one woman. In Africa it was legal. It was built in and our whole social customs were arranged in such a way that it was cool. After getting here and supposedly getting freed Black men have always had another woman out there. He just didn't let momma know about it at home. So it has always been going on but I will say that the Black men will have to gather in much wisdom in order to deal with it.

3. I'm very adaptable and as I see it now I don't see the problem. I hear there's a male shortage. I haven't felt it yet. I can see it happening. I think a lot of Black sisters who are unattached and have the need to have a male relationship or a male companion, then it might be necessary but I see conflicts in that too because I don't think that the goal of marriage or any relationship should be simply companionship. I think there has to be other motives involved. I think there has to be a common ground such as one to one. I don't see anything

> against it. It could be very touchy. That's getting into a whole new realm and I'm trying to expand my mind to cover all the possibilities. I can think of two women friends, and our lives are taking on pretty much the same direction, and I can see my living in that type of polygamous situation with them. But now I can say that because I know them and I can't see where there would be any conflict. We love and respect each other that much where we want the same things, or pretty much the same things out of life which is the liberation of Black people and I can't see where it would pose any problems. The men I go out with are pretty much oriented that way too but then not knowing someone is different. I don't know how it would work living in the same apartment. I think everybody should be polygamous, even women. I think it gets to the point that if one man does not satisfy all the needs of a woman—and the same way one woman will not always satisfy the needs of a man—when it gets to that point I don't think there should be a binding or strangling relationship that does not allow for each individual to satisfy their needs.

A few women clearly favored the polygamous situation. Some even had adopted that form of marital relationship. One person saw a polygamous relationship as putting an end to the frustrations of a monogamous situation.

> Polygamy exists today even though there are legal one to one marriages. They're informal arrangements but they meet a need and they exist. I think we ought to publicly acknowledge them so that we can eliminate some of the frustrations that emanate out of attempting to have a one to one relationship in a polygamous situation. There is such a shortage of men. They have to be shared.

Another gave polygamy her stamp of approval as long as a man could economically support more than one woman.

> I believe he should have as many as he can afford. If he can handle two, handle two.

Of those who admitted to living in a polygamous household one, a 21 year old college student who is also a Sunni Muslim, stated:

> According to the scriptures and the Bible polygamy was instituted quite early. Under Islam a man is able to have four wives and if he feels that this will help him then by all means I would agree to polygamy.

Another woman, a 24 year old southerner with one year of college commented:

> (I) most definitely, most definitely (believe in polygamy). For one thing I'm living in it and I don't think that most men, as well as most women, can deal with as many people as they think they're capable of loving. And people are capable of loving more than one person.

Another group that adheres to polygamy, other than Muslims, is Ron Karenga's US organization. Four women from that group constantly spoke of the sense of community instilled in members of the organization, a sense of community with strong emphasis on interdependence and mutual love. Headed by a former graduate student in political science at U.C.L.A., US carves out a definite role for women within the framework of the organization. This role is stated in terms of inspiration, education, and social development. As one of the four women interviewed put it:

> Well as Maulana Ron Karenga teaches us the role of the Black woman is inspiration, education and social development. Inspiration in terms of inspiring her man to go on to build a nation and all. Education would be

educating her children for inspiration and information about Black people. And social development would be getting out into the community and letting other people know what we're doing and giving them advice and helping them. And social development also in terms of developing our own habits and etiquette. Like developing these things ourselves like if we feel like we want to use napkins, we'll use napkins. Or if we feel like we want to use finger bowls to dip like it was done traditionally to cleanse our hands before we eat a meal—all these things—even as far as showing deference to Maulana in terms of the meals. Before we eat each meal we say all praises due to Maulana; all praises due to Maulana Karenga. That's something that's part of our customs and conception of what's important in terms of the Black female role.

The above quote not only reveals the specific role assigned to the women in US but also the clear impact and influence of Maulana Ron Karenga on his followers. It is not surprising, then, that with such influence Karenga could lead the women of his group to accept polygamy as the most valid form of marital relationship. One woman summed up Maulana's views on polygamy:

Just as Maulana teaches us in terms of our house system, the family system, the man has any right that does not take away from the collective benefit of the family. The man has any right you see. Also Maulana teaches us that no one woman could fulfill all the needs of a man. No one woman is that bad that they could fulfill all the needs of a man because men can see so many beautiful different things in different women. It would be like these different things could complement a whole relationship.

Not surprisingly perhaps, Maulana teaches his followers that polyandry is an unnatural and unacceptable pattern. As one US woman asserted:

> That's another thing Maulana teaches us. In terms of the Black woman there's more stability with the Black woman. The Black woman has to have a feeling of security which she could only have in a relationship with one man.

It is probably true that other cultural nationalist groups have resorted to polygamy. If and as the cultural nationalist movement grows, the incidence of polygamous relationships probably will increase. And, if it does, no doubt it would equally be true that nothing new or decidedly revolutionary had taken place. As one 62 year old southern, still active community organizer said:

> That's one thing that never crossed my mind. Ever since Solomon had 300 wives and 700 concubines I know no man is not going to have no one woman at a time so I never think about that.

We have wandered through a maze of subjects involving personal relationships. We now return to the theme of our chapter: liberation can be a trick bag. While some in the Black community may decry traditional marriage and opt instead for mutual understanding or simply living together in lieu of a formal marriage ceremony, all in the name of freedom, the question remains —as posed by many women—will this represent freedom or liberation from responsibility? That is, will men with increased freedom feel no compunction about walking out on women and/or ignoring the needs of children they helped create. Moreover, while some view the pill as a liberating force, in the sense that freedom from a constant process of nine month pregnancies may mean more time for "revolutionary" activities, others look upon it as an oppressive mechanism which through evil side effects not only can incapacitate one in terms of performing activities for the Black struggle, but also effectively preclude the production of additional troops for the "revolution." Furthermore, polygamy may indeed allow more freedom to experiment and experience different lifestyles. Yet it is equally apparent that the introduction of polygamy (of course without legal sanction) into Black American society may also cause personal and psychological conflict as well as augment the economic strains on Black men. If then freedom from responsibility, physically incapacitated women, and forms of personal and psychological conflict as well as additional economic strains become a reality in the Black community as a result of: 1) abandoning traditional patterns of marriage; 2) utilizing the pill as a birth control device, and 3) adopting polygamy as a way of life, then liberation may truly represent a trick bag.

The case for liberation (in terms of personal relationships) as a trick bag may have been stated too harshly and too sharply. Yet it is clear that the women involved in our study are not accepting numerous forms of liberation at face value simply because they may be in vogue. On the contrary they seem to be analyzing each form of alleged liberation to determine whether or not its colors are really false.

CHAPTER III

# Traditional Political Animals? A Loud No

*Against a background* of urban riots and rebellions, and a deep-seated fear of Blacks by Whites, Richard Nixon entered the White House as the thirty-seventh President of the United States. His success at the polls occurred without the cooperation of most Blacks since about 90% of the Black vote went to Hubert Humphrey. Unlike Lyndon B. Johnson, Nixon made no apparent effort to include a Black person in a cabinet position. Nor did he extend an "open" invitation to any "Black leaders" to come periodically to the White House to talk over pressing problems confronting the Black population. Indeed, with respect to the Black political leadership President Nixon initially adopted a closed-door policy and refused repeatedly to meet with them, a fact which led all twelve Black members of the United States House of Representatives to boycott the 1971 State of the Union address. Only after the boycott did President Nixon agree to meet with the Black congressional caucus.

While some "Black leaders" may have chastised Nixon for his cool attitude and non-productive endeavors with respect to Black people, the women of our study employed very vivid and colorful terminology in describing their feelings toward the Nixon-Agnew

Administration. Nixon was called everything from "a bunch of shit," to an "ass hole," to "a dirty old man." And Agnew's labels ranged from "monkey," to "honky," to "son of a bitch." Some typical comments follow:

1. Nixon—that's my hound dog. I can't stand the guy. I'm going to be frank and honest with you. He's not helping no one but Nixon himself.
2. Nixon: I think here too is a bunch of shit. I think the most swinging thing that's happened—there've been two or three things. One when some of his cabinet started to resign and got other jobs. Two is when that little gal last week—Princess Anne—came to town. I think that's the most dynamic thing that has happened since the Nixon Administration. When that kid went up there on the hill and these old men started shuffling her around as to where she ought to go and she pulled her arm away from them, I thought that was very significant. The fact that they had her lined up to go to some library showing thing at the White House and she said I don't want to go there, I want to go where the riots were; the word is bad but she knew what she meant and she knew the street. When those two limousines from the White House took her—and they had to take her because how do you tell the Princess she can't go where she wants to go in America? They had to take her and when the car was driving fast she said slow up I want to take a picture; slow up more. And they had to slow to a snail's pace. I thought that was beautiful. That was magnificent. While Charles is all charming and Mrs. Nixon is trying to make sure there's a romance created there, an international romance, this kid was always left alone and I'm glad they didn't find her an escort because America will always remember that.

3. Nixon, I think he's an ass hole. There's no better word to express it.
4. Well, since I'm on tape I won't say it but you do want my honest opinion? Really I do think they (Nixon and Agnew) are two crazy motherfuckers.
5. President Nixon is a pig. He's what capitalism is. He's what it represents.
6. I think Nixon borders on fascism. I think he's deliberately attempted to organize a really dangerous right around him. Socially all his friends are pro-fascist pigs. The attempt to get Haynsworth and then Carswell into the administration proves he's a really dangerous person.
7. I think he's an ass hole. I think he's a motherfucker. Nixon's not thinking about us but one must always be thinking about him.
8. I think Nixon's just an example of White America, what they represent: white supremacy, middle class values, narrow isolation philosophy about other countries, just all the negative things that anybody has written about White middle class America seems to me to be Richard Nixon and everybody that supports him.
9. Agnew? What is my attitude toward the monkey? A monkey would have more sense than this guy. I mean a monkey even has sense enough to clean his tail when he go to the washroom or else whatever he does. Agnew ain't got that kind of sense. He don't have the sense he was born with and I don't see how he got in the White House in the first place, as Vice President.
10. Agnew? He's a nut. I know he's supposed to have this 135 IQ but after all that's not very high. I have two sons with a higher IQ than that. Mine too was higher than that. But I don't see why he keeps going around talking about a 135 IQ—so what? That doesn't prove anything. It doesn't prove that a per-

son has the attitude and outlook that's going to help people. You can be a genius and still not have the attitude and outlook that's going to help people. This matter of going around and flinging high phrases—anybody can hire him a good writer and do this. I feel that if his speeches are an indication of his attitude then we're in a sorry state.

11. Agnew is nothing but a down right, no good, low lifeted racist and is only doing his job as far as the power structure is concerned, reflecting what they want him to reflect: the right wing views and to frighten Whites more to make them think we, Black people, are their enemies and that the power structure is their friend.
12. In one sentence Agnew's a front for nothing. I don't think he's actually nothing.
13. Agnew is a fool, a racist fool.
14. Agnew is a honky.
15. All I know about him (Agnew) is that he's a good friend of Nixon's. Well, he's just another dirty old man to me.
16. (Agnew's) so funny. He deserves all those little watches and all those little tee shirts. It puts him right where he belongs: in a play pen. He's a child. He's a child in an adult body. You laugh at him and forget him. I don't think he really has any political influence. I however think he does have political influence on the crackers and wasps in Ohio.
17. He's a fool. That's all. (Agnew)
18. Agnew's a pig.
19. Agnew's a joke. He's unbelieveable really. Do I need say more?
20. I'm sorry. I think Agnew is an ass. That's all I can say about him.
21. (Nixon and Agnew)—they're two big idiots.
22. I don't have any feelings about Agnew at all. He's just another Mickey Mouse, Jr.

A few women suggested that President Nixon was mad or insane, or power mad:

1. He's the President of the United States and he represents the silent majority that deals with patriotism and all that. Sometimes I get the feeling that the man's insane. I watch him on tv. He just looks like some people who are just out, just gone that I know. Then a lot of times he acts like a little kid. That whole thing in terms of Carswell. Like he got mad when they didn't approve his people and stomped his foot and then he says your job is not to choose but to approve what I do. They just laughed at that. He doesn't act like a mature adult. I think the man has a lot of problems that have been evident in his whole political career since the Eisenhower days since this tremendous scandal about him taking payolla from the people in San Francisco—being bought lock, stock and barrel by the business people out there.
2. First I thought Nixon was an idiot but really now reading some more things about the mass media and rereading 1984 I think he really might be less of an idiot and more of someone that's shrewd and who has the key for bringing this country into a total suppression of all the people or bringing people into World War III. I think he's mad in a strange way. His madness is toward what someone called saving face. He has a mania toward saving face and he would kill himself to save face. I think the danger is he would do the same thing to the whole country.
3. It's really sad. I don't think the man has all of his senses. I think we are in a very dangerous situation.
4. He's power mad. I feel that the man is very entrenched in the glory of power. I haven't seen him operating as a human. He's operating like a kid you give a bunch of toys for Christmas. It's difficult for

him to see the toys as toys. He's so far out on the ego trip, now the toys are his.

Still others advanced the theory that someone else is pulling the strings for Nixon; that is, others are exercising effective political power even though Nixon ostensibly holds the reins of legitimate power. Big business interests were most often identified as the controlling force acting upon Nixon. Yet someone even suggested that Governor Reagan of California represented the real force in the American political system.

1. Like all administrations they are controlled by big business and he's only doing what the power structure tells him to do. He's only a lackey.
2. Nixon actually is only a figurehead. He's part of a system that's out to destroy us. We've been a sore spot to these people here for a long time. I think Nixon is following the policy.
3. Shit. I think he's going to screw everybody up in terms of foreign policy. I think those that are beckoning to him because they feel he is in sympathy with them domestically and so they are giving him the red light on certain foreign policies. It's like he goes to the highest bidder. Nixon is bought off so he's a puppet on a string so far.
4. Nixon isn't even the man in power. Neither is Agnew or Finch. They are mouthpieces that do the work of those that are out to repress Black people in this country.
5. Well, President Nixon, he's just a puppet to Reagan. Reagan rules the United States.

An overwhelming majority of women felt that Nixon had done nothing to help Blacks. On the contrary, some women were convinced that Nixon's ultimate plan is to send Blacks to concentration camps.

1. My feelings about him ain't nothing. I just don't say nothing about President Nixon. He's just done told

us so many different things wrong until it's just awful. He's done a good job on poor Black people. President Nixon didn't keep a word he said he was going to do for the Black people. He just ain't right.

2. Nixon and his administration have lived up to and probably surpassed everything that a lot of Black people felt he was going to do which is essentially to support what he calls the silent majority of people and his emphasis on law and order and the protection of property which has always been a very consistent position with him. I don't think there is any question that he cares nothing about the interest and welfare of Black people in this country and has demonstrated time and time again that his position is going to be one of containment and if necessary extermination. I think this is very clear.

3. I don't trust him at all. I don't trust him if I was a radical White student. I don't trust him if I was a peaceful, submissive militant Black person. I think he's one of those subtle racists. He cut back all the funds across the board for jobs and poverty, housing, everything he cut back—the Headstart and everything. I think he's really cracking down on the Black community, especially ghettoes because it's getting real bad and he isn't doing anything to alleviate it. I think it's going to come a time sooner or later that the next riot that they have, if they have a large scale riot like the summer of '64, I think he's really going to start shooting people down 'cause they started already and he's going to give the order. Remember when they had the segregation of the schools and they turned over the bus with those children and he hasn't come out and said anything about that. He's taking his time with the desegregation bit in the south. And his partner Agnew with his comment: 'you seen one ghetto you seen them all!' If there ever was a President that's ready to put Black people in concentration camps he's the one,

       'cause he has the backing of the so-called silent majority.
4. (Nixon's) really more anti-Black than I expected him to be and I didn't expect nothing out of him. I expected him to be anti-Black but I guess I didn't expect him to be so open about it.
5. The Nixon Administration stinks. They are all a bunch of fools. They have nothing for the Black man. They're not giving the Black man anything. They don't want to have nothing to do with the Black man. As a matter of fact, they're all racists. That's all.
6. As far as Black people are concerned, they are full of shit, like every other administration. As far as White people are concerned, they exemplify their system.

Some women saw the Nixon-Agnew Administration in a favorable light in terms of its ability to radicalize people. As one woman said:

> The Nixon Administration will serve to radicalize a great deal of people. And I think I'm glad Nixon got in rather than Humphrey because I think it will serve to heighten the differences between Johnson and the present administration. I hope more people will wake up as a result and see the seriousness of the situation.

Other women confessed that they had nothing to do with Nixon since he was not the president of Blacks. Most of these women simply "tuned out" the Nixon Administration completely. One woman admitted that she would not give one second to mourning the death of Nixon.

1. To show how much I've turned him off, I don't listen to him on the radio, on the TV, when he comes on. I don't read any statements that he has made in the newspaper. I don't care. I have no interest in

what he is doing and saying because it's so way out.
2. I hate him. I can't even look at the man on television.
3. If he (Nixon) was to die today it would not be one minute of mourning for me and I hope a whole lot of more feel the same way.

Quite a few women believed that Vice President Agnew represented or was the embodiment of Nixon, saying or doing nothing without the approval of the President.

1. (Agnew) is the mouth of Nixon and more than that. He is the next movement of the right. He never knew he could have it so good up there. And now that he's gotten used to it, if he didn't believe it before, he believes it now.
2. I feel whatever (Agnew's) expressing he's been specifically designated to express. I think that's his purpose. He is like the mouthpiece of the things that Nixon would not be able to say and get away with. I think Agnew is a very intelligent person. They realize what they're doing.
3. I actually don't think Agnew think at all. His thoughts I don't think has ever really been projected. I really would hesitate to say what he really thinks because I believe before he goes on a speech Nixon write it for him, or he sit down and have an all night briefing session with him. I feel if he has any feelings of his own he's afraid to buck the administration any way.

Some women were quick to point out their belief that Nixon and Agnew were dangerous individuals who had to be taken quite seriously. This was true, most believed, because the Nixon Administration is quite bold and willing to take actions which might have been looked upon with horror some seven or eight years ago.

1. Nixon and Agnew—yuck! Chet Huntley denies this but Life quoted him a couple of weeks ago as saying

that Nixon frightened him. Well Chet Huntley might not have said it but I say it—Nixon frightens me because this man is very much concerned with Richard Nixon period. It is surprising with his Quaker background. You would think that a bit of the Quaker humanism—and there is some humanism in the friends' theosophy I guess you would call it—you would think that some of that would come out but you never see any of it. Nixon frightens me because he makes these little jokes—'I am the President,' type thing that David Frye did him up brown.

2. Agnew is an ass. He's not a very intelligent man at all. They always say an empty wagon makes a hell of a lot of noise. I think he's allowing himself to be used by the President. I think he's falling very much into the qualifications for the Vice Presidency in that you are supposed to parrot or say those kinds of things that the President wants to say but it is not politically advantageous for him to say it. Nixon gets his speech writers to write things Nixon wants to say or Mitchell wants to say and the ass repeats like a parrot what he is told to say. As a matter of fact I think he is so (un)intelligent he really wouldn't have any opinion on almost anything because he doesn't have the intelligence to form an opinion. When a man has to go through and publish his IQ and that whole bit then that means there's some question there as to his intelligence, and I don't think he has any. I think he's dangerous though. Dumb people in positions of power are always dangerous. This country would be in very dire danger if something happened to Nixon and Agnew became President. That's one of the worst kinds of catastrophes I could think of.

3. And Agnew I think is even more dangerous because Agnew is Nixon's alter ego. Agnew is really the old Nixon. He is mouthing what Nixon really wants to say and thinks but Nixon as President can't. So

# Traditional Political Animals? A Loud No

Nixon is really putting on a facade. He is the new Nixon but Agnew is the old Nixon. This Agnew is dangerous because he is appealing to the baser instincts in man's nature. I don't like Republicans generally. Those that you see in the media, the newspapers, the TV, you notice them. They all have narrow eyes, thin lips, and they very seldom smile. I think so often about a quote from Shakespeare: "let me have men about me that are fat, sleek-headed men. On such a sleepy night yon Cassius has a lean and hungry look. He thinks too much. Such men are dangerous." But these fools don't even think. Agnew: the only qualifications he could list for President of the USA was that he was President of the PTA of some school in the suburbs.

4. Agnew? Is it allowed? I think he is a blooming idiot. I think people should take him seriously. He is dangerous, very dangerous.
5. It's been thrown out that (Nixon) will cancel the '72 elections. Just as an attorney he really knows better. This Manson thing (about Manson being guilty) which I think he put out there to see what the climate was. That was nothing but a test case and if that can be acceptable, which it seems to be, because of the extreme nature of that, he can do whatever he wants.

In an effort to see how deeply ingrained the disaffection of Black women for the national administration might be, we asked them to indicate their attitude toward Nixon's Family Assistance Proposal and toward former Secretary of Health Education and Welfare, Robert Finch. In terms of the Family Assistance Proposal (designed ostensibly to assist lower socio-economic levels of the population which include a heavy proportion of Blacks) we felt that a positive reaction to that guaranteed income package would negate many of the negative comments on the Nixon Administration—especially with respect to the treatment of the Black community. Of those who had heard of the proposal (and many had not) the overwhelming majority merely confirmed the disaffection of Blacks for the Nixon Administration. The Family Assistance Proposal was scored time after time as a grossly inadequate crumb thrown out to appease the Black populace. As some women contended:

1. That's jive time. It's very superficially dealing with the needs of poor people. When he talks about guaranteed income or a base of $1600 bucks in this inflationary time he's—it's being stupid. I mean 1600 bucks ain't even poverty. It's like desperation. It's like people starving to death. I don't think he is sincere because when he talks about people working and then he cuts back on employment, he cuts back on federal programs that would provide employment, then it's jive time. If you want people to work you're going to have to give people a job. I think what it was was people from various elements of this country putting pressure on him to come out with dealing with social welfare and he got some of his "brain childs" to come up with something that might look good on paper, might sound fairly decent but means nothing.

2. I think this income thing is a joke. It's a joke. It's a hoax and every other thing you want to call it. There's a gimmick to that thing. Whatever they say it takes to maintain a family your size, whatever you're making or whatever you're lacking the government is supposed to give you what's missing provided that you take on whatever occupation they find. Now fuck the fact that you may not be able to swing it. If you don't do it you don't get the money —not to mention that the amount of money that they've designated per size of family is not enough anyway. He's not doing anything for Black people. He doesn't have the slightest intent of doing anything for Blacks. He's a poor redneck. Now what has a poor redneck ever done for a Black man?

3. It's just a whole lot of talk. Now this guaranteed income, the reason it looks so pleasing to some people like in Mississippi in the South, it's more than what they have now but for the people out here in California, and in New York it's less than what they have now. But what he intends to do is supplement that. He intends for every able bodied person to be out there working. Now with the state of the economy as it is now, where are these people going to get a job? These people are old. Some of them are crippled. Some of them are mothers who don't have anybody to keep their children and mothers without any skills. It looks good: we're going to guarantee every mother or every able bodied person a job. It sounds good but where are you going to get a job?
4. I think it's something he's throwing out here just like the poverty program to pacify the people and make them feel that they are getting somewhere under this present system. Just like the poverty program it will not be a success.
5. I feel like (Nixon) should go home and live on it a couple of days. It doesn't even take a week, just a couple of days. Then the whole thing would be changed.
6. Now you know Nixon spends more on his dogs feeding them and we're supposed to be a little above them. We should be entitled to more than that. It's just not worth a damn.

We chose to question the women about Robert Finch because he was pictured in some quarters as the 'good guy' of the Nixon Administration, that is a 'good guy' in the sense that he was viewed as more in tune with the social needs of Black people. Yet most women had never heard of Robert Finch or had not heard enough to comment one way or the other. Those who did make a statement on Finch were divided in their evaluation of him. Some accepted the 'good guy' image and felt that Finch had tried to help Black people.

1. I heard quite a bit about him helping the Black people with this program they had. I think he's a nice man.
2. I think Finch was an idealistic man. I think that he wanted to do a lot of things and he would have done a lot of things if his hands had not been tied but his hands were tied and Finch could not and I say it's the best thing that he's no longer there.
3. Finch was the type of person that was helping the Black people. That's why he was fired. Any White man that helps the Black man is either killed or taken from his job.
4. His job has probably made him more liberal. He's now been made a minority and he's beginning to see how it feels. And one thing about White people, they're not used to being mistreated and they come out fighting. We haven't heard the last of him. If he leaves that administration he'll be the one to tell all.
5. I think he was a little White boy who was just trying, who really was coming from his principles, dealing on that whole level that they taught him when he was a kid and the stuff he read in the constitution, on the level you can't do it if you're White. You're not supposed to do that. They call you nigger lover like they used to call folks Indian lovers. He was coming from a straighten HEW line. This is what HEW is supposed to do and this is what we were told. 'No, that ain't what you're supposed to do. You're supposed to keep them niggers in check, not give them niggers more money, not fund this program and that program.'

Others concluded that Finch was just another White man who could not be trusted. Moreover, they viewed him as incapable or unwilling to go against the wishes of Richard Nixon.

1. All I know is that he got burned by his buddy. I understand he wasn't as big an s.o.b. as Mitchell is

but I'm sure he's done his little tricks in his day too. I'm not really too concerned about White folks.

2. I think he kept the same type of double image of trying to be a poor struggling liberal but under the attack of all these moderates and conservatives. I think he was just the President's boy and he was there. There was no way possible he could have brought off any significant health, education and labor reforms because Nixon himself didn't want them to go through and the people he had given him to work with weren't going to approve them and put them into practice. So he was put in a hamstring type of position and he was demoted and now put into a position of Presidential advisor. It just adds to that thing of giving false illusions to the American people and he let himself be used in that way. I just see him as being someone who is aiding and abetting the eventual increased suppression of people.

3. I never met the guy. I never seen the guy. All I know I hate the guy. He does so many things that just don't agree with my way of being and my way of thinking. I understand he's White. A lot of things that really need attention to and a lot of proposals that's sent in to him to get rents and this type of thing, they always come back without any help for it. He's out to help just me and my White folks and that's it.

4. I think Finch is just like the rest of the little puppets Nixon has around. When things got too tough for him he cut out like most of them do. He's secretary of HEW and we want to talk with him. We were advocating this guaranteed income and a lot of policies that can be set by him but he just didn't want to deal with it. He was afraid of the people for one thing. He was afraid of Nixon. He didn't want to lose his white collar job so we in turn went down and took over the office. I think Finch began

to realize welfare rights was organized. We have a membership of 45,000 people across the country. He knows that we are beginning to speak up for our rights and he just got scared. He even had a heart attack or whatever that was that put him in the hospital. I think we did it.
5. Finch is not a liberal. Finch is a Californian and a Reagan man. He ain't no different from all them other exploiters. He's a tool of the military-industrial complex. He was never a liberal. He was a liberal to Reagan but shit, what is that? He's to the left of Reagan and not to the left of Nixon. He has no guts. When it was finally demanded that he meet with his people he had a nervous breakdown.

It is apparent, then, that most women surveyed have written off the national political administration and dismissed any possibility of Nixon, Agnew, or any member of the cabinet being helpful to Black people. Some women were so disenchanted with the national political scene that they refused to comment on it. Then, too, several women abstained from offering remarks about national politicians—apparently because they feared their words would end up in the wrong hands and result in possible reprisals against them.

Upon viewing the total rejection of White politicians on the national level, we were anxious to see how the Black women would assess the contributions or potential of Black politicians in terms of improvements in the Black community. To this end we asked the women what they thought of Senator Edward Brooke, James Farmer, Adam Clayton Powell, Clifford Alexander, Shirley Chisholm, John Conyers, and Charles Diggs.

*Senator Edward Brooke*

Beginning in 1950 Senator Edward Brooke launched his political career in the state of Massachusetts where he had migrated after World War II to attend law school. Unsuccessful in his first try for the Massachusetts State Legislature Brooke tried again in 1952 and once again suffered defeat, although by a narrow margin. After another defeat in 1960 in a campaign for Secretary of State in Massachusetts, Brooke began to make his mark as Chairman of the Boston Finance Committee. In this capacity he was able to unmask a great deal of public corruption and to receive the applause of 'honest-minded' citizens for a job well done. Primarily as a result of his work on the finance commission Brooke, in 1962, became the elected Attorney General for the State of Massachusetts. He performed so well as Attorney General that he confidently announced his decision to seek the United States Senate seat to be vacated by the retirement of Leverett Saltonstall. After emerging victorious in a primary contest Brooke went on to wage a successful campaign against Endicott Peabody whose mother was one of those participants in civil rights activities in the South.

Despite his long exposure on the political scene, albeit mainly in Massachusetts, many women in our survey had difficulty with the name of Senator Brooke. Almost invariably the "e" in his last name would be substituted with an "s" so that instead of Senator Brooke, he became Senator Brooks. Even one woman with a doctorate from an Ivy League institution referred to him constantly as Senator Brooks.

The attitudes toward Senator Brooke varied, with most women being negatively critical, or at least skeptical of his impact on the concerns of Black people. A few, however, were positive in their comments. These positive attitudes stemmed from those who recalled that Senator Brooke had done some favors for people. A few in the South remembered and appreciated his efforts in Mississippi following the violence at Jackson State College.

1. He impressed me very much when he (went to) Mississippi after the killing on the Jackson State campus. Through him and others like him I believe we have done more toward placing responsibility than would have been done had not such a person as Senator Brooke (gone to Mississippi).
2. He's o.k. I really liked him. I believe he made his appearance in Mississippi during the violence at Jackson State College and he did a lot of talking for

the Black students and got (them) through a lot.
3. I believe he has done the best he could under the circumstances. But I also understand that he (went) to Jackson State College when the slaughter of the Black students took place.
4. He's been in there for a while and he's probably done a few small things. I personally had a friend who was in the service and wanted to come home for some reason—I think his wife was having a baby—and Brooks was able to arrange something. But that's was able to arrange something. But that's such a small level. That's one person you're doing something for, one Black person and Brooks has been in office enough to accomplish something. I really don't feel about him as a Black man. He's a Negro that we have. I don't think of him as being somebody who has achieved something.

A few others thought that Brooke had improved over the last two years or so and could be seen as working for the betterment of the Black man's condition.

1. I have been more impressed and I have been willing to respect him more in the last couple of years than when he started off.
2. Very interesting. Right away I kind of think things about Black Republicans. But I began to respect him very much with—I don't know which one it was—the Haynsworth or Carswell nomination. He surprised me, pleasantly so, in being as vocal and speaking up. This is why I'm very leery of saying this man is a Tom. He shouldn't be here. He shouldn't be there 'cause a lot of times these people can grow and they just have to see the light.
3. I like him personally. I think he could do more in his own town but I realize he has a lot of opposition because being Black and in his position he's getting

hit from the White side as well as the Black side. It's awful hard when you're in a political position or high executive office to please everyone. I believe he's working for betterment of Blacks. I believe he can do more but still he's in a position as most Black men and women are in. They have a certain amount of fear because they're there and if they do a lot they're going to be kicked out. For some reason they feel they're part of the first and they've got to be good and behave in order for other Blacks to make it.

4. I don't know of any particular point I can remember him for in terms of the Black community but lately I think he's expresssed a lot of alarm at what the administration he's worked so much with over the past years has been doing. I think he's really made some strong statements about Nixon and his pro-right approach.

Still a few others felt that he was effective nationally even though this might not be obvious. Yet, some who did recognize his effectiveness hastened to add their opinion that he still allows himself to be used in certain instances.

1. I don't know too much about him. I'm glad to see a brother a senator, having a Black man in that high position again in the country. He by no means is revolutionary and has never purported to be but I think that he functions on his level in terms of effecting some change for his constituents. And that's all he's required to do.
2. I think he's a marvelous person. Being a Republican, I think he's not let the present administration dictate to him policies. I think he's still maintained his Blackness in a white situation.
3. I like the way he uses power when he has it: very quietly and very elegantly and nobody knows what

hits them; and he's probably one of the quiet heroes of the Senate. At the same time he has allowed himself to be used in horrendous ways and that's unexcusable. Maybe in the future he can do more in a way his own people know he's doing more than at the present. Otherwise he will be crucified in his own way for not doing enough and maybe he really has.

But most of the comments about Senator Brooke were negative from a Black perspective. That is, most women seemed to agree with the label affixed to Edward Brooke by Chuck Stone: "Mr. Non-Negro Politics." (Chuck Stone, *Black Political Power in America*, revised edition, New York: A Delta Book, 1970, p. 171). A number of women denied his Blackness—preferring to call him "Negro," or "colored," or "White." Many concluded that he was not Black because of his marriage to Remigia Ferrari-Scacco, an Italian woman. The hostility to this liaison spilled over in the words of several women.

1. Well Edward Brooke is a nice boy. He comes from a well to do family. He went off to Italy and married an Italian broad, has two beautiful White daughters. He should be happy. I think of Edward Brooke like I do any other liberal White man.
2. I'm not very impressed with Edward Brooke probably because of his wife. She's what—Italian?
3. I don't have anything to say about—especially Edward Brooke. I read a poem by Don O. Lee once and it was: Edward Brooke sat at his desk crying and slashing his wrists because someone had called him Black. I think that's the sentiments I have toward him. He recognizes no ties as far as I'm concerned back to the community in terms of his position.
4. Edward Brooke is a very responsible *Negro*. I'd give him C minus. He is the type of leader that Charlie likes. A Negro is a person of African ancestry who

thinks and wishes subconsciously, perhaps consciously too, that he were White.
5. Senator Edward Brooke is a colored man. He is not a Black man, not to me and I do not have very much respect for him because Brooke has denied his race all along—married his little White woman. His kids have known nothing but White. He hasn't had anything to do with Blacks. Maybe I hold a grudge but ever since I heard him speak on nationwide TV at the Republican Convention where he made this statement out of his effort to back—he got up there on that podium and my dear colored man did say that he thought that people should back Goldwater and accept his platform and he did say how the platform could be advantageous to colored people and I heard the man say that. As far as I'm concerned he can go to hell, fifty times and back again. Now recently you'll hear him say the Blacks here, there and the other. The only reason why Black is coming from the lips of that man is simply because of the fact that in this day and age everybody knows he's a nigger first of all. He's not going to make it unless he acknowledges his race. Everybody knows that if you're Black you got to talk Black or else you're lost.
6. He's married to a White woman. That's quite a contradiction. He couldn't be a Black politician married to a White person.
7. Edward Brooke is a White man. He's more Nixon than Nixon is. The tragic thing is that he thinks he has to be that way. He doesn't know he can be Black.
8. Any Black cat that's fucking a White woman at night is off my list. I don't even want to consider him. I don't even want to discuss him. He does not exist. I don't like him. He does not exist for me. You write him off. He's with them. It's time for Black people to choose sides. He's already chosen

> sides so you don't consider him Black. He's Mr. Brooke, colored man. He belongs over there with them.

One or two women even expressed shock when informed that Senator Brooke was not biologically White. As one woman said.

> Senator Edward Brooke? Ain't he White? Well honey that's what I think about him. I haven't even looked at him. I hear him talking and he talks so much like a White dude I thought he was.

A few women chastized Brooke for trying to make it in the system. Still others accused him of a lack of concern for the masses.

> 1. I think he's a rather frustrated man now really. He feels that you can make it within the system just like many of the others. He gets angry when Black people are being repressed. What he doesn't know is that repression is a matter of routine in this country and this is what he ought to know. If he thinks there is any way in the world he can change this system with one Black man in the Senate he's off his rocker.
> 2. (Senator Brooke is a) bootlicker. He's someone who's not going to do anything to change their position. He's not worried about the people. He's worried about his job.

A couple of women had written Senator Brooke off completely saying he meant nothing to them and that he simply represented his constituency which, as of 1960, included only 2.2% Black people. (Stone, 1970, p. 172)

> 1. I heard of him, seen him on TV but he doesn't mean a darn thing to me.
> 2. I think he's representative of his constituency.

It is clear, then, that Brooke is not looked upon as any kind of leader in the Black struggle. Moreover it is equally apparent that the women in our study do not perceive Senator Brooke as being in a position where he can siphon off money, jobs, or other items for the amelioration of Black people. In other words not one woman looked to Brooke as a means of achieving "pie" or even "beans" from the system, let alone as a way of "liberating" resources from the grasp of the establishment.

*Adam Clayton Powell*

Three marriages and twenty-six years after making a grand entrance onto the political scene Adam Clayton Powell finally seemed vulnerable. As a youthful enthusiast and young minister he fought many battles including that against employment discrimination in Harlem, that to force the New York Transport Workers Union to admit Blacks, and that to end treatment of Black soldiers in World War II as inferior beings. The climax of his career came in 1961 as he assumed the chairmanship of the House Education and Labor Committee. Of his tenure as chairman of that committee Chuck Stone has written:

> In his five years as Chairman, Powell's Committee passed 60 major pieces of legislation which included increasing the minimum wage, fair employment practices, aid to elementary and secondary schools, manpower development training act, antijuvenile delinquency, vocational rehabilitation, school lunch program, barring discrimination in salaries paid to women for the same work performed by men, Federal aid for library services and the war on poverty. Few could dispute his skilled admiralship in steering a bill through the hidden reefs of Congressional whims and neuroses. (Stone, 1970, p. 198)

Even President Johnson felt compelled to congratulate Powell on his fine record as Chairman of the Committee:

> The fifth anniversary of your Chairmanship of the House Education and Labor Committee reflects a brilliant record of accomplishment. It represents the successful reporting to the Congress of 49 pieces of bedrock legislation. And the passage of every one of these bills attests to your ability to get things done. . . . Only with progressive leadership could so much have been accomplished by one Committee in so short a time. I speak for the millions of Americans who benefit from these laws when I say I am truly grateful.
> (*Stone, 1970, p. 198*)

The beginning of Powell's "demise" may be traced to Mrs. Esther James, a Harlem resident whom Powell ungently called a "bag woman" while a guest on a TV program. When Powell refused to retract his statement Mrs. James commenced legal action which resulted in a monetary award originally set at $211,500 —$11,500 in compensatory and $200,000 in punitive damages— but later lowered to $46,500—$11,500 in compensatory and $35,000 in punitive damages. (James v. Powell, 14 N.Y. 2d 881, 19 N.Y. 2d 249).* Powell's failure to honor the court action soon led to contempt citations which "forced" him to steer clear of New York —first only during week days—and then even on Sundays after a criminal contempt citation was handed down against him.

In addition to the James' matter Powell experienced problems with his own Education and Labor Committee. Disagreement with his policies and actions led to a revolt on the committee which saw his ouster as committee chairman. A series of Drew Pearson articles purporting to "expose" Powell's personal behavior—for example, "junkets" with female secretaries and the failure of his third wife to receive her pay checks, even though they were being cashed, as well as trips to Miami and Bimini with Corrine Huff—did not help take the pressure off Powell. A House investigation of Powell in late 1966 led not only to the loss of his

---

* After Powell made a transfer of some real property to avoid an attachment the Court added $75,000 in compensatory and $500,000 in punitive damages. Eventually, this additional award was struck down on appeal.

chairmanship of the House Education and Labor Committee but also the refusal to seat him in January 1967 even though he was a duly elected congressman from New York.

Despite partially successful judicial litigation which resulted in a decision that Congress should not have excluded him, Powell was not able to regain his position and stature either in the Congress or in his congressional district. Then, too, the redrawing of congressional district lines by the New York State legislature added to Powell's constituency residents of New York's Upper West Side, a racially mixed conglomeration as well as a relatively high socio-economic mix. Powell was defeated in the Democratic primary by Charles Rangel, a Black man who went on to win Powell's congressional seat, without serious contest, in the November 1970 election. Powell was held ineligible to run in that election as an independent.

As in the case of Edward Brooke, attitudes towards Powell on the part of women in our survey ranged widely. It is interesting to note, parenthetically, that no woman had difficulty recognizing the name Powell. In other words all women were familiar with Powell whether they were from the East, West, Midwest, or South. This ease of recognition seems to confirm Chuck Stone's characterization of Powell as "Mr. National Black Politics."

Several women commented upon Powell's physical health and seemed to view him sympathetically as in the twilight of his career silently suffering from a serious, dreaded illness.

1. It's sort of sad. I feel sort of sorry for the man because he looks sick to me now. When you see him on television and everything he just looks sick.
2. Probably if Adam had gone on as Whitey he could have been President because he knows how to wheel and deal. He's kind of a tragedy of an active man who can't face his own ending so he has continued to grasp for power after physically it's impossible if what I have heard is true.

Others felt that he had been forced to abandon his career because he was Black and too powerful.

I think Powell is a bit ahead of our time so I don't know about him like say our parents might know about him but I have to speak on what happened to him as far as his political career is concerned. And I must say that I think the man was put down because he's Black. Powell wasn't doing anything more than any of those White congressmen were doing but since the man's Black and since he did wield as much power as he did, the White man is smart. He's not going to let Black people get too much power. The minute they see there's a possible threat to the White power structure they're going to blow it away or try to. I think that's what happened with Powell. He did a lot of good things and shit, the man is Black and as long as he's Black I can't say too much against him especially since he's tried to do good for his people. Sure he was out for himself and gained quite a bit for himself. There was nothing wrong with that because it was the White man's money. That's who holds it all.

Several women displayed a generally positive attitude toward Powell pointing out what he had achieved for Black people and how he had dared flaunt his virtues before the White power structure.

1. I love Adam. He's a devil. He's loud and wrong but I love him because he's just a loveable old devil. His committee work was very good. His absenteeism was bad. Adam is very ill now. I don't think a lot of people know it. I suspect he has more cancer than was announced.
2. As much as Adam Clayton Powell might be hated by the White community I still respect him because I think he did a lot for Black people, as much as he could possibly have done.
3. I admire Adam Clayton Powell. He did an awful lot as far as getting bills when he was the Chairman of the Education Committee and he did an awful lot of organizing and getting bills through

> the Congress. He's a very flamboyant person. Sometimes I wonder if his mistake wasn't being too flamboyant although he was crucified for doing the same thing the White man did.
> 4. I liked (Powell). So many things he did I didn't like because wrong is wrong and you can't do nothing to make it right but he was a Black man and he was in office. But he had a lot of nerve and he did this because the White men were doing it too. I don't think he did it because they were doing it. I think he did it because Adam wanted to do it because this is the way it seems like he is made up and that's wrong. He shouldn't have been doing these things. If he was going to do it, he should have used a little more discretion with it. But I admired him when he fought back. I really dig the man. I respect him because he's standing up saying yes I did this and I'm a man and I'm a Black man and I'm going to stand up to it and when he got ready to tell Mr. Charlie off, he'd tell him. So I dig this about him.

One woman even saw Powell as a continuing symbol for Blacks even though his positive contributions may have diminished over the past couple of years.

> I think he tried to put some things through but whether in recent years he has done anything is questionable. But since I don't view that as the potential of any kind, I was very disappointed that he wasn't re-elected because I think he's more of a symbol. I don't think he has any power but I think he is a symbol in that since White people have come down on him so hard it's unfortunate at this particular time that he was defeated; well he still has a chance. I don't think Rangel's going to be able to do any more.

Another woman regarded Powell as a "true politician:"

I often say he's stealing in the name of the Lord. He's a true politician and in terms of Black people you can't dispute his record in Congress. He has voted right all the time and I think he was one of the most powerful men in the Congress. I think a lot of the fact that he didn't take more initiative and do more is that Black people were not considering the importance of his position and pushing him to do some things of a political nature. Black people were asking him very petty things: get my daughter in Howard University; but no one pressed Adam, as far as I know, for a political position say that supported Black nationalism or panafricanism or anything like that. Yet in his power he did a great deal about finding out about Africa himself and understanding the White man's situation. He understands the White politician better than any other Black man alive today and what makes him tick. I see the White politician in a way as a prostitute.

Yet other women were not as complimentary. Women in this category, as a rule, thought Powell could have done much more for Blacks instead of retreating to Bimini. But the sharpest criticism came from those who accused Powell of denying his Blackness.

1. He's been shucking and jiving for a long time. In the 1970's here's a gal named Shirley Chisholm working her cane off up there and he's still going to the Bahamas and wherever else he wants. The people in Harlem said man, we're getting us a ticket together but we don't want, we got to get rid of you because we got to get some workhorse in there.
2. This is one of these "White" racists. I really feel he is a racist. Maybe other people have a different view than I do. To me he's a racist that tried to get in and get on the good side with the Black man. He really don't know how. He always tried to fool the Black man into something. He used the Black man so that he could get his position. That's the

type of person he is and he ain't good enough for my footstool.
3. I think he's doing a good thing. I don't think he's Black in any way. I think he's Italian and he figured he could not make it being an Italian so he figured he'd become Black. And I think he has done his thing, did what he wanted to, made the money he wanted to, and he's still hollering and preaching but I don't think he's really for the cause.
4. I have mixed feelings about him because first of all he says he's not a Black man. Then again he says that he is a Black man and if I'm not mistaken I read an article not too long ago where he said he is not a Black man. And there was some conflict between he and his wife. I believe he disowned her in some ways or another. If he is a Black man I don't go for a Black man denying his color because I think Black is beautiful.

In contrast to the comments on Senator Edward Brooke, at least some women thought that Powell had managed to use the system to channel some few benefits to the Black community. Nevertheless, some women also pointed to the ease with which a man like Powell could be eliminated from a position of power which allowed him to use some of the system's resources for the betterment of the Black community.

1. Well, they kicked him out of Congress but I think he was one of the best Black leaders. He did a lot of things wrong but he was the first one who channeled so much money into Harlem, HarYou, and he got jobs for Black people at 125th Street. Everybody in Congress most likely has taken some graft or stealing. I think that was the first guy who came up there and kicked him out. I don't think that girl Esther James got up there all of a sudden and said she was going to sue him. I think someone pushed her into doing it. Since he was for the first

time pushing all that money, money into Harlem and the first congressman the people rallied around, I think they had to destroy that image. Old people in Harlem can sit back and remember when Adam Clayton Powell got them jobs. Adam Clayton Powell was around when they didn't have any congressmen. Last year he didn't campaign and won. This year he almost won too.

2. I don't know that much about Powell but I think it's funny that he managed to steal all that money from out the White man's nose and then when he got caught threatened to set people up. He had them going. He was together.

It seems, then, that a few women recognized that vulnerability to destruction by the White power structure increases as the power of a Black man like Powell augments itself. In this respect perhaps parallels can be drawn between the case of Adam Clayton Powell and Kwame Nkrumah, deposed leader of Ghana.

*Shirley Chisholm*

"Fighting Shirley" from Brooklyn, New York was the most frequent image painted by the respondents when asked what they thought of Congresswoman Shirley Chisholm. She had "fought" her way through the very competitive Brooklyn College in the forties, "fought" again to secure employment in her chosen field of education, "fought" to help establish the Unity Democratic Club in the Bedford Stuyvesant section of Brooklyn in the very early '60's, "fought" first to secure the nomination for a New York State Assembly seat in 1964 (she met hostility from many quarters, for example a 70 year old man lashed out at her with the following questions: "Young woman, what are you doing out here in the cold? Did you get your husband's breakfast this morning? Did you straighten up his house? What are you doing running for office? That is something for men.") and then secured a smashing victory in the campaign with 18,151 votes to 1,893

# Traditional Political Animals? A Loud No

for the Republican Charles Lewis, and 913 for the respected Liberal Simeon Golar. Then in her greatest "fight" Congresswoman Chisholm emerged from an operation for a "massive tumor" to wage a battle for the United States Congress against the nationally prominent James Farmer. In a crushingly successful contest Mrs. Chisholm outpolled the Republican Farmer with 34,885 votes to Farmer's 13,777. Ralph J. Carvane, running on the Conservative ticket, brought up the rear with 3,771. With this victory "fighting Shirley" surged into the national spotlight as many, out of curiosity maybe, sought to understand how a small woman could have won such a solid victory over the former leader of CORE and the master rhetorician and debater. (For further information on the life of Shirley Chisholm see her autobiography: *Unbought and Unbossed*, 1970.)

The image of "fighting Shirley" evidently had seeped into the minds of most of our respondents who were familiar with Congresswoman Chisholm. Of those who were acquainted with her most comments were laudatory, ranging from "together" and "the most" to "beautiful" and "a fighter."

1. Oh, I love her. O my goodness, here is a woman after my own heart. She is just great. One thing about her, she comes up with a little different approach. She doesn't ape somebody else for one thing. She feels deeply. She comes right from the thing which many brothers do. Some of us on the higher rung of the ladder did too but they erased it. But she, I think the woman has very strong convictions. I really think she ran for that job to try to get that job to do something for her people. Of course it's too bad that she won't be able to do it in Congress because out of 435 congressmen, we've only got nine, and they say it's a possibility we can elect up to nine more. That's only 18. It will be past the year 2000. Frankly I don't think we are going to make it out of the seventies, to get anywhere near a partially meaningful number.
2. I think she's groovy from all that I've seen on TV

and what she talks about. I think she's got a lot of good things that are going for her if they let her do it.
3. I've read a little about Shirley Chisholm and I think she's a dynamic little woman. I feel she, in contrast to Edward Brooke, would be an example of more of what we would want out of a politician who is working within the system.
4. Shirley Chisholm is a beautiful gal. You have to respect her because she's honest and honorable.
5. Shirley is my kind of girl. She's a fighter. She's outspoken. She's fearless. A for Shirley.
6. I think she's a great woman and I have been in conference with Shirley Chisholm. And I really think she wants to change (the system) and she would work in whatever direction she can. I feel she would do all she can to bring about a change in the direction that she can do it in. Shirley Chisholm can't do it by herself. It'll take more Black women and more Black men to work together. With togetherness we can achieve something but divided among ourselves we can't.
7. I think she is a fantastic lady. She is a very vocal lady. I can't really argue with anything that she has done up until this point.
8. I think she's the most. I heard her speak. I was in . . . . I tried to get a chance to see her but I couldn't. I admire her greatly in everything she does. I like the way she talks. The fact that she is a woman makes me feel good I guess. She is unabashed and unafraid. She's just everything that I would like to be.
9. Wonderful. I think that's the beautifulest Black woman I ever saw other than Miss Bethune. She is standing her ground. She couldn't care less about how they feel about her. She couldn't care less about the salary she is receiving. She is still stepping. She is going on and saying the same thing.

She said one thing to get elected and she's saying the same thing after elections.
10. She's sort of my idol in the sense that she does hold a national office in Congress. I have nothing but admiration for her. At the same time I think she reflects the ideal of Black femininity. She not only vocalizes in terms of Blacks in general but she also is able to voice the concerns of Black women and I think this is very important.
11. Beautiful. That's a beautiful sister. Oh, get down. She is so beautiful. One day she came here and I followed that woman around. She landed at the airport and X and some other people brought her to the Z and she spoke at a luncheon. She left the luncheon and went to the D to a women's tea or something and I went. She left the tea and went to a reception. Then she left there and went to E and talked to a group of students. This woman started at 11:30 and just constant; I was super tired and she looked like she'd just stepped off the plane. Her hair was still in place. Her dress was still immaculate. Her voice was still clear and she was rapping some beautiful stuff. I read an article in the Black Scholar about her, women's liberation, and she was hitting on a lot of points we talked about today: how the racism and sexism are involved together and the women's roles. She's beautiful.

A few women expressed admiration for Congresswoman Chisholm but in the same breath raised serious doubts about whether she could accomplish anything in the system.

1. Again because I don't believe this system is good, that it can function for our best interests, becoming a politician or infiltrating in that sense is going to be effective. You might win a little game here and there but certainly not in terms of a big over-

all change or revolution. You just become part of the system.

Then there were some women who, expressing no admiration for Shirley Chisholm, simply insisted that she needs to learn that Black people cannot make it in the system.

>    1. I think Shirley Chisholm has a lot to learn as far as Black people are concerned. I guess she feels that within the present society Black people still can make it through law, the changing of law. But Shirley Chisholm like other Blacks within the legislative power will have to learn that we cannot make it that way. They have been making laws for us all our lives and up under this present system that's all they are going to do. People do not make the law. Laws are made for us and Shirley Chisholm is one who is going to have to understand that herself.
>    2. I'm not impressed with Shirley Chisholm at all. She is a Black woman so to speak. I think when Black people excell to such high positions I'll say right on to them but I don't tend to think you can work within the system to destroy it. Overall, people like Shirley Chisholm and James Farmer, they don't deal with the problems of Black people.

Still a few others thought that Shirley Chisholm might have started thinking too much of herself, even to the extent that she will not listen to others, especially to youth.

>    1. I met her and I think she's a very interesting person but I don't know if I believe her. I just don't know. I think somewhere along in the conversation I think she was saying that she was like a little god. I'm going to do this for my people. I can't explain it. Maybe in my mind I thought she was a Black person first and a politician second. Maybe it's the other way around. And there's nothing wrong with

with that. She doesn't bite her tongue. That's for sure. And she says what's on her mind. I really don't know what it is that concerns me. Maybe it's that she's a politician first.

2. I thought she started out real good but did I read an article by Anderson who took Drew Pearson's place? He was saying that she had accepted so many engagements to speak and in accepting these engagements she had made so many thousands of dollars for her own personal use. I think she started off real nice and her intentions were good but I think a lot of times when people get into positions like that then they think of themselves. So I think she's doing all right and she's voting nicely and she hasn't missed any votings. I guess she's voted the way her people want her to vote but I still think she's thinking of herself like many of us do when we get into certain positions.

3. I liked her more before I got to meet and talk with her. She's all those great things and she wants to talk for youth but she's got on this talking thing so she won't let youth talk to her. She was here several months ago . . . and being in two of the things the only Black persons she and I started talking and it was . . . she'll be great as long as she maintains an open communication line between the people she's representing. Otherwise she's so dynamic she tends to take over and that's worse than someone who can't comprehend to begin with.

A couple of women expressed the belief that Shirley Chisholm talked quite well but failed to follow through with actions. As three women said:

1. I like her. I think that she's outspoken. I haven't looked at a lot of the issues that she's spoken out on except where she challenged the Democratic Convention and challenged the way the Democratic

Party—the way she challenged them and said basically there was no difference between them and the republicans. A lot of times I heard her speak loudly and become emotional but she doesn't really seem to follow through with actions. I wonder if she's going to do any more with this.

2. As far as Shirley Chisholm is concerned I don't feel she has done as much as she could have for the Black people. I feel that, I don't know, she's more or less a symbol but she's not really doing anything. I don't see anything that she's doing. She makes a lot of great speeches and she tells Black people what they should do and the things that need to be done but I haven't seen any bills that she's introduced or anything that she's done constructively to help Black people.

3. I don't think these congressmen or congresswomen are able to do any too much. She gets up and she makes her speeches. And she's applauded and she's hailed as the first Black congresswoman and all that stuff. These little kids out here haven't fared any better as a result of her being the first Black congresswoman.

It was with great fanfare and publicity that Congresswoman Chisholm successfully rejected a position on the House Agriculture Committee. This challenge and rejection seemed to disturb several women who felt that Congresswoman Chisholm had not pondered the importance of the Agriculture Committee—especially its connection to the food stamp program and school lunches. As one woman indicated:

I think Miss Chisholm's hands been tied. They put her on no important committees where she could make a contribution. However I feel that it was very wrong that she didn't get into the Department of Agriculture, because you have to dig into these bureaucracies before you know what's happening there. For example, she

could make quite an impact on school lunches. All of
the lunches for schools come out of the Department of
Agriculture and I know just plenty school systems where
they don't even have a cafeteria much less warm lunches
for kids who need them. In suburbia, beautiful cafeterias and the best of school lunches prepared.

Then, too, several women were quite disturbed to see that "fighting Shirley" had signed a statement in favor of Israel—an act which was viewed as a clear contradiction to her alleged support of Black causes in the U.S., especially those touching, even remotely so, on revolutionary action.

1. Shirley Chisholm was cool with me until she came out and signed the Israel declaration. I thought she was following a correct line until she did that. I was very much taken aback when I saw her name.
2. She doesn't consider herself a Tom. Obviously when you run for office you must feel that you can do something in that office. You can't say they are opposing their people but they may not understand what has to be done to help them. She seems to try not to get into a proper congressional woman bag. She seems to want to keep who she is. Then anyone who could sign to support Israel when she comes from Brooklyn where the Jews are trying to close down Ocean Hill Brownsville—that's just a poor understanding and Jews are not our friends. In her mind I think she's committed but whether that will have any effect I doubt it.
3. I have a lot of respect for Shirley Chisholm. I think that she's certainly done or made, or just brought a lot of the questions of repression, the questions of poverty in Black communities to the fore. I think she is a very fine force but unfortunately I think she is not a very political person. That's obvious from her change in her supporting activities. For instance she supported, along with other women, and helped

raise funds to get Joan Bird out of jail, a political prisoner and part of the New York Panther 21, and in the same breath she went out and supported funds and military arms to Israel which is working in the interest of the bourgeoisie and not in the interest of Black people. So I think that she really doesn't have a good clear cut understanding of the way things work.

A few conclusions may be drawn from the attitudes expressed about Congresswoman Chisholm. First, although a great many respondents knew of her, an estimated ten or fifteen percent had never heard of her. This was true mainly for those respondents who were geographically removed from the East coast. That is, of those who had heard nothing about Shirley Chisholm, most resided in the South and West. Second, and more important perhaps, is the indication that some Black women are casting a constantly watchful eye on Congresswoman Chisholm to determine exactly what she is doing for Blacks while working in the political system. Third, and equally important, some women have already concluded that Congresswoman Chisholm erred in her decision to work within the political system. Her endeavors within the system are viewed by some as incorrect because of a conviction of the futilityof plowing one's way through the man's system.

*John Conyers and Charles Diggs*

What was most interesting about the responses to inquiries about Congressman Conyers and Diggs is that even though both had been in Congress for a much longer time than Shirley Chisholm (Diggs since 1954 and Conyers 1964), most Black women in the survey had never heard of them. Moreover, Diggs was often confused with the late William Dawson of Chicago. Of Diggs and Conyers the latter was viewed in a more positive light while the former was often pictured as the spoiled issue of a Black bourgeoisie who acceded to his position by some unwritten right of succession. In light of the results to be revealed in Chapter 5, Pan-Africanism:

What's That?, it is interesting to note that Charles Diggs has served as chairman of a House subcommittee on Africa. As part of his work on that committee he traveled to Africa, especially some areas of southern Africa, to investigate liberation movements there. One investigation resulted in a little publicized and rather superficial House subcommittee report.

Most of the comments on Congressman Diggs were negative. A few were lukewarm and none were glowing or purely affirmative. As some women said:

1. This man could do so much more. This man has become so sloppy in having things handed to him all his life that he's just kind of totally irrelevant. Now when somebody prods him he says oh, yes. How could he go over to South Africa and say it's great and then go back and of course he's great on it but he can't afford that kind of sloppiness.
2. Diggs fronts a lot behind this committee on Africa. We were not impressed with him at all when he came here. He could not look at anybody's face when he was answering questions. He has not done that much. He has not pushed for much change. Diggs is just sitting up there making a buck.
3. I don't know too much about him except he's from Detroit. Although he's been up there a long time people still don't know the name Charles Diggs as they know the name Edward Brooke or Shirley Chisholm.
4. I don't think Diggs does anything.
5. Diggs is an old stalwart. Diggs is another person who doesn't have to worry about his constituency. Nobody seriously runs against Charles Diggs. He's coming around. He used to come from a very, very elite Black bourgeoisie kind of thing. You didn't see Diggs down at that get down campaign level in terms of really with the people but he functions. He functioned as a congressman and you could write things to him but he wasn't available in terms of

being a person that you could send a complaint to if you got beat up on the street. They wouldn't do anything about it. The last time I heard him speak he talked about South Africa and he talked about the U.S. government pulling all diplomatic ties etc. from it. He's just coming around. Like again Brooke; he's not coming from any kind of revolutionary or against the system change. He's talking about changing within a system but he's talking about change.

6. He's a landmark here and if he weren't there I think we'd all feel a little lonely that he weren't and I think he led the way. I think he has been brave and has all the attributes of a Black leader. I do admire him very greatly too.
7. Pretty good. You can count on him sometime. I think he's beginning to understand a little better. He's going to arrive one day.

As for Conyers, a few comments were complimentary in the sense that they pictured him either as effective now or having the potential to be so.

1. John Conyers is a man turned on politically. If you want a way created he's the one you go to see.
2. He's very outspoken and I think if he continues to stay in Congress he's going to be one of our outstanding Blacks.
3. John Conyers is beautiful. John Conyers is moving in beautiful fashion. John Conyers was an unknown, young cat running for Congress. He ran against Richard Austin who had been in the district before who was an incumbent, well known man and also just knew he was going to win. Conyers started in January and election was in November. He was also wise enough to get Women for Conyers. Almost a thousand women organized kaffee klatches, teas and bridge parties and babysitting pools. They raised money. They got their husbands out there and voted.

These women in that district just got together and he won by 27 votes. Do you know the next time John Conyers ran for Congress he ran unopposed. Nobody democratic and nobody republican would dare to run against him. They knew they would not win. They knew it was a waste of money. The UAW machine didn't even run a candidate against John Conyers. He's building a political machine. His administrative assistant is running for state senator. He's building a base. John controls a lot of things. John pulls a lot of things because his own position is secure. Nobody can run against him this time either so he has the power to deal from where he is. He also is wise enough to make coalitions with other Black people. He's also a very beautiful man. He works all the time. Not only he works but his office works. Like you can call if the police beat you up.

Most of those who commented upon Conyers saw him as maybe helpful in initial stages of problem resolution but rather shaky when it came to following through with positive actions that could do more than just enhance his political career.

1. He's a statesman and a showman and he gets things done. Yet Black people have to be careful to keep him on his feet. I guess that's a hazard of that job. He has an excellent staff and that's his saving grace.
2. He's not even a shrewd politician, just a politician. I don't think he has any convictions, or any real sincerity. Everything he does he does with such obvious political purpose. I've seen him play tennis with people and at the same time say to them well, don't forget about my petitions or don't forget about my campaign. I don't think he relaxes himself to the degree of being a man among the people. He spends a lot of time giving the image of being a Black congressman that's up and trying to solve all of the

problems of Blacks in the country. But a whole lot of times when he was out getting his picture taken doing image types of things, there were bills going on in Congress that he should have been there to vote on because they had more to do with the conditions of Blacks.

3. Conyers talks very well. He makes a good speech. He makes people feel happy. I remember some of our students tried to enlist his aid in helping them bring about a change in the schools. He talked to them very nicely and referred them to someone else. Of course it did nothing. Conyers is a politician.

4. I had an interview with him. The first interview I was really impressed. The second interview he didn't show. The third interview was nothing. Some of the kids from the freedom school went down and we wanted to know why the funds had not been passed for the fiscal year for the D.C. public schools because we didn't have any supplies. He smiled and grinned and was very sweet. I always had an impression of Conyers that he was going to help out but when it got right down to talking to him and finding out how things were he left us in the wayside. He wasn't there and we needed him and he knew we needed him. He told us in fact well, you need me; I'm here. We set up appointments. It wasn't like we just charged into his office. We set up appointments weeks in advance, went down there and he wouldn't show. Three times he didn't show. That was ridiculous.

A few people were totally negative in their assessment of his worth. As two women said:

1. I just can't say anything good about him.
2. Poor Mr. Conyers until the Detroit riots was just another Tom. Remember him hopping up on the car and them Black brothers booing him off? That

# Traditional Political Animals? A Loud No

> to me right there was an indictment: "Brother, you ain't been doing your thing so don't come down to this ghetto and hop up on this car and tell us what to do." I've never been to Detroit. If Conyers had really been sensitive to the Black community, I don't know that he would have prevented the riots but he sure could have walked among the brothers in some safety. They indicted him. I dig what they are saying.

As in the case of Shirley Chisholm, some respondents were bothered by Conyers having signed a statement sympathetic to Israel.

> 1. I think he's committed but he doesn't understand what he's dealing with. He signed that thing to support Israel and I think that's really silly.
> 2. I have mixed feelings about him and Shirley. When the thing of Black Americans in support of Israel came out, Shirley was here and kind of said that the people who were against it were coming up with a whole lot of emotional reasons but no facts. That was kind of like Whitey's saying if you are against the war in Vietnam, you're a communist. I didn't appreciate that too much because I knew I wasn't being emotional. I thought there were some real basic problems in terms of supporting Israel and being Black.

One thing is clear about both Conyers and Diggs. Even though their own constituencies seem to have enough confidence in them to re-elect them repeatedly to the U.S. Congress, Black women surveyed for this study do not view them as Black politicians working for a Black cause. If in fact Conyers and Diggs conceive of themselves first as Blacks engaged in a struggle for the survival of Black people, that message has not been communicated to the Black community at large. And if Diggs views himself as a major contributor to the body of Black knowledge on Africa or even a major distributor of information on Africa—especially African liberation movements in southern Africa—as well as a major formulator of policy on Africa, then again word has not spread to the Black community to any significant extent.

### James Farmer and Clifford Alexander

To determine how Black women felt towards Blacks who achieved relatively high positions in the national executive we included the names of James Farmer and Clifford Alexander in the list of Black politicians. Farmer, until his recent resignation, served as Assistant Secretary of Health, Education and Welfare. Alexander was appointed to the chairmanship of EEOC (Equal Employment Opportunity Commission) under the Johnson Administration and continued into the early days of the Nixon reign until he was forced to step down as a result of pressures from the late Senator Everett Dirksen of Illinois and Nixon himself.

Although EEOC is the major national governmental organization assigned to handle complaints of employee discrimination and also to take the initiative in ferreting out such bigotry, at best only about two per cent of the women interviewed had ever heard of Clifford Alexander let alone the EEOC—this despite the widespread publicity given to Alexander's fight with the Senator from Illinois and the Nixon Administration, a fight allegedly begun because of a deep-seated feeling that Alexander was stepping on too many toes by vigorously trying to terminate discriminatory hiring and promotional practices in industry, the entertainment world, and other fields. Of those women who commented on Alexander a couple were quite enthusiastic about him, two were cautiously positive in their evaluation of him and his leadership role in EEOC, and one doubted his "gut" commitment to the Black cause.

1. He was with EEOC. He resigned. I admire him because he was able to stand up and say what he thought about the administration. I think in his job he was trying to—I can't remember exactly what his job was. He was hired to do a job but when he tried

to do it he was doing a little too much as far as . . . he found too much racism it seems in the area that he was exploring. So this got to be a hangup and I guess he got little directives saying cool it. So he was the type who couldn't work under the circumstances like this and he was big enough not to be an Uncle Tom and just said well if I can't do the job, forget it.

2. I dig him. I like the way he did his job and got fired as a result. He was able to accept the consequence for his actions and his actions mirrored his integrity and I dig integrity.

3. It's funny about him too. I had very "boug" friends in New York who kind of liked him. So when I first heard that name and when he was first in the administration it had all kinds of positive connotations. Then other friends of mine kind of said he was dragging his feet and he hadn't really established his own strength but then when he kind of I think resigned in the manner he did I started thinking well, he's an example of the Black man who has had the fruits of the establishment more or less who can more than anyone else forget where he's coming from but who in today's world still must come home and at least he's made the right decision—at least from my point of view—in coming home. Now it won't be as strong as what some of my friends would hope for but at least he didn't opt out and take the lumps as they were coming.

4. All I know about Alexander is that he was with EEOC and there was some difference when Nixon came in about who was going to run EEOC. From what I understand he's a very bright young Black man and he'll probably go places. I don't know what the accomplishments of EEOC were under his administration.

5. He's a very charming individual and very handsome man. He's a sort of Johnny come lately in that he

really does not know Black people and he really doesn't have the soul that Black leadership requires and this is the result of his background.

In light of this very sparse recognition of Alexander's name and his work in EEOC, one is led to ponder Chuck Stone's early evaluation of Alexander's appointment to EEOC:

> Of the forty-four largest federal independent agencies, only one—the Equal Employment Opportunity Commission—is headed by a "Negro," Clifford Alexander, Jr., a colorless and mediocre lawyer who was previously a Deputy special counsel to the President with no precise administrative abilities. Typical of the excessively cautious Federal civil servant, Alexander climbed slowly through the ranks by becoming a faceless Negro who neither made controversial comments nor militantly condemned the injustices against Negroes in American society.
> (*Stone, 1970, p. 69*)

Although this portrayal may seem rather harsh when one recalls Alexander's open clash with the Nixon administration, still it is a compelling one in terms of his performance under the Johnson administration. Clearly, employment discrimination has aroused the continuing interest of Black people. Had Alexander been doing an effective job of lowering numerous barriers to Blacks in employment, no doubt the message would have traveled to many and varied Black quarters. As it is, in retrospect, as far as Black women in our survey are concerned Alexander might just as well not have been Chairman of EEOC.

James Farmer evoked more responses than did Clifford Alexander numerically speaking, albeit not too many more. Very few women pictured Farmer in a favorable light. Only one woman seemed to feel both that he was effective in his work and that his image as a Black man remained intact.

> I think he's a good man, a very good man. I think he's been representative in a situation where he didn't have

to be. He reminds me of Robert Weaver. Under the pressure that he had to bear in his office he was still able to maintain the dignity of Black people. This I say is true of James Farmer. He's in a situation; I think he's a token but he's still maintaining his dignity as a man and as a Black man. He hasn't lost his identity. This is good.

One woman was not sure how she should evaluate Farmer at this stage of his career and simply adopted a "wait and see" attitude:

> I expected a great deal of him when he went into the administration. I haven't heard any more from him since then. I don't know what's happening with James Farmer. I'd expected a great deal. I had met James Farmer and he certainly wouldn't remember me but I have met him and I heard him speak various times and I thought he was a man who understood the problems of Black people and I'm waiting to see if he's going to do something about them.

Another woman explained that she would just as soon see Farmer draw the HEW salary as a "honky:"

> I listened to a report that he did for HEW last year and he recognized the problems. I think if he really could do something he really would. I'd just as soon see him get the money (for the job) as to see some honky get the money. It's just unfortunate that he can't do anything. Let's face it. I'd rather see a do-nothing nigger from Mississippi get Eastland's salary than to see Eastland get it, even if he wasn't doing anything.

A few women painted Farmer as a pathetic figure with whom one must sympathize because of his own personal shortcomings.

> 1. Poor Farmer. He's not been successful, completely successful in anything he's done. It's a shame. Maybe he ought to go back to the ministry and get himself

a good church and settle for that. He was effective with CORE but he got them in so much debt—this impressive office downtown. I think it was Fifth Avenue. He left them in such a terrible financial situation. And then he was supposed to be in some type of government project they set up. They even rented the offices and that government job fell through. That never materialized. It was some kind of educational thing. And then Nixon appointed him to HUD and of course he hasn't been able, I don't know if he is capable or not, but he hasn't been able to do anything there. So this man might be a good man but he has never achieved any success in what he has done. And I just say poor James Farmer. It's a pity. He's a good lecturer and public speaker. He hasn't really made too much of a contribution to Black people.
2. Jim is a very difficult person to talk about. I do admire him but then his values are all screwed up because he's married to a White woman he keeps in the dark. He worked very hard for CORE. The Jews got mad with us because we said they helped oppress the Blacks too. I don't think Jim could be the effective public leader that Malcolm or Stokely or any of those guys could be because he's just not that type of personality. He's a good behind the scenes man.
3. I think he got tired and he got confused. He got vulnerable. He got tired and he got beaten and he got vulnerable. But apparently he's beginning to see the light of day and find out he can't work with the White establishment and the dear old republican administration. He's going to get his ass out of there. Thank the Lord. I think there's a place for him. I think he has a lot of expertise but marches are over.

"One should recognize Farmer's contributions during the civil rights movement even though his actions are now misguided and directed on the wrong track," was the way several women expressed their attitudes toward Farmer.

1. Nowadays we complain about the previously popular civil rights leaders as being antiquated and not knowing what's happening but these were the people who got us up to the small level that we are. We really would be in bad shape if we were starting from nothing. But they have made some accomplishments. But I do feel as most people feel now that they have reached their limit and their methods have become outdated. He feels that working for Nixon he can accomplish something as far as helping his people. I think he is sincere. He doesn't really see that this is not the way.
2. I think it's a very frustrating experience. Farmer has been quite an admirable person in many respects. How he can sit there and take the crap is really beyond me. I just don't see how much good he's going to be able to do because he should know, if we should know here, he should know that by working with them that there is just so far that the administration intends to go, that the system intends to go. They do not intend for Black people to come up to equality, as every person since the turn of the century has made clear. You know Lincoln wanted to ship us to Central America, and his political advisors warned him that it would not be expedient.
3. He's an idealist and he comes from the idealist period which means that he carried his influence most during the King operation. I think he's idealistic in that he's trying to be a vanguard in this administration and there is a need for vanguards but I think the vanguard has to be very honest with Black people and have to be very honest with themselves. And I don't think he has been honest with Black people nor himself. Like for instance the kind of optimism he comes out with sometimes—I think it's un-

founded. He seems to want to go through the system to get things done whereas I would approach a job like his with trying to circumvent the system whenever possible. I think he's running up against a heck of a lot of walls with trying to maneuver within the system instead of trying to find a way to change. He's come out with a heck of a lot of optimistic bullshit.

4. I sort of put him in the category with Roy Wilkins: somebody whom I have to give credit to for having served a very useful purpose in the progression of things but who have been sort of left standing as the parade goes by.

Most women, however, were not at all kind to Farmer and were quick to hurl accusations at him which ranged from "sell out" to "Tom," to "disgraceful man with a White wife," and "fool."

1. I really don't know. He's a Tom.
2. I knew Farmer. I was in CORE and worked in the South. I met him a couple of times. No, I don't admire him at all. I think he made a big mistake. I think he sold out.
3. That man's totally confused. He's irrelevant. He should be eliminated in some way. Retire him if possible. He's an opportunist. He's confused about his Blackness. He's always got to hang around White people. He even treats his own White wife like she's—he's one of those when you get a personality that hasn't found himself how can he respond to a total group? He was in CORE and the rest through an accident—I think oratory skills or something like that and it's never gotten any better. And those that have had the dubious experience of working with him can't help but have a kind of contempt for this man.
4. I feel that James Farmer is another lackey. I know I would never have accepted any position like that

and I think that any Black person like Farmer, given Farmer's record, his historical record, is nothing but another lackey for the Nixon Administration in helping them to control the factors out here.

5. I worked for national CORE after being in the civil rights movement for a couple of years. I have a very low opinion of him. I think he's a very used man and he's used again and again and again. He fought for a while against the White Jewish socialist element in CORE but he did it very paperly. I've never been satisfied with him. At first I loved him. I just think he's not very much of a brother.

6. I don't know what's happening with that poor brother. He used to be in CORE and CORE was essentially an integrated civil rights organization. I try not to have a thing about brothers who are married to White women but it just clicks in my head in a certain kind of way. Like maybe he loves her but wow really! And now his whole syndrome in terms of being just some kind of puppet almost for Nixon and all these people—no, not Nixon but that administration, in dealing with that administration. I just see people who don't have Black folks on their minds at all and he being a Black person I can't understand it. I think he's going the way of being bought off, or maybe getting tired. Maybe he's bone weary and he just wants a little niche in life and they're going to give it to him.

7. Farmer is an integrationist who's getting his piece of the pie and he's rationalizing it away in terms of he's doing something for the good of all Black people when he's just getting his piece.

8. Paid by the pigs. A lackey.

9. He's a Black man who hasn't given up on the system. I think that is more obvious than that he is married to a White woman. He's nothing but a fool.

10. Right now I suppose I might feel that he is a traitor since he works with the Nixon Administration.

11. He's got his price. He's bought for a price. Blacks with White wives fall into a bag. They all give the excuse of joining the establishment because they can do more inside than out. But what has he done? He has to prove it to me.

It is clear, then, that by being in the Nixon Administration Farmer lost a lot of face or legitimacy with the Black community, at least in the eyes of the Black women included in this study. They are saying that a Black man, supposedly strong enough to head an activist CORE (Congress of Racial Equality) cannot enter an administration hostile to Blacks and expect to maintain a firm footing in Black circles. Even his recent resignation from the HEW post may not serve to erase the image of "traitor" and "sell out" which is embedded deeply in the minds of many Black women.

There were some Black women who refused to comment on individual Black politicians. Rather, they preferred to make general statements about Black politicians. The theme of most general statements was the utter powerlessness of Black politicians who were sometimes called pseudo-politicians or figureheads. As some women pointed out:

1. They have no power really because they are going to elect or allow just enough Black people in those kinds of positions to still appease Black folks because as long as they got a Black mayor some place you're going to have some Negroes, or Black folks, say, well, it ain't so bad. We got four or five colored mayors and so and so and so and so and so. As long as they can do that it will appease a lot of us and sort of keep us untogether which I think is the whole basis of their control over us, that we are so divided. We are just not together on a lot of things that we should be. The only way I can see that Black folks have political power is to have a Black President and a Black Vice President. Like they have to monopolize. Otherwise I can't see where politics is the way that permanently can help us.

2. I do believe that Black officials' hands are tied. I really think that Hatcher's, Stokes. . . . If it's still White controlled and it's not Black controlled and community people have very little to do with how the system is run, then it gets worse after Blacks take over because it deteriorates more. The institutions get poorer because the Whites will not come forward and support them. If the true story is told I think you will find Hatcher has not been able to do, and Stokes has not been able to do what he thought he would do because the office without the power is just no good.
3. In the last three years have conditions changed that much for Black people since this new crop of Black legislators have been in power? They just don't have any power. The whole role of the politician, he is indebted to so many people he cannot sincerely go about bringing change for a greater number of people. He can only institute changes if the powers that be allow him to make these changes. He has to cope with a whole administrative staff that might not have his best intentions. The politician has a power base. He has his party. What party do Black people have that they can rely on to see them through storms?

One has only to look at national statistics available on Black politicians to confirm the state of powerlessness. For example, *The Black Politician*, a Journal of Current Political Thought estimated that some 1500 Blacks hold elective office in the United States. This represents approximately three-tenths of one percent of a total number of U.S. elected officials estimated at 500,000. (*The Black Politician*, Vol. 2, #1, Summer 1970, p. 18). Although the Joint Center for Political Studies counted up to 1600 Black elected officials, the total number still is infinitesimally small compared to the total number of U.S. elected officials. (*JCPS Newsletter*, Vol. 1, #1, December 1970, p. 8) In terms of Blacks elected to the U.S. Congress, in addition to Senator Edward Brooke who continues to serve in the U.S. Senate, twelve Blacks are now seated in the U.S. House of Representatives. Six are returning as a result of November 1970 election victories: Shirley Chisholm (N.Y.), William Clay (Mo.), John Conyers (Mich.), Charles Diggs (Mich.), Augustus Hawkins (Calif.), Robert Nix, Sr. (Penn.), Louis Stokes (Ohio). Six are newcomers: Parren Mitchell (Md.), Ron Dellums (Calif.), George Collins (Ill.), Ralph Metcalfe (Ill.), Charles Rangel (N.Y.). Twelve out of 435 congressional representatives may reinforce an image of powerlessness. And yet the boycott of President Nixon's State of the Union message to Congress in January 1971 by those twelve Black members of Congress was viewed as enough of an exercise of power to hasten the long awaited meeting between the President and the Black caucus. The meeting, eventually held on March 25, 1971, included a Statement to the President which purported to outline concerns of the Black American population. In addition it made recommendations in behalf of the Black community. These covered three broad areas: 1) Economic Security and Economic Development, 2) Community and Human Development, and 3) Justice and Civil Rights. (For the full text of the "Statement to the President of the United States By the Congressional Black Caucus, March 25, 1971" see: *The Review of Black Political Economy*, Vol. 1, #3, Winter/Spring 1971, pp. 101–119.) Among the more notable recommendations were: "permanent job creation programs," "a guaranteed adequate income system of a minimum of $6,500 a year for a family of four," "short-term financial assistance" to "local communities," the creation of "a non-profit quasi-public, publicly funded development bank for consolidation of present programs intended to assist minority business" with "an initial appropriation of 1 billion dollars," "child development legislation," an increase of federal aid to Black colleges, more public housing funds, the declaration of drug abuse and addiction as "a major national crisis," the appointment of black federal judges and other legal officials," "full implementation of the 1970 Report of the U.S. Commission on Civil Rights," and the allocation of "at least 1% of (the U.S.) annual gross national product for international aid, with priority attention to Africa."

In another attempt to exert itself as a powerful force with which the Nixon Administration must contend the Black Caucus demanded a response to its Statement and Meeting with the President in less than two months—presumably to coincide with the May 17 anniversary of *Brown v. Board of Education*, the historic school desegregation decision. On May 18 the Administration released a report, variously described as 112 and 115 pages, which soon was characterized by the Black Congressional Caucus as "deeply disappointing." (*New York Times*, May 24, 1971) In the eyes of Congressman William Clay of Missouri the Nixon reply constituted no more than a reiteration of current civil rights and aid to the poor policies. Said Clay: "We already contend that those policies are having a devastating effect on the lives of poor and black Americans." (*New York Times*, May 24, 1971)

Thus while the initial boycott of the 1971 State of the Union message undoubtedly was perceived by many as a clear exercise of power on the part of the Black Congressional Caucus, still the result of that first thrust did not really reflect a significant element of influence or power flowing from the Black Caucus.

There are signs, however, that the Black Congressional Caucus intends to move toward a coalescence of power. This may be seen, for example, in the effort to raise substantial funds for a permanent Black Caucus staff. Furthermore, the budding interest in running a Black person for President has not escaped the attention of some Black Congressional Caucus members. In this connection one may see soon the emergence and consolidation of various potential power aggregates, for instance the civil rights-religious bloc represented most clearly by the Rev. Jesse Jackson; local politicians like Percy Sutton and Basil Paterson of New York, Carl Stokes of Cleveland, Richard Hatcher of Gary; aspiring politicians with some community as well as pecuniary backing, notably John Cashin of Alabama; the educational guild typified by the new breed of college President—for instance Dr. Charles Hurst of Chicago; and "floating" national Black personalities with the capacity to marshall large sums of money.

Upon all these events the "together" Black woman no doubt would cast a somewhat cynical glance. Had they known of the Nixon response to the Black Caucus statement when the interviews were conducted the overwhelming majority probably would have dismissed it cynically as not even amounting to the proverbial "drop in the bucket." As for talk of a Black presidential candidate the attitude of the "together" Black woman probably would cause her to denounce the pouring of huge sums of money into the political arena in pursuit of an impossible goal instead of pumping those assets into some worthwhile project in the Black community at large.

Once in office many Black politicians—especially mayors—find themselves presiding over a bankrupt system. Thus, for example, Charles Evers of Fayettville, Mississippi had to wage a national campaign to try to make his city solvent and Hatcher of Gary, Stokes of Cleveland, and Gibson of Newark have all had to become fundraisers. Many of the mayors are caught in the webbing of the Nixon Administration's "new federalism." Under this arrangement federal funds for cities are sent first to state governors whose job then is to rechannel them to urban centers. As Richard Hatcher explains the "new federalism:"

> The concept of the "new federalism" is simple: instead of federal monies going directly to the cities, the monies would first go to the governors and then to the cities. But why is this being done? According to Jerome Cavanagh, former Mayor of Detroit, Vice President Agnew gives his answer in typically unvarnished language which I quote from the November, 1969 issue of Harper's Magazine: ". . . The governors in the main are Republicans and the Mayors of the big cities are Democrats, and (that) the Administration was going to put the money through the governors."
> (Richard G. Hatcher, *"The Black City Crisis,"* in *The Black Scholar*, Vol. 1, #6, April 1970, p. 56)

Of course with the anti-Black orientation of the Nixon Administration the "new federalism" represents even more of an albatross for Black politicians.

Another theme of the general statements on Black politicians is that they simply are not helpful to or working for Black people.* As some women pointed out:

1. The Black politician is not accomplishing what he should for the Blacks.
2. I have very little pure respect for any of the Negro politicians that we have because they work for the establishment and the establishment works against me and my people. This is what is so misinterpreted. Negroes feel that if they get some of the money, if they get some of the wealth, if they get their nice house, then everything is cool. This is not what Black people want. This system is very corrupt. Everybody who receives the money and moves in this situation becomes corrupt too. They want to change the very basis of the system because in this misinterpretation now has set up a conflict between what is called Negroes and Blacks. Negroes maintain that Blacks do not have the right to claim that they want an entirely different system to govern them. They have this right. Any Negro that wants to stay within the system and attempt to get whatever they feel the White system has to offer, has that right. But by the same token, those who want to desist and back away and form their own, it's part of their constitutional right to do so.
3. I think obviously that Hatcher did at least concentrate on Black people in his campaign. I haven't kept up with his record. I know that Stokes is not very popular, is not looked on as anyone doing that much for Black people. I just don't think the system is going to allow anybody in a position in the system to make it relevant to Black people. The Black

---

* There is a general underlying assumption that Black politicians, especially those elected to the United States Congress, are not representatives of a more narrow constituency defined by the boundaries of a congressional district or a state, but are representatives of a much broader constituency of Black people in general.

mayors may not be bad because they may teach people that it doesn't make any difference whether you have a Black mayor. Then maybe they'll move to something else. I don't think in any legal way there's going to be change in the country because if the law is passed it has to be executed.

It is becoming apparent rapidly that Blacks are apt to be much more specific in terms of the kind of assistance they expect from national Black politicians. And much of it is of a political nature. That is, one may be requested to speak out strongly against inimical state budget cuts whose conscious or unconscious target may well be large segments of the Black community. Or one may be imposed upon to mediate a dispute between factions of one community board or another. Or, the national Black politician may be approached to support Black candidates who too aspire to national political office. In connection with the latter one might ponder for a moment whether the position of the Black Congressional Caucus on the one hand and that of the "together" Black woman on the other might not be diametrically opposed. For instance, while a candidate epitomized by a Victoria DeLee of South Carolina might excite the "together" Black woman, this same aspirant to the political arena might receive a lukewarm reception, or even be ignored completely, by members of the Black Congressional Caucus. Briefly, Victoria DeLee, self-described as a grass roots candidate with advanced degrees in poverty, hunger and malnutrition ran in a special election in South Carolina to fill the First Congressional District seat vacated by the death of Mendel Rivers. Prior to posing her candidacy Mrs. DeLee, an extremely dynamic, honest and sincere woman, had placed herself squarely on the battle lines of South Carolina—suffering personal abuse, threats to her person, a narrow escape from her burning house, all as the result of her persistent endeavors to desegregate the schools of Dorchester County, South Carolina, to mobilize Blacks to assert their political influence, to fight for the rights of Indian children, and to operate a day care center. Yet for some of the Black Congressional Caucus, Mrs. DeLee apparently proved an unstated embarrassment, probably because she lacked the formal education (high school and college) to which members of the Caucus were accustomed and because she did not speak in the polished, sophisticated tones utilized by noted Black orators. Hence Mrs. DeLee received little assistance from the Black Caucus in her race for the South Carolina First Congressional District seat. Only one Caucus member, Parren Mitchell of Maryland, ventured into South Carolina (with his aide George Mainor) to help Mrs. DeLee campaign. The only other support was traceable to Congresswoman Chisholm who issued a statement endorsing Mrs. DeLee. While it is true that many of the Caucus members may have shied away from Mrs. DeLee because she ran on the United Citizens Party ticket—a Black oriented party—rather than under the rubric of the Democratic Party, still all available evidence seems to favor the theory that Mrs. DeLee constituted an unstated embarrassment to the Caucus because of her lack of formal training. This theory appears to be true despite the fact that most members of the Caucus took pictures with Mrs. DeLee and met with her to listen to her appeal for support.

If the "together" Black woman did decide to involve herself in traditional politics, apparently she would be quite amenable to embracing a political aspirant who, like Victoria DeLee, closely typified the Black community to be represented. The same probably could not be said of a Black Caucus member who still, circumstantially at least, seeks to support candidates emanating from the Black middle class.

This theme of the lack of assistance given to Black people by Black politicians is interesting in light of Kenneth Clark's attempt to portray Black politicians as the new leadership of the civil rights movement:

> Negro elected officials have, in a significant sense, become the new leaders of the civil rights movement in America.
> (Kenneth B. Clark, "The Present Dilemma and Challenges of Negro Elected Officials," p. 10 in *The Black Man in American Politics. Three Views*. By Kenneth B. Clark, Julian Bond, and Richard G. Hatcher.)

Black women in our survey so far either reject Black politicians as the "new leaders of the civil rights movement," or are convinced that the civil rights movement is outmoded and a thing of the past.

We discovered in our survey that the majority of women (104) identified with no political party. Only two claimed to be Republicans, sixty-six Democrats and six Independents while several others claimed affiliation with various third party groups: thirteen Black Panther Party members, four in the Peace and Freedom Party, and two Communist Party members. Nor did the women tend to participate in other aspects of traditional politics such as working in political clubs or engaging in formal debates and discussions about candidates and issues. Some admitted, however, that they did engage in formal discussions about candidates and issues. What is striking about the results is that some women were completely unaware of certain Black candidates in their own areas who were waging vigorous campaigns either for national office (U.S. Congress) or some state or local post. Then, too, some women could not identify local Black elected officials. One woman tried vainly to recall the names of all the Black councilmen in her area:

> Let me see, there's X and—what are their names? Well X is the minister of a large congregation here and he is a minister that I don't think at this point is teaching or preaching anything relevant to Blackness right now and—oh, what's the other Black councilman's name? Well, any way neither one of them I think are doing as effective a job on the Council as they could be doing or as they should be doing as Black councilmen.

Despite voter registration drives across the country there is no indication of a guaranteed Black voter turnout. Many of the women in our survey, for example, indicated that they simply did not vote:

> 1. I arbitrarily decided to register two years ago. I tried it out on 14 or 15 propositions. Most every-

thing I said yes on ended up being no. It didn't make any change in my life. It hasn't made any change in my immediate environment, except they're going to put more buses and cars out there because they think the ghetto is a great place to use as a traffic thing. I don't believe in voting. I don't think it makes any difference.
2. I did not vote in the last election for President because there was nothing to select. The same was true of the gubernatorial race here last time.
3. I wouldn't vote even if I was old enough to vote. I believe in forming your own Black political club. I think a Black party is necessary, a Black revolutionary party. I think it's important for us to organize politically.
4. The voting age went to 18. Big deal! I wouldn't give them my vote if they got on their knees and begged me for it and told me they would do this and that for it. You vote for the democratic, the republican, the international something party and what is it? They all three of them are out of that capitalism bag. They not thinking about you. If Black people start thinking of themselves as a strong forceful group of many people around the world instead of just we are the Black people of America and sit here like this, we could sway the vote either way if we had someone we knew could do the job.

One of the laments of Andrew Young who ran recently for U.S. Congress in Georgia was that Blacks did not vote. Out of 75,000 Black registered voters in the congressional district which Young sought to represent, only 35,000 appeared at the polls on election day.

Blacks, especially in the South, have decided to form various third party groupings, perhaps as a means of arousing Blacks to vote. In Newark, New Jersey, for example, a political coalition of Blacks and Puerto Ricans nominated Kenneth Gibson for the office of mayor and participated in his successful campaign. In South Carolina the United Citizens Party, led by John Harper, was spawned to stimulate greater Black participation. The NDPA (National Democratic Party of Alabama) or "The Eagle Party" appeared in Alabama as John Cashin tried to defeat George Wallace for the governorship of Alabama. That party won victories, however, in Greene, Macon and Lowndes counties. And in North Carolina the NCCFMRPP (North Carolina Committee For More Representative Political Participation) emerged in 1968 at the urging of gubernatorial candidate Reginald Hawkins. What is clear about most of these third party efforts is that they were launched in order to circumvent or negate local regular party forces who were noted for their resistance to any kind of Black political gains. What is equally apparent, nonetheless, is that many Black people—including those women in our survey—are not persuaded by these or other Black political efforts. If, then, Black people, masses and middle class alike, do not see the desirability of supporting Black politicians, then penetrating questions ought to be raised about the feasibility of spending thousands of dollars in Black election campaign efforts. If "together" Black women are not prepared to be "traditional political animals" and further, if their support is desirable, then new approaches to politics by Blacks are in order.

## CHAPTER IV

# Of Marx, Mao and Uncle Sam

*Marxism-Leninism,* and even Maoism to a certain extent, have had an appeal not only to West Indians and Africans but also to Afro-Americans despite the latter's entrenchment in a definitely capitalistically oriented country. Ever since the Russian Revolution of 1917 and the rise of international socialism and communism, African peoples (Black Americans, West Indians, and continental Africans) have been touched by its influence. Harold Cruse mentions the flirtation of West Indians and Black Americans with Marxism in his *The Crisis of the Negro Intellectual* and devotes a chapter to "Marxism and the Negro" in his *Rebellion or Revolution.* George Padmore's *Pan-Africanism or Communism?* is also enlightening on this subject. What was so appealing about the Marxist-Leninist doctrine as far as African peoples were concerned? A brief glimpse into the Marxist-Leninist doctrine might serve to answer this inquiry. Karl Marx was indignant and angry about the brutalities of the industrial revolution. Hence he wanted to emancipate man through a pattern of revolutionary action designed to cure society's ills. Lenin, an ardent follower of Marx, was a professional revolutionary who began his activities as a youth and who wrote profusely about the evils of capitalism and the virtues of socialism.

Marx condemned capitalism because he believed its main motive to be an interest in money and material gain, a motive which allegedly leads to the exploitation of one class—the oppressed or proletariat or working class—by another—the ruling, bourgeoisie or capitalist class. In a capitalist society, he argued, man is transformed into a "crippled monstrosity;" that is, labor becomes forced, alienated and meaningless. Alienation, or estrangement, means in essence that man does not feel or view himself as the acting agent in the world; he does not develop his mental or physical capacities. Rather, man is miserable. He is physically and mentally debased.

A socialistic or communistic society, according to Marx and Lenin, would cure the ills of a capitalist society. This would occur because money and material gain would cease to be the major, motivating force of man. Hence, the exploitation of man by man would cease. Moreover, man would no longer produce in a competitive way but rather in an associated, cooperative manner. Instead of production governing man, production would cease to be the private property of certain individuals and thus would be under the control of man. Furthermore, freedom and democracy could prevail because there would be no classes, no state and no exploiting capitalists.

With this brief background in mind, it might be interesting to explore the impact of Marxism-Leninism upon a continental African, an Afro-American, and a West Indian. In undertaking this task our focus will be on Kwame Nkrumah of Africa, Angela Davis of the United States, and Frantz Fanon of the West Indies.

### *Kwame Nkrumah: The Leninist Czar??*

After the toppling of the Nkrumah regime in February 1966, Ali Mazrui's article entitled: "Nkrumah the Leninist Czar" became quite popular. (*Transition*, Vol. 6, No. 26, 3-1966, pp. 9–17). Mazrui's contention is that:

## Of Marx, Mao and Uncle Sam 187

> There is little doubt that, quite consciously, Nkrumah saw himself as an African Lenin. He wanted to go down in history as a major political theorist—and he wanted a particular stream of thought to bear his own name. Hence the term "Nkrumahism"—a name for an ideology that he hoped would assume the same historic and revolutionary status as "Leninism." The fountainhead of both Nkrumahism and Leninism was to remain *Marxism*—but these two streams that flowed from Marx were to have a historic significance in their own right.

Why did certain African leaders in general and Nkrumah in particular come under the influence of socialism? This influence may be traceable in part to the educational formation of African leaders. Several Africans studied under Harold Laski of the London School of Economics. Laski's thinking was not only socialistically oriented but his impact upon African scholars was so significant that he was invited to address one of the Pan-African conferences which W. E. B. DuBois had convened between 1919 and 1945. In France, Africans from the French territories were exposed to courses on Marxism at the University of Paris. Moreover, the French socialist and communist parties had organized study groups on the African continent for the purpose of introducing African students, workers, and potential leaders to Marxism-Leninism. In addition to the influence of educational formation, that of African social traditions may have led several African leaders to look upon a socialist path as a natural one. Traditional African societies, it has been argued, embody socialist concepts. That is, there is communal land tenure and not individual, private ownership of land. Moreover the principle of cooperation, hospitality and the sharing of resources pervades the society. Then, too, the key role and responsibility as provider for all people is assigned to one entity, the chief. Further the influence of socialist states, or aspiring socialist nations, may have led several Africans to choose the socialist path. Many continental Africans believe that their problems are much more similar to those in the Soviet Union, China, Cuba and other allegedly socialist states than those in western countries. As a result, they tend to conclude that it is easier to catch up economically with China and the Soviet Union than with the United States and other western countries. Finally, the writings of Lenin, particularly on imperialism and self-determination, may have attracted many Africans to Marxism-Leninism. Who could deny the impact of: "The right of nations to self-determination implies exclusively the right to independence in the political sense, the right to free political separation from the oppressor nation;" or, "Imperialism is the highest stage in the development of capitalism?" (V. I. Lenin, *Selected Writings. National Liberation, Socialism and Imperialism*, New York: International Publishers, 1968, pp. 113, 110). Lenin, in very simple terms, made his case against imperialism and capitalism. He contended that imperialism found its way into underdeveloped countries after capitalism had been transformed from its free competition stage into its monopoly phase. In the highest stage of capitalism, termed imperialism by Lenin, capitalist decay begins to occur and the nationals within the imperialist-dominated country are destined to wage and win a war against national oppression. Victory in the war against capitalist powers would mean self-determination, that is, political separation from foreign control. To many aspiring African leaders these thoughts were not only welcome but seized upon as an inspiration for a continuing struggle against the colonial powers.

Nkrumah, too, came under these general influences as well as that of the Afro-American W. E. B. DuBois who had begun to talk about the virtues of socialism by the time he had met Kwame Nkrumah. By 1948 Nkrumah was accused by the British of being "imbued with a communist ideology" and of wanting to form a union of west African socialist states. After Nkrumah rose to the Presidency of Ghana he talked about the implementation of African socialism. Later, after the early sixties, he seemed to abandon the concept of African Socialism and tended to write and speak only about socialism or Nkrumahism. For him the key elements of socialism seemed to be: 1) a pivotal role assigned to the state which was viewed as the "main entrepreneur in laying the basis of national economic and social advancement;" 2) the commencement of national economic planning which would lead to socialism through the establishment of a mixed economy (state enterprises, foreign private enterprises, joint-owned enterprises, cooperatives, Ghanaian private enterprises), the creation of new economic institutions, the modernization and diversification of agriculture, the utilization of the state as the main source of capital development, the guarantee of basic minimum standard of living, etc; 3) a change in social attitudes such as the conversion of trade unions from consumptionist to productionist functions, and the establishment of a minimally stratified society by the elimination of the bourgeoisie element. (See: *Some Essentials of Nkrumahism* by the Editors of Spark, New York: International Publishers, 1964, pp. 50–69).

Before he could really move his country far along the socialist path, Nkrumah found himself removed from power. It is interesting to speculate why, if socialism is so in tune with the functioning of traditional African societies, Nkrumah the socialist was rejected from his leadership position and K. A. Busia, apparently the capitalist, eventually accepted in Nkrumah's stead. It may be that Nkrumah enmeshed himself so deeply in what Jean Ziegler calls the counter-revolution in Africa that he could not extricate himself from the tentacles of international capitalism. For Ziegler the counter-revolution consists of moves by international economic interests designed to stifle the revolutionary paths of African states. (See: Jean Ziegler, *La Contre Revolution en Afrique*, Paris: Payot, 1963). Of course Nkrumah's book *Neo-Colonialism: The Last Stage of Imperialism* (London: Nelson, 1965) did not help to capture the confidence of international economic forces. In *Neo-Colonialism*, which Ali Mazrui sees as Nkrumah's effort to write a book equal to Lenin's *Imperialism: The Last Stage of Capitalism*, Nkrumah identified the international economic forces he thought were inimical to African progress and economic independence. Nor was Nkrumah's Seven Year Plan, introduced in 1964, viewed kindly by the international economic community. The plan was designed to increase the rate of economic growth and to nationalize all production. This would have meant an increase in the development of the state and cooperative sectors of the economy, and the removal of all colonial remnants and influences on the Ghanaian economy. Finally, Nkrumah's establishment of his Winneba Ideological Institute was not greeted enthusiastically by external, international forces nor internally by certain interest groups such as the military, members of the bureaucracy, chiefs, market women, and cocoa farmers. The aim of the Winneba Institute was to train Ghanaians to become good socialists. Hence public or civil servants were required not only to take but to pass a course in socialism.

Despite Nkrumah's fall from power his commitment to socialism has not diminished. In one of his messages to the Ghanaian people he decried the "complete dismantling of the socialist sector" of the Ghanaian economy and asserted that it was "being handed over shamelessly to foreign capitalists." (Kwame Nkrumah, "A Call to the Workers of Ghana," in *The Struggle Continues,* London: Panaf Books Limited, n.d., p. 5). As Nkrumah persists in his dedication to socialism as a correct path for African states so too, in various forms, do Sekou Toure of Guinea, Julius Nyerere of Tanzania, Leopold Senghor of Senegal, and perhaps a few other African leaders.

*Angela Davis: Committed Communist?*

    i move on feeling and have learned
        to distrust those who don't
    i move in time and space determined
        by time and space feeling
    that all is natural and i am
    a part of it and "how could you?" they
        ask you had everything
    but the men who killed the children
        in birmingham aren't on
    the most wanted list and the men who
        killed Schwerner, Chaney and Goodman
        aren't on the most wanted list
        and the list of names
    unlisted could and probably would include

> most of our "finest leaders" who
> are wanted in my estimation for
> at least serious questioning so
> we made a list and listed it
>
> (First stanza to "Poem of Angela Yvonne Davis" by Nikki Giovanni, October 16, 1970, printed by Afro Arts Inc.)

Just as several African leaders admitted the attraction of socialism for them so has Angela Davis publicly announced her commitment to socialism and communism. And from various quarters of American society has come the question: "How could you?" . . . "You had everything." No doubt the same question was hurled often, accusingly, at Paul Robeson.

It is, perhaps, a bit presumptuous to analyze Angela Davis' commitment to communism so soon after her projection into the all-consuming public eye. Yet this one case study may afford some insight into the attractiveness of Marxism-Leninism to a Black female candidate for the Negro intelligentsia. It should be noted, however, that only Angela Davis really can explain the magnetism for her of the Marxist-Leninist doctrine as espoused by the Communist Party.

Middle class, Black, brainy, aloof. These are terms which invariably crop up in any description of Angela Davis. Born and raised in Birmingham, Alabama, Sister Davis led what her father called a "comfortable" existence. (San Francisco Examiner, August 17, 1970). Both parents, in the tradition of many Black middle class families, not only worked but had "respectable" occupations. Frank B. Davis operated a service station which he had purchased and Mrs. Sally Davis taught school in Birmingham. Like other middle class Blacks, Angela's parents elected to attend a Congregational church where young Angela participated in the Pilgrim Fellowship. Still in the tradition of Black middle class families, the Davises sought to give their children every advantage despite the unpleasantness stemming from a White, race-oriented American society. Needless to say, it was important to the Davises to shield Angela, her sister, and two brothers from the gruesomeness of the bombing which took the lives of four little Black girls who lived in Birmingham. No doubt the importance of education was instilled in each of the four Davis children as they were probably informed that education did not terminate with a high school diploma but continued to the level of college and beyond. Indeed Mrs. Davis may have impressed this thought upon her children by her own act of attending New York University during a few summers in order to acquire a masters degree. It is not surprising, then, that Angela Davis led the way for her sister and brothers. After attending an integrated Parker High School in Birmingham for two years, she transferred to the Elizabeth Irwin School in New York as a result of a scholarship granted her from Quaker sources. Again this was not an atypical occurrence for children of the Negro middle class as many of them journeyed northward in search of the kind of secondary formation which would facilitate entrance not just into any higher educational institution but into one "of class." Upon graduation from the Elizabeth Irwin School Angela accepted a scholarship to Brandeis University, a place where she would be exposed not only to profound and competent instructors, but also to the competition of classmates noted also for their high intellectual potential. How Brandeis did or did not change her thinking is not altogether clear. It is apparent, however, that despite her major in French, in her senior year Angela registered for a course offered by Herbert Marcuse. Marcuse, who was born and educated in Germany, has studied Marxist philosophy deeply and attempted to "update" it for application in the middle and late twentieth century. His writings, all published by the Beacon Press, include *One Dimensional Man, Reason, and Revolution, Eros and Civilization,* and "Repressive Tolerance" (in *A Critique of Pure Tolerance* with Robert Paul Wolff and Barrington Moore, Jr.). It may be interesting to note that Marcuse dedicated his "Repressive Tolerance" (1965) to "my students at Brandeis University." The aim of the essay, in his words, is to examine "the idea of tolerance in our advanced society." Portions of this essay may have aroused more than the passing interest of a shy but intellectually gifted student from the Black middle class. In one passage he points out the dangers of the educational system in its form of repressive tolerance and the necessity of transforming a concept of self to cope with such repression:

Education offers still another example of spurious, abstract tolerance in the guise of concreteness and truth: it is epitomized in the concept of self-actualization. From the permissiveness of all sorts of license to the child, to the constant psychological concern with the personal problems of the student, a large-scale movement is under way against the evils of repression and the need for being oneself. Frequently brushed aside is the question as to what has to be repressed before one can be a self, oneself. The individual potential is first a negative one, a portion of the potential of his society: of aggression, guilt feeling, ignorance, resentment, cruelty which vitiate his life instincts. If the identity of the self is to be more than the immediate realization of this potential (undesirable for the individual as human being), then it requires repression and sublimation, conscious transformation. This process involves at each stage (to use the ridiculed terms which here reveal their succinct concreteness) the negation of the negation, mediation of the immediate, and identity is no more or less than this process. "Alienation" is the constant and essential element of identity, the objective side of the subject—and not, as it is made to appear today, a disease, a psychological condition. Freud well knew the difference between progressive and regressive, liberating and destructive repression. The publicity of self-actualization promotes the removal of the one and the other, it promotes existence in that immediacy which, in a repressive society, is (to use another Hegelian term) bad immediacy. . . . It isolates the individual from the one dimension where he could "find himself": from his political existence, which is at the core of his entire existence. Instead it encourages non-conformity and letting-go in ways which leave the real engines of repression in the society entirely intact, which even strengthen these engines by substituting the satisfactions of private and personal rebellion for a more than private and personal, and therefore more authentic, opposition. The desubli-

> mation involved in this sort of self-actualization is itself repressive inasmuch as it weakens the necessity and the power of the intellect, the catalytic force of that unhappy consciousness which does not revel in the archetypal personal release of frustration—hopeless resurgence of the Id which will sooner or later succumb to the omnipresent rationality of the administered world—but which recognizes the horror of the whole in the most private frustration and actualizes itself in this recognition.
> (Marcuse, 1965, pp. 113–114)

In another passage in the same essay Marcuse asserts his conviction in the right of "extralegal" resistance:

> But I believe that there is a "natural right" of resistance for oppressed and overpowered minorities to use extralegal means if the legal ones have proved to be inadequate. Law and order are always and everywhere the law and order which protect the established hierarchy; it is nonsensical to invoke the absolute authority of this law and this order against those who suffer from it and struggle against it—not for personal advantages and revenge, but for their share of humanity. There is no other judge over them than the constituted authorities, the police, and their own conscience. If they use violence, they do not start a new chain of violence but try to break an established one. Since they will be punished, they knew the risk, and when they are willing to take it, no third person, and least of all the educator and intellectual, has the right to preach them abstention.
> (Marcuse, 1965, pp. 116–117)

This encounter with Marcuse may have guided Angela Davis to her decision to undertake graduate studies in philosophy at the Institute of Social Research at Johann Wolfgang Goethe University in Frankfurt, Germany, an Institute which reflected a Marxist orientation in its course offerings. After a two year stint at the Institute,

Sister Davis returned to the United States and enrolled in the Ph.D program at the University of California, San Diego where she placed herself under the wing of Herbert Marcuse in the writing of her doctoral dissertation which treats "Kant's Analysis of Violence in the French Revolution." (*Newsweek*, October 26, 1970, p. 21).

While still in the process of completing her dissertation, Angela was hired to teach philosophy at U.C.L.A. Shortly after beginning her task as an acting assistant professor of philosophy, her connection to the Communist Party was revealed and subsequently she was fired from her position. After taking court action she was reinstated and continued her teaching assignments which included a course in "Recurring Philosophical Themes in Black Literature." At the end of the 1969–1970 academic year, the Board of Regents refused to renew her contract on the basis of her speeches, many of them made in behalf of the "Soledad Brothers" (three Black inmates accused of killing a guard in January 1970 at the Soledad State Prison in California) as well as the activities and outlook of the Black Panther Party.

Sister Davis' subjection to the judicial process for allegedly criminal reasons is now well known and need not be developed extensively here. She was charged with five counts of kidnap and one count of murder for her alleged role in the courtroom seizure as hostages of a San Rafael, California judge and some jurors, and the subsequent death of that judge (Haley). Indicted under a California law which makes any secondary persons involved in an alleged crime just as guilty as the primary individuals, she has been accused of purchasing four guns which were utilized during the courtroom seizure. After leaving California before she could be questioned by the local authorities Sister Davis was charged with flight to avoid prosecution and placed on the FBI's "Ten Most Wanted" list until her capture in New York City on Tuesday, October 13, 1970.

Just how deep was Sister Davis' commitment to the Communist Party is not clear. Nor is her attitude obvious toward the tension between the communist ideology and the Black movement, or between "white radicals" and "black radicals" (see Cruse, 1968, pp. 139–155). What is discernible is that Angela belonged to the Che Lumumba Club of the Communist Party of Southern California.

The name selected for the club is rather curious since, despite American efforts to picture Patrice Lumumba as a communist or communist lackey during his tenure as Prime Minister of a newly independent Congo, he never really displayed the same commitment to Marxism-Leninism as did say Kwame Nkrumah. Moreover only after repeated efforts to gain assistance from the Eisenhower government, and only after his disenchantment with the United Nations Mission in the Congo, did Lumumba turn for assistance to the Soviet Union. At any rate Sister Davis worked in the Che Lumumba Club with others including Franklin Delano Alexander who was a member of the Communist Party U.S.A. until his expulsion in 1968 on the ground of being "too militant." Both Franklin Alexander and Angela Davis identified and worked with predominately Black organizations—Alexander with SNCC and Davis with the Black Panther Party. What is not crystal clear about either of these two persons is to what extent their commitment to Marx's analysis of the class struggle took precedence over their dedication to the exposure and elimination of racism in the United States; or to what degree they had managed to reconcile the two in their own thinking. Only after this point is clarified will one be able to respond to the inquiry, Angela Davis: committed communist?

### *Frantz Fanon: Neo-Marxist?*

One of the more recent ideological influences on socially aware Blacks has been the social and political thought of Frantz Fanon. Unlike Marx, Lenin, and Mao, Fanon was Black and this factor in and of itself seems to lure many Black potential ideologues to his writings. Those Blacks who cast aside Marx and Lenin on the ground that although they may have been correct in their basic analysis of the evils of capitalist society, still their solutions were inaccurate in that they could not help but reflect the biases of White racist society, often turn to Fanon. Moreover, Marx and Lenin themselves, the argument runs, could be viewed as White racists for in their entire works little mention is ever made of Black people or areas of the world inhabited by men of African descent.

In fact the treatment of Third World people by Marx and Lenin is quite cursory and superficial outside of some basic comments on Sun-Yat-Sen's situation and the possibility of emphasizing in China the role of the peasantry and the possibility of passing over the capitalist stage of development.

But Fanon could not be accused of being a White racist, and therein lay his appeal. Like Aime Cesaire, Frantz Fanon was a West Indian from Martinique. And like Cesaire, Fanon traveled to France to study and there encountered in its stark form the racism of European society which led him to write in 1952 *Black Skin, White Masks (Peau Noir, Masques Blancs)*. It is in this work that he writes bitterly, accusingly, and angrily about discrimination against Africans, West Indians and Afro-Americans residing in France. "Look, a Negro!" or "Dirty Nigger" or "Mama, see the Negro! I'm frightened"—this is how Fanon saw French society's reaction to people with Black skins. (Fanon, 1952, 1967, pp. 109, 112–113). Initially Black reaction was to don a White mask until hit with the emergence of a new consciousness as a result of indignities heaped on Black men. Then armed with this new consciousness, a gradual transformation in Black thinking occurred— from an assimilationist mentality to an assertion of Black worth and value.

After completing his medical and psychiatric studies in France, Fanon secured a position as Head of the Psychiatric Department of the Blida-Joinville Hospital in Algeria. The years between 1953 and 1961, when he died in December from acute leukemia complicated by double pneumonia, were filled with a tremendous work load as he attempted to care for the physical, psychological, and psychiatric needs of those actively committed to the Algerian war. Yet Fanon still had the time for the creative role of ideologue and was able to fashion and set down his thoughts prior to his death. Fanon was not a classical or a traditional Marxist but his writings did reveal a Marxian contour or strain as well as a "commitment to socialism." (David Caute, Frantz Fanon, New York: The Viking Press, 1970, pp. 76, 82). It is clear from *The Wretched of the Earth* (New York: Grove Press, 1963), published first in 1961 as *Les Damnes de la Terre*, that his experiences in Algeria served as the primary source for his thoughts. But his visits to other African countries such as Ghana, and his brief experience in the United States also helped to round out his philosophical views.

Fanon the ideologue conveys essentially three ideas which have been found attractive and quite acceptable to the Black "revolutionary" sector. In the very first sentence of *The Wretched of the Earth* he writes: ". . . decolonisation is always a violent phenomenon." (Fanon, 1963, p. 29). Violence for him is not only a "cleansing force" in that "it frees the native from his inferiority complex and from his despair and inaction," but it also "makes him fearless and restores his self-respect." Moreover violence is a means through which society's masses may learn and comprehend "social truths." (Fanon, 1963, pp. 73, 117). This view of decolonization has had a definite effect upon Afro-Americans who believe they are in a colonial situation in America and hence who contend that violence, or violent acts, are necessary before their liberation through decolonization can take place.

The second Fanonian idea upon which Black Americans of a "revolutionary" bent have pondered is the condemnation of the "national bourgeoisie" and the "glorification" of the peasant and lumpenproletariat. In classical Marxism, the urban working class or the proletariat is viewed as the major force to lead the transition from capitalism to socialism. For Fanon, however, the peasant and the lumpenproletariat are seen as more capable of guiding the transformation. In this respect Fanon divorces himself from the classical Marxist. Moreover, his views also represent a theoretical divorce from those of Trotskyists, Stalinists and Maoists; for as Caute points out: "Neither Troskyists, Stalinists, nor Maoists have ever departed *in theory* from this concept of the proletarian vanguard; they have never admitted the possibility of a viable peasant revolution." (Caute, 1970, p. 76). Fanon reflected a basic distrust not only of the European working class but also of the indigenous proletariat. (Caute, 1970, p. 77). Yet his description of the peasantry uses complementary and glowing terms. When the "urban militants" are forced back to the countryside, he writes,

> These men discover a coherent people who go on living, as it were, statically, but who keep their moral values

## Of Marx, Mao and Uncle Sam

> and their devotion to the nation intact. They discover a people that is generous, ready to sacrifice themselves completely, an impatient people, with a stony pride. . . . The men coming from the towns learn their lessons in the hard school of the people; and at the same time these men open classes for people in military and political education. The people furbish up their weapons; but in fact the classes do not last long, for the masses came to know once again the strength of their own muscles, and push the leaders on to prompt action.
> (Fanon, 1963, pp. 101–102).

Fanon felt that the decolonization effort would move from the countryside into the urban centers. In the urban phase of the struggle the lumpen-proletariat as opposed to the urban working class, would represent the key to success. As Fanon said:

> In fact the rebellion, which began in the country districts, will filter into the towns through that fraction of the peasant population which is blocked on the outer fringe of the urban centres, that fraction which has not yet succeeded in finding a bone to gnaw in the colonial system. The men whom the growing population of the country districts and colonial expropriation have brought to desert their family holdings circle tirelessly around the different towns, hoping that one day or another they will be allowed inside. It is within this mass of humanity, this people from the shanty towns, at the core of the lumpen-proletariat, that horde of starving men, uprooted from their tribe and from their clan, constitutes one of the most spontaneous and most radically revolutionary forces of a colonised people. . . . This lumpen-proletariat is like a horde of rats; you may kick them and throw stones at them, but despite your efforts they'll go on gnawing at the roots of the tree.
> (Fanon, 1963, pp. 103, 104).

In assigning such a pivotal role to the lumpen-proletariat Fanon clearly deviates from Marx who castigated this group as perhaps the lowest element of society. Yet, at the same time he encourages Black American "revolutionaries" who contend that pimps, drunkards, drug addicts, and all kinds of hustlers are capable of joining and even leading the battle against "colonialist Amerika" or Babylon.

The third idea from Fanon which has captured the interest of Black Americans is the necessity of a revolutionary party. It is true that Fanon was clearly opposed to certain one party systems existent in Africa at the time he wrote The Wretched of the Earth. This is why he stated, for example, that: "The single party is the modern form of the dictatorship of the bourgeoisie, unmasked, unpainted, unscrupulous, and cynical." (Fanon, 1963, p. 133). Nevertheless he did believe in the absolute necessity of a revolutionary party. This party together with the masses (peasants) and socially conscious intellectuals would represent the force for the transformation and reconstruction of colonized areas. As Fanon said:

> In under-developed countries, the bourgeoisie should not be allowed to find the conditions necessary for its existence and its growth. In other words, the combined effort of the masses led by a party and of intellectuals who are highly conscious and armed with revolutionary principles ought to bar the way to this useless and harmful middle class.
> (Fanon, 1963, pp. 140–141).

The Freedom Now Party and the Mississippi Freedom Democratic Party may have been fledgling efforts to create a revolutionary party in the spirit of Fanon. Closer to Fanon, however, is the Black revolutionary party which James Boggs envisioned in his "Manifesto for a Black Revolutionary Party" (Philadelphia: Pacesetters Publishing House, 1969). Bogg's party would seek to destroy the "present white racist-capitalist government" and would represent one aspect of a National Liberation Front.

In summing up Fanon the ideologue David Caute writes:

> Fanon was a socialist; an enemy of capitalism, colonialism, and neocolonialism; a revolutionary; an anti-racist

who believed in the efficacy and humanist value of violent counterassertion; an opponent of authoritarian and elitist government, whatever its nominal label; and a champion of the poorest men on earth, the peasants of the Third World.
(Fanon, 1963, p. 106).

These words capsulize the reason for the strong impact of Fanon upon Black Americans such as I. A. Baraka, Stokely Carmichael, and many others who are deeply involved in the struggle against the oppression of Black people wherever they may reside. And though most Black Americans had never heard of Fanon in 1961 as he lay dying in a lonely hotel room, by the time of the urban riots and rebellions in various American cities, Frantz Fanon had become a household word for many of those deeply involved in the Black struggle in America.

*Black Capitalism*

Despite the influence of Marx, Lenin, Mao, Nkrumah, and Fanon upon Black Americans the proponents of capitalism were not yet ready to yield. Thus after the advent of Black power, many in the American business sector began to emphasize the possibilities of a Black Capitalism. In this endeavor they were joined by an aspirant to the highest executive-administrative level as Richard Nixon, during his campaign for the presidency, began to reveal his support for Black Capitalism as a means of gaining at least some degree of support from the Black community.

Not every individual who espoused greater Black control in the economic sector talked in terms of Black Capitalism. Some referred to it as "Black economic development," "getting a piece of the action," "minority entrepreneurship," and "Black nationalism." (See Darwin Bolden, "Economic Nationalism: The Case of the Afro-American," in *The Black Prism: Perspectives on the Black Experience*, edited by Inez Reid, New York: The Faculty Press, 1970, pp. 125–130). In its July 1967 convention in Oakland, CORE revealed that it too had begun to move toward some form of Black

Capitalism. At the meeting, Roy Innis of Harlem CORE cited the creation of the Harlem Commonwealth Council, Inc., a "small business investment corporation" designed to implement a "program for the gaining of control or the creation of institutions" in the Black community. A short time after the Oakland Convention Floyd McKissick suggested that Black people should begin to take control in various areas having a direct impact upon their welfare. He contended, for example, that "ownership of business in the ghetto must be transferred to Black people—either individually or collectively." (Robert L. Allen, *Black Awakening in Capitalist America*, New York: Anchor Books-Doubleday, 1970, p. 153). The launching of plans for Soul City, North Carolina represents McKissick's own effort to make his suggestion of Black ownership become a reality. At CORE's 1968 convention Roy Innis further elaborated his program for Black Capitalism (some people would insist that Innis is not advocating any form of Black Capitalism) in a position paper entitled "Economic Theory of Nationhood." The paper advocated "the complete takeover by Blacks of all economic, political, and social institutions in black communities for the purpose of fostering economic development of these communities." (Allen, 1970, p. 185).

In analyzing various Black Power conferences convened, one in Newark in 1967 and another in Philadelphia in 1968, Allen saw a clear "connection between the Black Power conference and corporate capitalism." He drew this conclusion not only because of the support for Black Capitalism which emerged in some of the sessions but also because the Wright Brothers, Nathan and Benjamin, secured financing for the conferences from various "white-controlled companies." (Allen, 1970, pp. 163–164).

While various quarters of the Black community were espousing Black Capitalism, others began to deny the possibility of its success in American society. Even Andrew Brimmer, a Black man seated on the Board of Governors of the Federal Reserve System, began to attack and reject the concept of Black Capitalism. Yet, if Charles Tate is correct in his analysis of Brimmer's position, Brimmer does not reject Black Capitalism because of the impossibility of making it a meaningful alternative in a white capitalist society. Rather, Brimmer's "larger purpose and objective is to persuade students, intellectuals and community leaders to abandon the concepts of Black Power, Black nationalism and Black self-determination that are gaining ascendancy in the ghetto and to pursue a strategy of integration instead." (Charles Tate, "Brimmer and Black Capitalism: An Analysis," *The Review of Black Political Economy*, Vol. 1, No. 1, Spring/Summer 1970, pp. 84–90). Others reject Black Capitalism not because it hinders integration but because they consider its viability a very remote possibility. This is true because of the difficulties which Black entrepreneuers have in obtaining loans from banks and the SBA (Small Business Administration). According to SBA statistics only about "3 percent of all U.S. business concerns are owned by non-whites." (Allen, 1970, p. 52) Yet, prior to 1968, the SBA made little effort to accommodate Black businessmen who requested loans. For instance, during most of 1964, out of 432 loans made by the Philadelphia branch of SBA, 7 were allocated to Blacks. (William K. Tabb, *The Political Economy of the Black Ghetto*, New York: W. W. Norton & Co., 1970). Even in 1968 the situation had not changed very much; for although SBA loans to minorities constituted 13% of its total loans, the business loss rate on SBA loans stood at 12% of the total loans granted. (Tabb, 1970, p. 47).

James Boggs sums up his belief in the impossibility of a viable Black capitalism in an article entitled "The Myth and Irrationality of Black Capitalism" (printed in *The Review of Black Political Economy*, Vol. 1, No. 1, Spring/Summer 1970, pp. 27–35 and in James Boggs, *Racism and the Class Struggle*, New York: Monthly Review Press, 1970). Boggs begins with the premise that "Black underdevelopment is a product of capitalist development," and therefore concludes that "In reality, Black capitalism is a dream and a delusion." Boggs further states:

> Today, in an effort to protect this capitalist system, the white power structure is seeking once again to re-enslave Black people by offering them Black capitalism. Now, scientifically speaking, there is no such thing as Black capitalism which is different from white capitalism or capitalism of any other color. Capitalism, regardless of its color, is a system of exploitation of one set of peo-

ple. The very laws of capitalism require that some forces have to be exploited.
*(Boggs, 1970, p. 29 in The Review)*

In light of the existence of these various poles of attraction: Marxism and Leninism, Frantz Fanonian socialism, and Black Capitalism, we were anxious to determine just what economic ideological position Black women would most likely accept. Hence, we asked the women in our study their opinion on what economic doctrine should govern the United States, their views concerning Frantz Fanon, Angela Davis, and "Mao's Little Red Book."

*Black Women in Search of an Economic Doctrine*

The majority of women interviewed favored socialism. It is interesting to note, though, that only a handful of interviewees expressed a deep ideological, doctrinaire Marxian commitment to socialism. Rather, most women seemed more caught up in a kind of generalized democratic socialism not traceable to any profound Marxist or Leninist approach. While most did not state their reasons for favoring socialism, those who did leaned toward the doctrine because they felt it would give Black people more of a voice in their destiny. Moreover, they believed that capitalism excluded Blacks—especially poor Blacks—from its fruits and rewards thereby necessitating experimentation with another kind of economic doctrine. A few of the women who espoused socialism carefully pointed out that they did not approve of the Soviet model of socialism because that brand tends to resemble capitalism. Selected comments follow:

1. Our society won't exist unless it becomes socialistic. There are too many poor people for it not to move to socialism—or it's going to be destroyed.
2. If you are talking about a system to benefit the masses it has to be something like socialism. Even if this is achieved in America I don't think Whites would be willing to accept Blacks as partners in that system. So I think that we have to plan that

ultimately our place is going to be in Africa. I'm conscious that many people won't do that and to do that many people will have to die. That's the only alternative that I see is that we get a land base with the economic resources where we can enforce a new value system for living which would be socialism.

3. The kind of economic doctrine that I would ideally like to see would be a socialist communal kind of economy where . . . but not one based on the same kind of lines as would socialism in Russia which is just turning into another form of capitalism.

4. I would consider a socialist society one in which the production and distribution is controlled and operated in such a way as to benefit the masses of that society. I would agree with Nkrumah that you don't have to necessarily establish capitalism to set up socialism. I think also included in that is that people on the local levels have some say in determining what it is that is in their welfare. The people have to have some say in what they want, what their welfare is instead of some people deciding because they are economists that they know what that should be. So basically that would mean that foreign investment is allowed only according to plan and that in the earlier stages you don't depend on that. I'm very much in favor as much as possible like self help programs of building schools and education.

5. The system is not geared to allow for the progress and inclusion of Black people. When you think in terms of what's wrong with the American system I think you must think in terms of capitalism and racism, which tends to work hand in hand. Capitalism is a system, is a dog eat dog, the survival of the fittest. Hard work, diligence does not even enter into the whole shebang. What capitalism thrives on is money and power. Just as capitalism is not go-

ing to respond or address itself to the needs of poor people, it doubly is not going to respond or aid or assist Black people for a very racist reason. You can't think in terms of improving the system. The only terms you can speak of is in terms of changing it. As to how it's changed I think thought should be given to socialism. Socialism could possibly address the problem of have nots but I don't know whether socialism is going to address the problem of racism because the thing about it is if you get rid of the criteria of money as being a kind of determinant in peoples lives then you're still going to have a hangup on a person being Black, a person being red, a person being brown. This is going to have to be dealt with.

6. We can't be capitalists. That's stupid. We can't even walk around and pretend we're Black capitalists. That'll never happen. I'm going on the assumption that a capitalist is a person who controls the means of production. The White man is greedy. He has his thing and he likes it that way. That's why inflation—that's why we're going to the moon: to look for markets on the moon. That's the only reason. I prefer socialism.

7. I sure don't like capitalism. I've had enough of that to know I don't like that. I don't know how socialism would work but to me it would seem better than capitalism. In other countries that I've read about it seems to be doing all right.

8. (I prefer) socialism. Let me deal from theory and what I have studied and that being somewhat of a Marxist Leninist theory. Given the capitalistic society which we are living under now, the present, they tend to make the people think that we are the government, that we make the decisions out here and the people have an opportunity to free enterprise and stuff like that whereas we know different. Socialism to me seems much better because under

socialism the people are controlling. You don't have like under capitalism about 300 people controlling the mainstream, controlling everything out here, whereas under socialism the people will be controlling. I feel that through struggle people learn and through struggle too they are going to end up with the best for them as well as—and furthermore I think socialism will provide much more for the workers. I feel that the workers would not do the same thing as the Rockefellers and the Gettys are doing because they would be the controlling factors.
9. That's hard to say. I would like to be a capitalist personally but I think that when you work with the people, socialism. I think as long as you have a capitalist society you're always going to have poor people and urban ills.

A few women concluded that neither capitalism nor socialism in a pure form would be feasible. Rather, they suggested a kind of hybrid system representing a cross between socialism and capitalism.

1. It seems to me that the capitalist doctrine has its advantages and certainly the socialist but I can't see it being one or the other, just that cut and dried. I feel that we can take a little of the socialism and mix it with a little of the capitalism and we might have a pretty good form of government. Under the capitalist regime that we have all lived in the same people kept getting richer. The poor people kept getting poorer.
2. I don't really know because there's really no pure economic doctrine I can see that's separate from a political doctrine. Looking at socialism and reading into some of the things, like into 1984 and the type of socialism that was operating there I really don't know. It seems like something midway between socialism and capitalism where people are free to do

what they want to, to do the kind of work they want to and not feel that they have to compete with another person just to be able to survive. Like if someone wanted to be a painter he doesn't have to be a painter by moonlighting and then carry on a corporate job in order to exist in the society. He should be able to be a painter and another man executive head but at the same time they both be able to go as far in the society as, well equally able to exist in the society without starving, having the basic needs in life. I think maybe I believe in a guaranteed income, and the uniform medical care for the country which is some of the things from socialism but not going into it as far as saying well everyone has to send their child to the day care center. Everyone has to do this. I don't believe in doing equality to that great an extent.

3. I think we are going to have a sort of social capitalism. I don't think that capitalism in its basic concept is going to work because the idea of just complete competition will not work in a society where there is discrimination and where there are all the things that work against a segment of that society. I feel that we have social obligations to people. Sometimes these people cannot fend for themselves. We can only do this by revising our capitalistic system so that we do have a social concept.

Still a few others expressed dissatisfaction with capitalism, yet did not choose socialism or a combination of socialism and capitalism. Those in this category generally refrained from affixing a label to their system. As some asserted:

1. I think that there should be an economic system where there are no people hungry and starving and dying in a country where food is thrown away, and pigs are killed and people are denied food stamps.

I think it ought to be an economic philosophy that says there's plenty for everybody and no one should go wanting because they don't have a dollar to buy it. The land was taken by a few people and it stayed in those general circles and those people control the resources of the country and so they decided that a dollar buys food and I don't think it should be that way. America should really attempt to enforce these historical ramblings about a government for the people, by the people which it is currently not.

2. I would like to see an agrarian society. I don't like industry at all. It does nothing for me. I think the important thing is to be happy and until you have a society that realizes this as the essential aim of life—that to be happy is to be alive; to be able to love is to be happy and to be alive. Anything, from the buck, to selfishness, to possessiveness, or fear of loneliness and independence that stands in the way of this happiness. I think you're always going to have a sick society. I think this society is an extremely sick society because it sells human flesh for paper.

3. I don't think the U.S. can adopt any kind of a system because in order to do so, it would mean the complete fall of the system that's being dealt with. I don't think communism is the answer. I don't think socialism is the answer. I think that within the realm of all of these we will eventually arrive at the most just economic situation; but the system used by our ancestors, the African, Asian version —the communal type situation in a form that has to be brought up to date I think will be what we will resort to but the main thing is that the very basic things of life that should be available to everyone, decent housing, food, should never enter the question. Now I don't doubt that in any system there will be those that excel but the level, the lowest level for which one can exist would have to be

elevated so this is something that I think our Black geniuses will have arrived at shortly because they're on the case.

4. That's a difficult question. I certainly think in this country as a whole and specifically for Black people whatever the system is going to be I certainly don't think it's going to be capitalism. Nor am I convinced that we can totally participate in a Marxist–Leninist system although I think certainly it has to be a system based on some kind of equity because I think one of the major hangups we have as a people is still this damn capitalistic system in which we are entrenched so that we as a people are constantly backstabbing each other in terms of someone having a little bit more and trying to get a little bit more by any means necessary, rather than trying to be liberated by any means necessary. And I think certainly part of that liberation will be that I actually have nothing if I'm not liberated until all of my people are liberated and that is inclusive, the whole economy, or Black economy and I'm not sure what that means, has got to be inclusive. I feel that it is very exclusive at this point. I think it will be one based on the idea that whatever we have we are going to share it or share in it, that whatever a Black person has he's going to be willing to make a commitment that's going to go beyond certainly just a momentary commitment.

5. I think it should be based on the land and the only thing I can think of at this particular point is the Arusha doctrine in Tanzania which I think being a rural people it's a thing we have to accept. And with all the problems that Brother Nyerere is having in setting it up I think we should be very sympathetic and have empathy for what he's trying to do; to try to see what inputs we can have in dealing with that, also dealing with the whole term coopera-

tives in their true sense, communes in their true sense. I'm not talking about socialism, collectivism. I'm talking about communes.
6. Communalism has in the past and always will work for Black people because we are a communal people.

A very few women sided with the capitalist system. Interestingly most of those who did were from the deep South. Even though a few southern women did choose socialism, most steadfastly expressed support for the capitalist system. It was almost as if they had read and digested *The Spirit of Capitalism and the Protestant Ethic* as they insisted that hard work under the capitalist system could produce results and that one who has not worked, or who has been employed at a lesser task, should not be rewarded monetarily or should not be given the same rate of pay as another with a higher position. Moreover a few of the women believed that socialism would paralyze initiative and therefore produce a society of "lazy" people. One woman even cited the alleged curtailment of civil liberties under the Soviet system as a reason for preferring capitalism. While one might have thought that a college education would free one from a kind of patriotic American view of socialism, this did not seem to be the case with the southern women since several of those choosing capitalism as the appropriate system had received some college training. Some of their comments follow:

1. Capitalism. I believe that if a man go out and work and make a living and get as much money and where the other man is just somewhere walking the street, I don't think it would be fair to share his money with someone else who is not even trying.
(*A 20 year old college sophomore from the South whose religious preference is Baptist*)
2. I don't believe in socialism and I'm not too much in favor of capitalism but since capitalism gives each man a right to—I mean there is a chance if you really want to you can if you like to, you might

have to work hard but there is a chance that you will have the same. I don't approve of socialism at all.
*(A 20 year old from the South with a 12th grade education and a Baptist religious preference)*

3. Capitalism. Capitalism is where a person will make a certain salary and my salary may be different from your salary because I don't believe if I'm a teacher and you're a ditch digger you're supposed to make as much money as I do.
*(A 22 year old college junior from the South whose religious preference is for the Church of God in Christ)*

4. I would say capitalism because socialism—if you will recall back when Krushchev was here visiting the United States and he wanted to go to Disneyland and Walt Disney would not permit him to come into Disneyland, he could not understand this and he asked President Eisenhower why was this. President Eisenhower, if I'm not mistaken, told him it was up to Mr. Disney to decide whether he should come in or not. In doing this he made this statement. He told Eisenhower that in Russia he ruled Russia and in the United States the people ruled the United States so we have here a chance to voice our own opinion and to debate on what we want whereas in Russia they have to accept what one person say.
*(A 26 year old southerner with one semester of college and a Baptist religious preference)*

5. Capitalism. To me socialism is basically for a lazy man and socialism in a socialized economy—if you don't go to work you know your family is going to provide for you any way and this could cause you a lack of incentive and keep you from going to work and I'd rather see a person work and get what he got himself than for the government to buy it for him.

> (*A 20 year old southerner whose religious preference is Baptist and who is a college senior*)

6. Capitalism. Under this doctrine of government people are able to advance. Everybody don't have to be doing the same thing and making the same amount of money.
  (*A 19 year old college senior from the South whose religious preference is Baptist*)

Although this is difficult to substantiate without further study, some of the southern women seemed to be afraid to mention any other doctrine but capitalism as a preferred one. Even one individual who chose socialism seemed to dare not reveal her reasons for that selection saying only rather rapidly when asked to explain her choice: "I'd rather not say." It was not at all astonishing to see that those southern women who did opt for the capitalist system generally had not read Mao's "Little Red Book" or the works of Fanon. Nor had they heard about Angela Davis.

If Black Capitalism is offered as another way of obtaining support for the capitalist system, most Black women are not ready to accept the niceties of any distinction between capitalism and Black capitalism. Only a very few, in fact a minute number of women, spoke up for Black capitalism:

1. I think that's a good idea especially here . . . especially since we got our first Black bank. I know it will work. I have every confidence that it will—even to the extent I'm involved in it.
2. If it could be done right, yes but that's like Africans taking over their own money. It has to be done quietly. It can't be done by places heralded for getting White money because that means the White man can look over it and estimate it—he's got all the accounting forms. Maybe you can spin off from that and then go into your own thing. But like the Jewish people, if we did have our own Black economic community, and I mean in terms of business

not just positions, we could participate in calling the shots even if they hated us.
3. Black capitalism has to be Black capitalism–socialism if you can envision that. He does not take the capital for himself. He takes it and puts it into a pool. Somehow we have to develop that kind of trust. So when the money is pooled, then you've got a plan worked out to do something.

But most women had only negative remarks when the subject of Black capitalism was mentioned:

1. I definitely am against capitalism—Black or any other kind. At one point I was thinking Black capitalism was good, but then I feel like it's only, it will be only exchanging one evil for another, Black capitalism for White capitalism. I feel that the Black capitalist won't be any more sympathetic or understanding toward the majority of the people no more so than the Whites.
2. Black capitalism do not exist. Black capitalism is another term which the power structure has put out here like moderates and militants to divide us and conquer us. Black capitalism is something from the state, from the president on down that was developed to make Black people think that free enterprise do exist out here. Now how can a person be a Black capitalist when he do not own any means of production out here? He still has to go back to the White man for anything that he might need. The only capitalists that exist are those people who control the means of production and our lives. I don't care what type of business a person might have because Black people only own beauty shops and insurance companies and things of that sort or either people might say that James Brown is a well to do man. He is not a Black capitalist because he do not have nothing to say as far as the con-

trolling factors out there. He just has some little token stuff that can be taken from him any time they feel it's necessary to destroy him.

3. I think it's a badly used term. And this is Whitey that did this. I think Black people must control their communities. They must control their destinies. They must have the say in everything pertaining to Black people. They've got to be the deciding factor. But when they go and term it Black capitalism this is what creates this resentment on the part of the people at the lower level because they say that all they're trying to do is get in the system. And I believe it was Rev. Jesse Jackson again who said that some Blacks are talking about the system. They don't want to destroy the way the system is operating. They just want to move the Whites out of the way so they can move in and do the same thing. This to me is what capitalism represents.

4. I don't think there is such a thing as a Black capitalist. A capitalist is a person who can maintain himself. He isn't a person who just sells one product or has one store. He's a person who controls the raw materials that come from another land that are transported on his ships, planes, trains whatever and sent to his factories. That's a capitalist and ain't no Black person own all of that. So Black quasi-capitalists, for lack of a better word, I don't mind them because Black people are always running around trying to get funding for certain programs from Chrysler, GM, and Ford and if there were a strong Black economic base feeding your own money back in, then you could request a donation from your own proprietors and your own store keepers and your own factory owners.

5. I don't dig Black capitalism. I think it's a White man's game. He ran a game on us and he sold us Black capitalism. I see Black business going down business by business by business 'cause we don't

have the resources or the knowledge for Black capitalism. Anybody who sold Black people that ought to be shot.

A very few women were not able to state their acceptance or preference for any kind of economic doctrine. Some appeared to have thought about the issue but as yet had reached no conclusion. As some women pointed out:

1. I'm anti-capitalism because I think the history of capitalism in this country and its development has gone into negative areas in that capitalism is more important than humanism. In other words I feel that capitalism is carried too far. Competition between people in work, education, what not is healthy, but when it's got to the point of it's more important than humans themselves, it's unhealthy. When a dollar is more important than a person's life, it's unhealthy or when it's all right to take away people's livelihood to make a dollar or make your business run it's unhealthy. So I'm anti-capitalism because it naturally develops to that level the more you get the more you want. And the more you are able to justify inhuman deeds to keep getting more. But I don't necessarily feel that socialism is the answer either.
2. Until we formulate something because we don't know exactly what is right for us at this point and when we talk communistically and socialistically a lot of people will get upset. Oh, they're communists. Like my grandmother—all the black people, the Black Panthers are communists and all this. I can see communistic overtones but they don't realize that this isn't their specific goal to take over the whole country and make it communistic. It's just that they want something different from capitalism. Whatever that might be I don't think anyone knows,

specifically, what might be better. It may turn out just as bad. But I don't have any definite ideas of what it should be or what we should strive for.
3. That one I really can't answer because I've thought that over very seriously and for everyone of them I think there is some problem or some hang up. When it comes to communism I think we can scratch that one completely. When it comes to the others I think there is a question where all of us are concerned. I think when it comes right down to the basics not all philosophies would be good but everyone would have the same economic opportunity throughout the country.

In summary, as far as economic doctrine is concerned most Black women studied clearly favored a socialist approach. This was true in general because they viewed that system as being more humane and capable of coping with the problems of all individuals—especially Blacks, and poor Blacks in particular—rather than caring for the needs of a very tiny select group who controlled the means of production. As one Black woman said in her condemnation of capitalism:

> My knowledge of capitalism suggests—or in my opinion capitalism as it works works for a minority of the population to oppress the majority. A few people only control the means of production and that means that we will have a working class that must submit to the small majority of people. I think I read somewhere where two percent of the population owns and controls everything, the monopolies and what not that are here. And I don't believe in the system. First of all it offers nothing to me. I'm not among the middle class who feel that they have something to gain under this system because you don't. I realize that. You can't get anywhere because of the way it functions. One is controlled by this economic system so that you will fall into a certain category, a working class category and you'll

never be in a position of ownership—not that I desire to be among that two percent but I don't think it's fair that they should.

## Black Women Take a Critical Look at Mao, Fanon, and Davis

Bobby Seale in *Seize the Time* (New York: Vintage Books, 1970) records how Huey Newton and other Panthers first became involved with Mao's "Little Red Book." Instead of viewing it as an ideological tome to be studied carefully and digested, initially they regarded it simply as a means of raising money to purchase guns for the Black Panther Party. Only at a later point in time did the Panthers begin to read and study Mao's "Little Red Book." While it is not clear how many of the Panthers really studied and accepted Mao's writings, at least the top leadership seems to have been deeply involved with the book. For example, Bobby Seale reveals the dedication of Huey Newton and others to the work in *Seize the Time:*

> You couldn't get around Huey. He knew the Red Book sideways, backwards and forwards. There are brothers in the Party that got to know the Red Book cattycorner. The brothers knew that book sideways, backwards, forwards, upside down. Turn that book any way you want to—they tell you in a minute. "The Red Book and what else? The gun! The Red Book and what else? The gun!" That's what Huey would say.
> (Seale, 1970, pp. 83–84)

As the result of the "unsolicited" publicity which the Panthers gave to the "Red Book" others in the Black community began to read it to determine how and if it could be applied to their situation.

Despite the popularity of the "Red Book," it's use does not seem to have filtered down extensively to the community of Black women who constitute our study group. Less than half of these women revealed a knowledge of or a familiarity with the "Red Book." Of those who were acquainted with it, most felt its content could not be accepted intact but that it should have selective application to the Black situation. That is, most saw the book as a text mainly for the Chinese. A few women deplored the fact that Blacks were quoting from the book at random—for instance saying that "freedom comes from the barrel of a gun" without placing that quote within the context of the whole revolutionary struggle. Although they had attempted to read the book, a couple of women said they had given it only cursory treatment or had not been able to grasp its meaning.

1. (Mao's Little Red Book) contains a lot of little sayings that are pretty good and applicable to the Chinese people but some of those things just aren't applicable to our situation.
2. The book is good for the Chinese. We can use some of it but we can't apply everything word for word to our situation. The mistake of the past is that we looked everywhere except to ourselves and to our own technique of skills. We are always trying to get someone else to apply their technique of skills to our situation. Words are cheap. You have to have actions to back them up. When a mother is hungry and wants to feed her children you can't show her a Red Book and tell her this is the way. In order to get a mass of people behind your plan you have to come up with something more definite than a Red Book.
3. I've heard of it and I've read it. I don't see any more in that than I see in a lot of other books that were put out by other groups to promulgate their own peculiar ideas. Some of the things in the book are of worth and some of it is just downright silly.
4. We used to go by the Red Book. We still go by the Red Book. But the Red Book applies to the times. You could pull out a saying that was relevant to you or that you could use and leave the rest. We

took our motto, our eight points, our discipline out of that. You can't use that—China who's been fighting the Japanese for 200 years—you can't use that. I think that each country has a different passage. Back in Marx's time it was different. The present is all racism.

5. I think he (Mao) is a very right on person. I think he's a good Marxist–Leninist and I think that he took Marxian theory and applied it very aptly to the Chinese people recognizing the fact that Chinese people had problems different from the ones that Marx described in his Manifesto. I got a lot from Mao when I was working with the Black Panther Party but at that time they applied it too strictly without recognizing the fact that we had different problems from the Chinese. I think there is a great deal to be gained from Mao, like comments that Mao has on discipline and how to be good communists. I know that can't be taken strictly but there are a great deal of suggestions that he gives for organizations that can be applied and need to be applied.

6. I know the brothers are dealing out of the Red Book. That's very masculine for me and I don't feel my role in the revolution calls for me to deal with it. The men will deal with this. The book itself, I do feel, speaks to the needs of a particular people in a particular situation. And in our particular situation here we've got to write a little Black book that would deal with how it relates to our liberation because Black people have a most different situation than any ethnic have been or will be and we have to deal with that accordingly.

7. Mao tse-Tung is a great revolutionary and he's written a number of very very good things which can help Black people I think. But I think the problem is that a number of Black revolutionaries have used the Red Book as a Bible and they tried to

export revolution from China to the United States. That's not possible. No book is a bible and no man is a god. What was good for China may not necessarily be what is right for this country. You have to experience things and gain from your experiences the tactics of the struggle and I'm just really opposed to using the Red Book as a bible.
8. I couldn't say one thing one way or the other about Mao's Little Red Book because it's nothing but a collection of sayings. And to me it's not better than any other collection of things that are just taken at random.
9. I think it was a book he wrote for the Chinese people. I disagree with Blacks who go around quoting it most of the time because they misquote it. They'll take out one section (like freedom comes out of a barrel of a gun). At the same time they'll attack people who believe in keeping a strong footing in education and in our culture. Within the Red Book Mao also talks about the necessity to maintain the culture of the people in a revolutionary struggle and the need for education. Most of the people who talk about the Red Book don't see the conflict within their own ideology. I think that rather than people relying on the Red Book as the handbook for their revolutionary struggle they really should try to develop their own Black book for revolutionary struggle.
10. I think the Red Book is beautiful. You have to read the whole thing. You can't come up and say look power comes from the barrel of a gun and learn that sentence and that's all. He also says a revolution can't be effective without culture. You have to read more than just the Red Book. I have a lot of admiration for the man because he managed to pull all those groups together in one vital force.
11. I started reading it once. He had some good ideas

about knocking off White folks but I never got deep down into it.
12. I have attempted to read it. I am not in any way on the level with this man and I'm not able to comprehend some of his theories.

Very few women in the study had read and understood Frantz Fanon. Several indicated that they had commenced *Wretched of the Earth* or *Black Skin, White Masks* but had become frustrated or annoyed by its complexity.

1. He's too deep. He's just too deep. That's all I can say. I just can't get through him. I have to study some more before I can even deal with him.
2. I started *Wretched of the Earth* but it's a hard book to finish. It's a beautiful book though it's really hard to read. I think it was really heavy and thinking through a lot of issues relevant to Black people.
3. I kind of like the man. I have friends who swear by him, and who say it will work. I don't really want to get too much into this but I just think if there is such a thing as a military visionary it's him. Now whether there are enough people around outside of him to not only understand what he's setting forth, and I'm not sure at times that I do, but to understand clearly 'cause he has his own disciples there.
4. I've read one of his books, *Black Skins and White Masks*, and I found it extremely difficult reading. There are lots of professional references to other psychologists and other psychiatrists that I don't think people—he didn't explain what their feeling was in summary. He just said Jung's theory is and if you didn't know what Jung's theory is you had lost something in that passage. You don't know what he's referring to. I have tried to read *Wretched of the Earth* but I just can't get into that. I think Fanon is very difficult. He wasn't writing for lay people. . . .

One woman felt that *Wretched of the Earth* had been introduced into the Black community before Black youth had developed their reading skills. The result was that many youth misunderstood and misapplied Fanon's theories.

> *Wretched of the Earth* was a good book but I think it was spread into the Black community too soon, to the youth. They hadn't learned how to read. It's a very heavy book. You can't even speed read the preface, Jean Paul Sartre's preface. This is one of the things that we've got to overcome—this business of the fratricide of the Black community and a lot of that I think was brought on by the passages in the *Wretched of the Earth*. Whereas in order for Black men to gain their manhood, they had to have the urge to kill. So the brother could read but he didn't go any further. This is very frustrating. They know they're supposed to be men and now they've read where they have to have the urge to kill to be a man and they're afraid of the man so they take their venom out. This is what has happened all through the centuries.

Several women had not only managed to wind their way through the labyrinth that Fanon's writings represent for some, but also enthusiastically endorsed his philosophical framework and even pointed to its impact on them. Some saw him as being much more valid for Black people than Marx and Lenin.

> 1. I'm very much impressed with Frantz Fanon. I think he was truly a Black intellectual and getting to the heart of some of the dynamics of the Black experience and their similarities in many countries outside of Africa. He even addressed himself to some extent to activities going on here in the United States. I think we really need to analyze and review his writings more than we are doing to see relevancies and go beyond what he has written.

2. I think Fanon phrased some very important questions for the movement. I think his whole concept of violence that frees them somewhat from their inhibitions and that violence is a cleansing force for oppressed people. I think it's an important notion. I don't agree entirely with all that Fanon says. I think he's a little too dogmatic in his approach to the problems of Black people. I do think that he has made an important contribution.
3. As a text it's great and I look at it basically as a textbook and you use what is applicable to your situation. I think it's much more valid than Marx, a very real 20th century kind of thing.
4. I think he was quite a guy. I think he was really developing himself before his death and that through his writing he has really contributed quite a bit as far as the movement is concerned given historical events as far as revolutionary tactics and how other revolutions were developed and stuff like that. I really like his writings.
5. I enjoy Frantz Fanon and I have a great deal of respect for him. I think that he is the only person that I've read who has given a Marxist-Leninist analysis as it relates to Black people and colored peoples.
6. I like the things he has written and I agree with what he has said about violence but at the same time some of the analyses he has made of what will happen after the revolution I'm not so really sure about. For instance in the *Wretched of the Earth* where he was talking about the have nots taking over the society and then the people that were cultural nationalists becoming equivalent to the bourgeois class and I see the possibility of that and at the same time I think he deemphasizes too much the importance of retaining the culture. But I agree that the only way people are going to take over the

# Of Marx, Mao and Uncle Sam

land is by violence. And you really do have to get a political organization of the masses.
7. After I read the *Wretched of the Earth* I was a revolutionary for about a year and I really found it very valuable as I was moving—trying to get my own personal philosophy together. I still feel that much of what he says has merit from where Black people have to move.
8. I think he was really analytical of the situation. He was Black. I think he could relate better than—see I'm not condemning Marx, I'm not condemning Mao. I don't want to say that because I really don't have enough knowledge of either one to make that kind of statement. It's just that I think Fanon could break it down better and related better to Black people because he was Black himself. He was studying a situation that he could see the racial overtones and consequences involved that Lenin or Marx couldn't.
9. I think that he was a fantastic brother—definitely one of the greatest Black minds to come out of Africa this decade, this century but I sometimes question the connection between—I recently started to read the *Wretched of the Earth*. There's a lot to read, decipher from it and take and apply to the situation here and in tactics rearrange for the situation here. But if you take it as written like a lot of people are trying to do, it doesn't apply. He was dealing with a majority, where Black people were in the majority and White people were in the minority and they happened to have more military set up. In this situation the Black people are in the minority and also White people have more military strength. But I think there's a lot to be gained from him. I've read three of his books.
10. I think he is an excellent writer. His perception of the race problem from the colonial standpoint and

> his descriptions of what I would call the Black middle class are excellent.
> 11. I think the current movement is as a result of having studied into *Wretched of the Earth* and Fanon.

As a footnote on Fanon, not one woman denounced him for having married a White woman. Perhaps this is an indication that most women were not aware of Fanon's decision to choose a White spouse. Yet one is left to ponder: if at least one or two women were knowledgeable about Leopold Senghor's marriage to a Frenchwoman, why didn't one or two women mention Fanon's marriage to a White woman? Further, one is forced to query whether Fanon's contribution of a meaningful political and social doctrine outweighed, in the minds of Black women, any "mistake" he might have made in marrying a White woman.

Most of the 200 odd interviews were completed before Angela Davis was linked to the San Rafael courtroom incident and subsequently placed on the FBI "Ten Most Wanted" list. This may have been the explanation for the large number of respondents who professed no awareness of Angela Davis or her entanglement with the University of California Board of Regents. Of those who were aware of her predicament, the reactions were quite mixed. Several women expressed a general admiration for Sister Davis and some even regarded her as a symbol for the Black movement:

> 1. I think she's a together sister as far as intellect and what have you. I can't say anything for her being a communist. I feel she has probably looked into it and she has decided she wants to deal with it. But I'm supportive of her. I admire her for her youth and being where she is today.
> 2. I think she's a liberated woman in her own way. I just give her a lot of credit for being a woman and speaking out and trying to get her opinions to the public and trying to get them to follow her. They got her for kidnap and murder. I don't believe that.
> 3. I'm sort of impressed with her in that she has been able to be a Black woman, have her own feeling and

kind of do her own thing. I'm not particularly in agreement with the communistic way of society but I don't think it's such a devil, a terrible thing that the rest of the world talks about.
4. She's found it for herself. I think that's hip. She ain't given up Blackness. She's making that adaptation. She might be light years ahead of us. There's a strong relationship with people who are entering the really militant or revolutionary stage where they see so much in communism as a catalyst for them to make that move over to revolution. I think if that serves the purpose for such then it's good. And I think a lot of people feel that way. She's heavy enough to know what she's doing. She's obviously given a lot of thought to it. She's helping a whole lot of other brothers and sisters get their minds together, and I can't condemn her for that.
5. I think she's a very beautiful sister really and I admire her because she represents to me what a Black liberated woman is in the fact that she would stand by her beliefs and goals to the extent of, or in the face of being fired.
6. So far so good. She's going to have a horrible year. I think she might provide the battleground for Reagan's next campaign and I think therefore she will become probably one of the leading symbols for the Black revolutionary movement for the early seventies.
7. I think she's great. She's beautiful. I've been personally in meetings with her and conferences. We've been on the same panel together and I think she's great. I love her. I just wish she was my daughter.

Others felt she was being persecuted unjustly either for being Black and an activist, or a communist, or a combination of the two:

1. She's being crucified by Reagan because she's Black. I feel that there's a lot of other professors on the

campus who are communist but just didn't come out and say they were. I admire her.

2. I can't say anything about her personally but as far as following the accounts I think she just got shafted. Any little thing you could bring about they would find because she was too outspoken as a Black woman. Something I find in this area too—if a woman speaks out men get turned off. They just can't take it. I think she was really just shoved out unjustly. She hasn't said anything that wasn't true and I think this upsets a lot of people. For someone to come out in the limelight like that and especially where she's working with those Regents you can't really say anything around them except hello, how you doing?

3. I think they really did it to her, Reagan and his boys. I'm sure that most of it was because she was Black and militant and vocal. And to top it all off she's talking about communism. I see her as being a very aggressive Black woman who doesn't let anything pass her by. I also see her as a competent philosophy professor.

4. I think it's a rotten thing they're doing because what she's only doing is presenting an alternate way and she's not really trying to convert anybody to anything. There are a lot of communists there and they know they're communists. But she's Black and she's a woman and she's an admitted communist so they feel they should get rid of her. I don't think she's the type of woman who's just going to say I'm not going to take it and go hide. She's going to have to get up and really speak out for everything.

5. I believe that if this is her thing, this is her thing. The only reason she is being fired is because she is a communist. She's got a good thing going. She speaks well and she's together. And that's what the White man don't want.

6. Any time people, especially Black people say what

they think, the way you feel about a particular subject if it is contrary to what the government says or however it is, they are communist, or you link them to some militant movement or violence or something like that. I don't know. I don't know why they should have that much to do with it. Hell, they got registered communists all over the United States. I don't think a communist could do no more to a mind than the mind is willing to let be done. I don't think a communist can come up and tell me to do this and do that and I'm going to do it if I know better. If communists can walk all over the United States saying what they want to feel, why not Angela Davis?

7. I admire her—the fact that she has a political, economical, philosophical ideology that is not popularly supported in this country—and really a sin among Black people. She stood by her thing. She stood up. That's what I like. She was probably fired because she was a Black communist. She sinned twice.

8. She seems like a sister who is definitely doing her own thing. She's obviously gone through the changes that Black people go through and declared herself a communist which—Black communist is like two and then Black communist who talks loud and teaches in Black Studies program and will not take no stuff off of Reagan and all those right wing(ers). I hope she stays in one piece out there 'cause I went to California. On one level it's very very liberal and on another level you could see that whole repression thing just knocking down people—no facade, no cover, just lock you up, put you in jail; you cannot get out. We will give you a trial, get up and say no he didn't do it—guilty. She's dealing in that situation and I hope the sister gets over and keeps her thing going. I read an article in Muhammed Speaks about a month ago I guess, an interview with her and the things she seemed to be saying seemed to be

very canned like books and some other things you've heard before but maybe that's just the terminology she wants to use.

Still others, while sometimes expressing admiration for her, deplored her alliance with communists or her alleged belief in a Marxist-Leninist-Maoist approach:

1. I heard Angela speak once at a Panther rally. If she believes in hard line Marxism or Maoism then I can't agree with her. That is not applicable to Black people in this country. We can't apply other people's techniques. We can try to but we can't apply them to a situation that is similar but totally different in a way. The Black man's situation in America is unique from any other place in the world and you can't copy Mao-tse-Tung tactics because Mao-tse-Tung did it and everyone looked alike.

2. I don't like a rhetoric person. I don't know why she joined (the communist party). I wouldn't condemn anyone for joining the party but I wouldn't do it myself because I don't think that's the answer. In those types of organizations you still have White people who are dominating Blacks. If it were possible for Black people to get in those leadership positions, that would be one thing, but I know it's impossible.

3. Regardless of whether Black people agreed with or could advocate communism I think that certainly our position should have been more supportive of her. It's another example of this country deciding who is expendable on somewhat technical and somewhat superficial kinds of bases. I guess when I think of Angela Davis I can't get real excited about her because I think of Paul Robeson who at no time actually verbally expressed his definite affiliation with the communist party and the kinds of things that happened to him in terms of total alienation in

this country. I suspect that the same kind of thing would not happen to Sister Davis, I would hope because Black people are certainly more actively supportive of Black people who are placed in that position but I would also question whether Sister Davis—well, I have not really heard that much that she has actually said in terms of whether she does follow a strict communist party guideline or not. I would have some serious questions for a Black woman to espouse this kind of ideology because I think she is probably several steps ahead of where most Black people are at this time. So if her commitment is to Black people—I guess that would have to be clarified for me which isn't and probably just due to my own lack of information is whether she sees this kind of a coalition with all people who are espousing the communist party philosophy or whether she sees it definitely as some kind of salvation, some kind of ideology which is compatible with and viable for Black people. I certainly think that we have to move toward a more socialistic type of policy but whether communism is going to be that philosophy I would question and at this point would even say that I rather think not.

4. If the two commitments are in contradiction that raises some very serious questions (i.e., Black woman and communist). When I see that I just have to wonder how does socialism work for the community of Black people and I haven't seen that.

5. I don't understand them (her communist affiliations) and I think as bright as she is she will not remain a communist.

6. The basic problem Angela has is her background which in the terms of the power structure is a very bourgeois background. Even though Angela was born in Birmingham, Alabama she left home at 15 years old. She went to a school that a regular grass roots Black girl could never go to unless they did

excel in academics like she did. The basic problem with Angela Davis is that, as I told her, Angela doesn't know anything about Black people. When you talk about Marxism-Leninism you're talking about White people and then to try to stretch and twist the arm of a Black situation to make it fit into a White picture—it just won't fit. Marx did not deal with race. He dealt with economics. I don't see Black people calling themselves Marxist-Leninists. When Marxist-Leninists talk about the class struggle they're not talking about Black peoples' class struggle. This class struggle includes the whole population of the United States. That's what we have to understand. I will never call myself a Marxist-Leninist. As far as Angela's teaching ability goes, she's an excellent teacher.

A few women were critical of Angela Davis. Some felt that she should have remained quiet and fulfilled the significant role of teacher.

1. She's crazy. I mean it's fine to be a communist if that's your kick. But she should have known when she got up and said she was a communist they were going to kick her out. I think it's a thing of self preservation for the time being. That's not to say that you sell your soul or don't admit that you are or how you feel about something but sometime I think you can achieve more from within than from without. She probably could have achieved a bit more if she had kept her mouth shut and stayed in.
2. I think she could have done better if she had kept her mouth a little bit closed. She could have helped her people more by remaining there and remaining as a teacher. I think she could have helped her people a lot more by staying there than to go on and be dismissed. Some of her ideas she could have kept to herself. Of course maybe she had to make a

stand. Maybe she was pushed in a corner and had to make a stand. I don't know too much about it. A lot of times in spite of the bill of rights there are some things better left unsaid.

3. For some reason or another she turns me off but I really haven't examined why she turns me off. It seems to me that most of the things she says are not particularly original. I haven't particularly been impressed with her viewpoint. Now as far as the position she's been placed in with the University of California I think that's totally unfair.

One woman thought that Sister Angela was much more committed to communism than to the Black revolution.

I think she's very brilliant. I think she is more communist than she is interested in the Black revolution. I heard her speak at a conference last year and she relates her whole theory of Marxist-Leninist philosophy to the current condition of Black people. And she's got a framework for how Black people can move within their philosophy and the revolution will come. It's very, very intellectual.

Another woman thought communists might prove useful to Black people.

I really don't know what she (Angela) was doing. I was reading the Zimbabwe Review and in it I saw an article about a convention in Russia and there's an extensive article talking about the support the Zimbabwe people are given by the communists in Russia, by the Russian people. It was weird to me because in my mind I feel that Russia and the United States are very close and they might very easily align and I really couldn't understand—for a moment I couldn't understand how Zimbabwe had made a statement like that just being thankful really for the support. That's understandable. It's useful. I think communist people can be useful to

> us. They have been and as long as we don't get too wrapped up in it it's all right to realize things might break. It may break in time.

Still another woman was convinced that Angela had stepped beyond the level on which Black people are now operating.

> Angela Davis seems to be hung up. She seems to be at a level that Black people haven't reached which is —I guess that's bad. Black people in general aren't at the stage that she is. Communism is more of a total view—all the people. Black people just haven't reached that level yet.

What is thought provoking about the varied reactions to Angela Davis is that while the majority of Black women leaned toward a socialist system, yet they were not willing to accept the doctrinaire approach of the communist party. Thus, the defense of Angela Davis by the Black community, as a general rule, comes not because of, but in spite of her communist party affiliation.

Due to the notoriety of the Angela Davis case and because of a desire to determine whether attitudes of Black women toward Sister Davis would change with news of her arrest, we drafted a short questionnaire which was completed by some 35 women in the original broad geographical areas of our study. This was done during the months of December 1970 and January 1971. Interestingly an even greater reluctance to talk and an increased level of suspicion greeted those whose task it was to distribute the questionnaire. Apparently those with the least reluctance to discuss the Davis case fell into the 26–35 age bracket. In this connection it is striking to note that those who preferred most to remain silent on the matter ranged in age from 16–25. Moreover most of the responding 35 women roughly fell into the professional class in terms of occupation.

While we make no claim as to the scientific nature of the sample, and while we recognize that it is far below the number of women in our original study, we do think it instructive to ascertain the attitudes of those responding on certain aspects of the Davis case.

Five main areas served as the focus of our inquiry: 1) Angela Davis' affiliation with the Communist Party, 2) Perceptions concerning the validity of Sister Davis' arrest, detention and any future sentence, 3) The ability of Angela Davis to get a fair trial in the United States, 4) Perceptions of Sister Davis' leadership role for Black people, 5) General attitudes toward Angela Davis.

Since Sister Davis' predicament in part is traceable to her affiliation with the Communist Party, and because Black people have never joined the Communist Party en masse, we sought to determine whether Black women were troubled by her working within the framework of the Party. An overwhelming majority (31) of the women questioned were not at all bothered by Angela Davis' membership in the Communist Party. Most women invoked natural or constitutional rights as a basis for not opposing Sister Davis' work in the Communist Party. That is, many thought Angela Davis had a right to join any organization she desired. In addition there was some sentiment that the Communist Party did not manifest the racism of most other American groups and institutions. Said some women:

1. Everyone is personally entitled to believe in what he wants. As far as political parties are concerned, that too is included. I do not believe the Communist Party will take up a racist format.
2. She is entitled to whatever political beliefs and or party she wishes to ally herself with.
3. Nothing is worse in the USA for Black people than racism. The Communist Party is not the real problem.
4. Niggers in this country can be whatever they want to be.

The few who categorically opposed Sister Davis' affiliation with the Communist Party generally did so on the ground first that the communists simply could not aid Black people and, second, that the Communist Party is alien to the American political party system. As one woman put it:

> Miss Davis cannot help her people in the United States under that party. U.S. is run on a two–party system—where one should work thru.

About two months after her arrest in New York Angela Davis gave an interview for exclusive publication in Muhammed Speaks (cf. Muhammed Speaks, January 1, 1971, pp. 3–5). The interview, arranged by Joe Walker, New York Editor of Muhammed Speaks, was conducted by Dorothy Burnam, one of Sister Davis' attorneys. Angela Davis was asked: "Why are you a communist?" Her response gives some insight into her commitment to "a socialist society free from racism" and her decision to become a member of the Che Lumumba Club of the Communist Party. She said:

> Before anything else I am a Black woman. I dedicated my life to the struggle for the liberation of Black people—my enslaved, imprisoned people. I am a Communist because I am convinced that the reason we have been forcefully compelled to eke out an existence at the very lowest level of American society has to do with the nature of capitalism. If we are going to rise out of our oppression, our poverty, if we are going to cease being the targets of the lynch-mob mentality of racist policemen, we will have to destroy the American capitalist system. We will have to obliterate a system in which a few wealthy capitalists are guaranteed the privilege of becoming richer and richer, whereas the people who are forced to work for the rich, and especially Black people, never take any significant step forward.
>
> I am a Communist because I believe that Black people, with whose labor and blood this country was built, have a right to a great deal of wealth that has been hoarded in the hands of the Hugheses, the Rockefellers, the Kennedys, the DuPonts, all the Super-powerful white capitalists of America.

## Of Marx, Mao and Uncle Sam 237

> Further I am a Communist because I believe Black men should not be coerced into fighting a racist, imperialist war in Southeast Asia, where the U.S. government is violently denying a non-white people the right to control their own lives, just as they violently suppressed us for hundreds of years.
>
> My decision to join the Che-Lumumba Club, a militant, all-Black collective of the Communist Party, flowed directly from my belief that the only path of liberation for Black people is the one which leads towards the complete and total overthrow of the capitalist class and all its various instruments of suppression.
>
> The Che-Lumumba Club is concerned with the task of organizing Black people around their immediate needs but at the same time of creating an army of freedom fighters which will overthrow our enemies. We realize that in order to accomplish this latter goal we must work in harmony with the progressive forces of white America who have seen the nature of the beast.

In response to the question "Have you ever had any doubt since you became a Communist about their ability to help Black people?" Sister Davis said:

> The Communist Party recognizes that Black people not only constitute the most oppressed collection of people in the United States but also that we are the product of the most militant tradition of resistance within the confines of this country. Therefore we as Black people are the natural leaders of a revolution which must ultimately overthrow the American ruling class, thus freeing the masses of the American people. Black people must free themselves.
>
> . . . .
>
> The Communist Party acknowledges the need for white people to accept the leadership of Blacks, especially white workers. If they are to free themselves

of their chains, they must realize that first and foremost they must struggle against all manifestations of racism.

Immediately after Angela Davis' arrest many Blacks began to protest her incarceration and to form committees for her defense. In light of these events we wanted to know how Black women felt about Sister Davis' arrest, detention, and even an ultimate prison sentence should she be adjudged guilty by the American judicial system. To this end we posed three questions: 1) Do you think Angela Davis should have been arrested? Why? 2) What do you think are the charges against her? 3) Do you think she should be sent to jail if found guilty? While five women felt Sister Davis' arrest was valid, twenty-four insisted she never should have been detained, four were uncertain, and two did not reply. As to the charges against Sister Davis, only five women listed those actually contained in the indictment against her: murder, kidnapping, conspiracy. One woman thought Angela Davis had been arrested for giving guns to others. But the overwhelming majority of women contended that she was arrested on trumped up and unfair charges, or because the FBI and California police needed a scapegoat. In response to the question "What do you think the charges are against her?" some women said:

1. Just about anything the courts might decide.
2. Bullshit.
3. Unbelievable charges. What will they think of next? They (white folks) will always be against blacks until we as black folks stop them, and the time is now.
4. It is a frame up to make her a spectacle and an example to other blacks should they "make the mistake" of following in her footsteps.
5. She is the example of what white folks is gonna do to too smart, bad talking niggers. She's the scapegoat.

One Southern woman who felt that Angela Davis should have been arrested wrote:

Of Marx, Mao and Uncle Sam 239

> She is being charged with ideas detrimental to our society.

To test how deeply the women felt about the validity of Angela's detention we asked them whether Angela should be imprisoned if declared guilty by the courts. While only five women felt the Davis arrest valid, ten maintained that she should be placed in prison if the jury returned a guilty verdict. As some women pointed out:

1. Yes, because this is the law.
2. Yes, I don't believe in double standards.
3. That's the law here. If the facts are true, yes.
4. If she is actually an accomplice to a murder she should be punished as such.
5. If we do not abide by the laws of the country we can expect to go to jail.

Parenthetically it might be noted that the average age of the above respondents was about 45 years of age.

Although twenty-four women insisted that Sister Davis' arrest was improper, only nineteen felt she should not serve any time in prison even if found guilty by the courts. (Six women did not respond to the question.) Some replies were:

1. That's the way whitey does things and I'm against that.
2. No, because she was a victim of circumstance.
3. I think she should be given a suspended sentence like some of the white folks who commit acts more vile than she.
4. No, I think if she is declared guilty it will only be because she is a communist.
5. No, because she is not guilty of any crime against people.
6. I don't believe in incarceration and punishment. To me, a Black person who shoots a judge and/or deputies is more like self-defense. Anyway, that law is dumb, because she wasn't there.

7. No, she didn't commit any crime.
8. No human being should be jailed for their political beliefs.

Of interest, perhaps, is the fact that virtually no one denied the validity of Sister Davis' arrest and detention on the ground that she is a political prisoner. Yet this is the neat slogan commonly attached to those Blacks who are detained illegally by an oppressive judicial and prison system. As Angela Davis herself pointed out during the interview for Muhammed Speaks:

> More and more Black people are being incarcerated not because they committed a crime but because of their political beliefs and the activities they undertake to bring our people together to struggle for freedom. Counterfeit charges are invented, outright frame-ups are increasingly becoming the rule.
>
> . . . .
>
> I am a political prisoner. The government intends to silence me, to prohibit me from further organizing my people, to prohibit me from exposing this corrupt, degenerate system by convicting me on the basis of a crime I had nothing to do with.
>
> . . . .
>
> The government intends to terrorize our people by railroading us into the electric chair, gas chamber and long prison terms. There is only one way political prisoners can be liberated, millions of people must serve notice to the government that they intend to use every weapon at their disposal to secure the freedom of their captive warriors, and eventually to secure the total liberation of Black people.

Much debate has occurred recently about the possibility of Black people obtaining a fair trial in American courts.* This

---

* See for example, Haywood Burns, "Can A Black Man Get A Fair Trial In This Country?" *New York Times Magazine*, July 12, 1970, p. 5.

issue has surfaced constantly in the Davis case. Thus, we asked our respondents whether they thought Angela Davis could get a fair trial. Only two people state, unequivocally, that Sister Davis could obtain a fair trial while twenty-eight felt that a fair trial would elude her, and five simply did not know. The most commonly cited reasons for Sister Davis not being able to get a fair trial centered on adverse publicity and the fact that Angela Davis is both Black and communist. As some women asserted:

1. No, because she is a communist first and a black woman second and this makes her suspect from the beginning.
2. Not until they rip off all the white folks.
3. In this country, society, no one darker than blue get fair anything.
4. She's black and too smart.
5. She is a communist and we are not friendly toward them.
6. The climate in our country today is such that it is difficult for the average white person on a jury to view a militant black female communist without prejudice.
7. Because of the way the system is they already have her down as guilty.
8. She has already been convicted by the press and public opinion. People who are afraid of communists always judge guilty anyone who has any connections.
9. It is highly unlikely that she will be judged by *her* peers. Court has always been hostile to Black people.
10. I believe the charges against her are political and also she is a Black woman in an imperialistic society.
11. I think they're so mad with her they're going to kill her—physically or psychologically.

Do Black women look to Angela Davis for leadership? According to our small sample Black women do not view Angela Davis in a leadership capacity. Only ten people considered Sister Davis a leader for Blacks in general, while thirteen definitely felt that she was not a leader of Blacks at all, and ten persons thought she might be at times, or for a small group of Blacks. Two women offered no opinion on the question. About the most novel comment on the leadership question came from a woman who suggested that Blacks have no leaders and that Angela Davis ought best be regarded as a "heroine."

The last area of our concern was to discover some general attitudes toward Angela Davis. We therefore asked our respondents: "Do you think the Black community should be: a) proud of Angela Davis or b) ashamed of Angela Davis? If neither, how do you think the Black community should feel toward Angela Davis?" The great majority—twenty-five women concluded that the Black community should be proud of Sister Davis. Two felt the reaction should be mixed—pride and shame; five gave other sentiments such as "sympathetic;" and two offered no answer. Some replies were:

1. If we can produce more Angela Davises we'll have it made. Margaret Walker Alexander said "Let a new race of men rise and take control." In responding to our life in a racist society that "control" is either over white society or among ourselves. . . .
2. I think Black people should feel by Angela Davis just like they feel by Marcus Garvey, Martin Luther King or any other Black that the white people want to rip off.
3. I think the Black community should be proud. There are certainly small amounts of obvious militant Black women. She was fulfilling her dream of awakening *her* people and hopefully the "Nation" cause Nation Time is here and now.
4. I think they should view her as a product of this society who is impatient and undesirous of accept-

ing the many compromises that must be made to become a "successful" citizen.
5. I think the Black community should be proud of Angela Davis because she has provided an alternative solution to our oppression.
6. The Black community should be proud of the fact that one woman has had the courage to stand up for her convictions in the face of the threat of losing her life.

The debate over whether Angela Davis' commitment to the Black struggle while giving allegiance to the Communist Party no doubt will continue. Yet, it is apparent that even those women who might have reservations about her alignment with the Communist Party still are convinced that Sister Davis has been victimized by an oppressive system which seeks to quiet or stamp out those who raise their voices in support of causes deemed by that system to be illegitimate. This victimization alone seems to be sufficient reason for Black women to assert a supportive stance in behalf of Angela Davis.

It would not be erroneous to assert, in developing a concluding statement for this chapter, that Black women still are in the process of thinking through their allegiance to any one economic doctrine. Most are able to articulate an appeal which socialism has for them. Yet, the strain of socialism to which they would attach themselves is not very apparent. What is perceptible is that: 1) those who have read Mao's "Little Red Book" deny its total validity for the Black community; 2) some women who have read Fanon vouch for the authenticity of his approach and its applicability to the Black American struggle; )3 while some view with interest the approach of some Africans who espouse a socialist approach—for example Kwame Nkrumah and Julius Nyerere, others have absolutely no awareness of Africa let alone what some leaders think about the possibility of implementing a socialist doctrine; and 4) some women are willing to support Angela Davis but not because of her ideological stance which reflects an acceptance of classical Marxism-Leninism.

CHAPTER V

# Pan-Africanism: What's That?

*The surge of Black consciousness* in America brought with it an adoption of certain styles of clothing and hair arrangements believed to be more consistent with an African milieu. Dashikis replaced sports coats, naturals were substituted for processed hair, and decorative beads became fashionable. Moreover, college students began to talk constantly of a "Third World" orientation. Since most of this was done in the name of "African heritage" we were eager to discover just how much knowledge Black women had about international phenomena as they related to the African continent and the Caribbean. As we approach this chapter it is crucial that we do so with a brief historical backdrop in order better to evaluate the responses which we received from the women involved in our study.

To say that all ties with the African continent were severed completely and abruptly upon the arrival of slaves in America is indeed an erroneous assertion. To claim that once in America, African people evidenced no further interest in the African continent is also invalid and fallacious. For although American society may have ridiculed anything labeled African and may have discouraged and indeed at times sabotaged Afro-American efforts to reflect the African culture or to return to it, African influences on Africans in America persisted as well as a strong determination on the part of some to make at least one voyage to the land of ancestry. It is not surprising that during the early existence of Afro-Americans in America, many Black organizations and institutions included in the title the word "Africa" or "African"—that is, for example, Free African School, African Development Society, Sons of Africa, and African Union Company.

There is some evidence that the cultural impact of Africa is much stronger in the West Indies, South and Central America than in the United States. At least one can say that the traces of African culture have endured longer in the West Indies, South and Central America, and on a much larger scale. For example the Haitian religion Vodun incorporates many African gods such as Duballa and Shango. Moreover, in places like Panama, Brazil, and Cuba "almost pure examples of African dance and music are still found." (Delores Kirton Cayou, "The Origins of Modern Jazz Dance," *The Black Scholar*, Vol. 1, No. 8, June 1970, pp. 26–31; p. 27).

Perhaps the most detailed early treatment of the survival of African cultural traits among Blacks in America can be found in the work of former anthropologist Melville J. Herskovits. Even though many of his colleagues disagreed with him upon the publication of his work and still voice doubt about its validity, Herskovits wrote in some detail about the retention of African cultural qualities in the Afro-American subculture. Other scholars, especially anthropologists, dispute any claim to African cultural traits having survived the crossing of the Atlantic Ocean. Still others take a middle position, arguing that some but not all African cultural traits can be found in Black American culture. For example, Johnnetta B. Cole contends: "Whereas we can document certain African retentions in music, folklore, and to some extent in religion, it is difficult and often impossible to establish the persistence of African traits in other areas of black subculture." (Johnnetta B. Cole, "Culture- Negro, Black and Nigger," *The Black Scholar*, Vol. 1, No. 8, June 1970, pp. 40–44; p. 40). Yet, having made this assertion, Cole goes on to say: "Regardless of the difficulty in establishing Africanisms, it is not therefore warranted to conclude that the subculture of black folks is simply a passive receptor for general American traits." (Cole, 1970, p. 40).

The links between Africa and Black Americans may be seen both in terms of historical events and cultural attributes but only the former will be stressed here. Contact between Afro-Americans and Africans on the continent persisted through missionary endeavors, educational efforts, colonization schemes, and the early Pan-African movement. Most of the Black Americans living in an early historical period expressed their continuing interest in Africa by becoming missionaries. For example, Paul Cuffe, sailor, shipbuilder and minister in the Society of Friends religious sect, made several trips to Sierra Leone in 1810–1811 and 1815. On the latter trip he took some 38 "free Negroes" to Sierra Leone. Henry McNeal Turner, a Methodist minister in the AME Church set up AME churches in Sierra Leone and Liberia. He even travelled to Capetown, South Africa in 1894 and there began to ordain African ministers. Serving also as Vice President of the African colonization Society he urged Black Americans to return to Africa, saying on one occasion: "But for the Negro as a whole, I see nothing here for him to aspire after. He can return to Africa, especially to Liberia where a Negro government is already in existence, and learn the elements of civilization in fact; for human life is there sacred, and no man is deprived of it—or any other thing that involves his manhood, without due process of law. So my decision is that there is nothing in the United States for the Negro to learn or try to attain to." (Adelaide Cromwell Hill and Martin Kilson, editors, *Apropos of Africa*. London: Frank Cass & Co. Ltd., 1969, p. 47). Two others who served in a missionary capacity in Africa were Alexander Crummell, twenty years a minister and teacher on the continent, and John Wesley Gilbert, a Methodist missionary in the Congo. Although he was ordained as a Baptist minister, George Washington Williams' mission to the Belgian Congo in 1889–1890 was of an investigative rather than a religious nature. Sent there by the United States government to examine reports of an odious treatment of Congolese people at the hands of Belgian corporate enterprises, Williams was so horrified by what he saw that eventually he dispatched a long sarcastic, cutting letter to Leopold II stating in part: "I was anxious to see to what extent the natives had 'adopted the fostering care' of your Majesty's 'benevolent enterprises'(?), and I was doomed to bitter disappointment. Instead of the natives of the Congo 'adopting the fostering care' of your Majesty's Government, they everywhere complain that their land has been taken from them by force; that the Government is cruel and arbitrary, and declare that they neither love nor respect the Government and its flag. . . . It is natural that they everywhere shrink from the 'fostering care' your Majesty's Government so eagerly proffers them." (Hill, 1969, pp. 100–101).

Educational efforts also served to keep the link between Afro-Americans and Africans intact. Several Negro churches financed the education of Africans in the United States. For instance, John Chilembwe was brought to the United States by Baptist Negroes in Lynchburg, Virginia who helped not only with his education but also gave financial assistance to his mission in Nyasaland (now Malawi) prior to the Nyasaland Uprising of 1915 which led to Chilembwe's death and that of some of his followers as a result of physical attacks against some European settlers. These attacks were an expression of their disdain and discontent concerning treatment suffered at the hands of Europeans. Then, too, Negro educational institutions as Wilberforce, Lincoln and Howard provided an education for many Africans. Some of them such as Kwame Nkrumah and Azikiwe went on to become leaders of their respective countries following independence.

Black Americans were also involved in colonization schemes relating to the African continent. Martin Delaney, trained in medicine and also a newspaper man, decided in 1854 to lead an emigration to Africa. In 1859 he led an exploring party to the Niger River Valley area in Nigeria and tried to obtain land there upon which Africans could settle. The African Civilization Society was formed by Afro-Americans in the 1850's with a stated objective of "the civilization and christianization of Africa, and of the descendants of African ancestors in any portion of the earth, wherever dispersed." (Hill, 1969, p. 157).

It is clear that most of the early Negro contacts with the African continent reflected, in some way or other, a western tendency to emphasize a religious and civilizing mission in Africa. It remained for the prominent scholar Alain Locke to decry such an approach. At one point he stated: "We now see that the missionary condescension of the past generations in their attitude toward Africa was a pious but sad mistake. In taking it, we have fallen into the snare of enemies and have given grievous offence to our brothers." (Hill, 1969, p. 352)

Beginning with the idea of Pan-Africanism most, although not all, religious and civilizing orientations were discarded. Historically, Pan-Africanism is a concept of more than one meaning or dimension. During the pre-1958 period of history Pan-Africanism could more accurately be described, in the words of Ali Mazrui, as Pan-Negroism or Pan-Pigmentationalism. (Ali Mazrui, *Towards A Pax Africana*, Chicago: University of Chicago Press, 1967). These concepts embodied the idea that all African people, including Africans in the diaspora (West Indians, Black Americans) were to unite and collaborate not only for purposes of recapturing a sense of identity but also to take steps for their liberation. Manifestations of Pan-Africanism in its Pan-Pigmentationalist aspect could be found in the Pan-African Congress movement, the negritude movement, and even the Marcus Garvey movement.

The first Pan-African Congress was convened by Henry Sylvester-Williams, a Trinidadian who served as legal adviser to several African chiefs and other African dignitaries. In 1901 he called a conference in order to "protest against the aggression of white colonizers and to appeal to missionaries and abolitionists to protect Africans from the evils of the colonial system." Sylvester-Williams died a few years later and the idea of the Pan-African Congress was not revived until after World War I when it was taken up by W. E. B. DuBois, the Black American historian and crusader. DuBois organized five international congresses on Pan-Africanism between 1919 and 1945. The first, held in Paris in 1919, was attended by 16 Afro-Americans, 20 West Indians, and 12 Africans. (W. E. B. DuBois, *Dusk of Dawn*, New York: Shocken Books, 1968, p. 262). This conference called for the "protection of nations of Africa" and some mechanism to "further the racial, political, and economic interest" of the peoples of Africa. (Hill, 1969, p. 312). The second conference was convened in 1921 in two sections—one in London and the other in Paris. Approximately 113 delegates participated—

41 Africans, 35 Americans, 24 "Negroes living in Europe," and 7 West Indians. (Hill, 1969, pp. 312–313). The 1921 conference strongly criticized Belgian colonial rule and called in general for physical, political and social equality of the races. The third conference was a relatively small one held in London and Lisbon in 1923. The key address in London was delivered by Harold Laski of the London School of Economics who had much influence on the economic thinking (socialist oriented) of Africans who were later to become leaders in their countries. The fourth conference, meeting in New York in 1927, had 208 participants and although there were representatives from the Gold Coast (now Ghana), Sierra Leone, Liberia and Nigeria, the African delegations were indeed small in number. Interestingly enough, little information is readily available on this conference. The fifth and final congress was held in Manchester in 1945. Considered the most successful of all the conferences, this one included among its 200 delegates Kwame Nkrumah (later to be elected President of Ghana), Jomo Kenyatta (now President of Kenya), Wallace Johnson (then a trade union leader in Sierra Leone), and Peter Abrahams (a delegate from South Africa). This conference, unlike the others, reflected a mass movement since representatives were drawn from the ranks of political, trade union and agricultural movements. Not only were the evils of the colonial system bared but the conference also resolved that the complete and absolute independence of Africa was the only solution to its problems and that of its peoples. Following the Manchester meeting a program of positive action was stepped up in Africa, a program that led to strikes, boycotts and other direct action.

Another manifestation of the Pan-Pigmentationalist aspect of Pan-Africanism was the negritude movement. Representing a kind of cultural-philosophical-literary resistance to colonialism, the negritude movement accomplished several things. First, it mobilized an intelligentsia which gave a philosophical or ideological contour to the anti-colonialist drive. This was done in the form of individual writings and through congresses convened in Paris and Rome (1956 and 1959) and attended by Africans, West Indians, and Afro-Americans. Second, the movement enabled the elite to voice the inconsistencies and inadequacies of Black assimilation into western society. And third, the movement gave the elite a means of mobilizing masses for the nationalist drive by helping to resolve the identity crisis resulting from years of oppression during the colonial period.

The origin of the concept negritude is not altogether clear. Leopold Senghor in his *Liberte I: Negritude Et Humanisme* (Paris: Editions du Seuil, 1964) identifies Rene Maran as the forerunner of negritude. (Senghor, 1964, pp. 407–411). After studying in France Maran, a West Indian, assumed a position in the French colonial government in Equatorial Africa. In 1921 he wrote a book entitled Batouala. In the preface he criticized the colonial administration and in the body of his work he depicted the first condition of negritude: racial pride. Although the book won the high French literary prize for the year—the Prix Goncourt—it also led to his forced resignation from service in Equatorial Africa. Another man identified as a forerunner of negritude is Etienne Lero, also a West Indian, who in 1932 wrote a manifesto called Self-Defense. In the manifesto he romanticized African attributes and contended that West Indian literature did not reflect the aspirations of an oppressed Black people. It is Aime Cesaire, however, who has been given credit for having first coined the word negritude. This Cesaire (a West Indian from Martinique) did in the years 1932–1934. He first portrayed the concept in a 1939 work called "Notes on Going Home" (*Cahier d'un Retour au Pays Natal*) in which he wrote about his return to Martinique from Paris and his finding himself once again as a Black man after having tried to escape his Blackness. It remained for Leopold Senghor (now President of Senegal) to develop and popularize the concept of negritude. He accomplished this not only through his writings and speeches but also at an early period through his collaboration with Aime Cesaire and Leon Damas (from French Guyana) in the founding of a newspaper called *The Black Student* which published much of the literature of the negritude movement.

Negritude, in its historical development and even today, represented an affirmation of Blackness. Or, as Cesaire remarks, it is the "simple acknowledgement" of being Black "which implies assumption of responsibility of destiny, history and culture." Senghor's definition is much more expansive as he views negritude as the total of cultural values of the Black world as they are expressed in life, in institutions, and the works of Black men. For him negritude is the spirit or soul of the "Negro-African civilization," a civilization or culture characterized by intuitive reasoning, a belief in a hierarchy of forces in the universe, a literature and art which is functional, collective and characterized by the fundamental traits of image and rhythm.

A third and final manifestation of the Pan-Pigmentationalist aspect of Pan-Africanism might be the Garvey movement, now a well known movement which saw the Jamaican Marcus Aurelius Garvey rise to great heights after the creation of his Universal Negro Improvement and Conservation Association and African Communities League (shortened to UNIA in America) only to descend into a state of exile after his conviction of fraud and income tax evasion resulting from an attempt to transport Blacks to Liberia on his Black Star line.

Following 1958 Pan-Africanism assumed a different connotation as it was most often viewed synonymously with the independence of African countries. Once African countries became independent Pan-Africanism seemed to mean political or economic unity either of the continental variety of Kwame Nkrumah or the regional form of Julius Nyerere and Leopold Senghor.

But while many on the African continent saw Pan-Africanism as meaning unity or cooperation on the African continent, several Africans of the diaspora began to revive its Pan-Pigmentationalist aspect beginning in the decade of the sixties. This became evident to some degree in the work of Operation Crossroads Africa (at least as far as its Black participants were concerned), a work study organization founded in 1958 by Rev. James Robinson as a means of allowing American students to work in Africa to establish links of friendship and cooperation. It was also evident in the work of Malcolm X and partly in that of the Panthers. Moreover, it could be seen in the exodus of West Indian workers and teachers from their small islands to some country on the African continent. Most recently the effort to revive the Pan-Pigmentationalist aspect of Pan-Africanism can be seen through the collaboration of Stokely Carmichael with Kwame Nkrumah and Stokely's efforts to convince Black Americans that the first step in their own liberation is the restoration to power of Kwame Nkrumah.

## Pan-Africanism: What's That?

It was against this historical backdrop that we decided to include in our probe questionnaire an international perspective section designed to gain insight on Black women's views on negritude, the Pan-African movement, Stokely's ideas on Ghana, Nyerere of Tanzania, the South African and Zimbabwean situations, the most admired African country, and the most admired Caribbean country. Nyerere of Tanzania and the South African and Zimbabwean situations were included because, at the time of the study, they were representative of events on the African continent about which "revolutionary Black people" (especially those with a Pan-African orientation) would have the most knowledge.

It is not an understatement or an exaggeration to summarize the overwhelming response to this section of the questionnaire as: Pan-Africanism: What's that? In other words, it was somewhat startling to see that very few of the respondents could speak knowledgeably or in depth about the African scene. Only a few who had taken courses in college or read articles on their own were able to reveal a sound knowledge and understanding of events on the continent. It was even more unsettling to see that despite the Black studies push and the college backgrounds of most of our participants, the American perception of the unimportance of Africa or the still uncivilized nature of Africa remained embedded in some Black women. Much of the little knowledge about Africa which Black women revealed had been acquired, not so much through intensive or even cursory reading about Africa, but through direct contact with Africans, or by watching news or special telecasts. Some were able to select an admired country mainly because of some kind of direct interaction with African students or Africans working in the United States, who had discussed their countries and culture. All of this may well indicate that colleges still are not offering good courses in African studies or that somehow Blacks are not finding their way into these courses. This general lack of knowledge about Africa may also indicate that the news media—Black or White—has failed in its effort to educate Black Americans about Africa. It also may reflect the failure of Black social, political and civic groups to launch programs designed not only to inform their respective members about Africa but also the Black community at large. Finally, this general lack of knowledge about Africa may be traceable to an attitude which says "T.C.B."—Take Care of Business at home, that is, in the United States since to look outward to Africa only detracts from the time needed to deal with the plight of the Black man in America.

As country after country became independent on the African continent, many Americans—Black and White—began to speculate about the various bonds or ties which might emerge from an association of African with Afro-American. Would Africans insist on having Black American Ambassadors, or would they be insulted by the United States Department of State assigning to their countries a Black American who was viewed in his own country as an inferior being? Would African students studying in America interact with Afro-Americans to such an extent that marriages between Africans and Afro-Americans would take place, or would Black American females refuse to even date African males? Would Afro-Americans look toward Africa as a new home base, or would they insist on holding fast to their own homeland? Had Harold Cruse's *Crisis of the Negro Intellectual* (New York: William Morrow & Co., 1967) appeared in the late fifties, doubts about any meaningful relationship between Africans and Afro-Americans might have crystallized. In the section of his Chapter 5 entitled "Ideology in Black," Cruse relates certain attitudes by Africans towards Afro-Americans and vice-versa. For example, he writes:

> Back in the middle 1950's, at an interracial party, a minor African official listened to American Negroes having a discussion on the possibilities of returning to Africa; he replied most indignantly that Africa did not want any of "you Negroes" over there, and proceeded to derogate the American Negro's attitudes, habits, and general condition.

(Cruse, 1967, pp. 422–423)

> In 1962, a very well-known woman jazz singer said, "The hell with Africans! They have their own thing going over there and they have little in common with us, and care less."

(Cruse, 1967, p. 423)

> "These American Negroes," say most Africans, "have no cohesion; they have no race consciousness; they don't identify with us Africans." But do not ask these Africans to facilitate or abet cohesion with the Negro by, perhaps, living too closely with him or by socializing more intimately than State Department protocol would allow. That would be an affront to their "new nation" status within the United Nations society. "We are Africans, not 'American Negroes.' They are ex-slaves, we are ex-colonial slaves (but in our own country)—that makes a big difference." Yet ironically deep down in the soul of many American Negroes, is ingrained the conviction that the African has just barely emerged out of his primitive-tribal past.!
> (Cruse, 1967, p. 434)

A theme of "Africans don't like us" could be detected in the responses of some Black women. Yet the number of those enunciating this theme was quite small in comparison to the total sample. Generally, three ideas were mentioned most frequently by those adhering to the "Africans don't like us" theme.

These were: the alleged arrogance of Africans, an alleged African belief in the superiority of Africans to Black Americans, and an alleged African desire to identify with Whites rather than with Blacks.

> 1. Most of the Africans I've met—they don't mix with our race. They go the other way. They feel that they are better than we are, than Black people. So I don't think that (Pan-Africanism) would be a good idea. Even White people like Africans better than they like Black people and some Africans will tell you they like White people better than they like us.
> (*An 18 year old recent high school graduate from the West*)
> 2. I think most of the African people I've run into— they really look down on the American Negro as far as saying they believe they are a little more. I feel

that to come together is going to take a lot of time. Then you have so many Blacks in America that won't stand up and say I am from Africa. They don't want to be called Black.
*(A 26 year old westerner with 3 years of college)*

3. My experiences with Africans is that they don't want us over there. We're not African. They don't want any Americans over there.
*(An 18 year old high school graduate from the West)*

4. I went to school with a couple of Africans and they tend to look down their noses at us as White people do. I'm not saying that they should be close to me because we're almost the same color. If the United States is good enough for them to leave home and come over here and get an education and if they can go to school with us and benefit from the same thing we're benefitting from at a small price, what they got to look down their noses for?
*(A 28 year old westerner with 3 years of college)*

In contrast to the "Africans don't like us" theme, several women denied the potential of a Pan-African perspective because they saw it as a "purely African phenomenon." Some women felt that Africans themselves are beset by problems in which Black Americans should not become enmeshed. Others rejected Pan-Africanism because of an attitude of T.C.B. Still others felt that Black Americans were too apathetic to make Pan-Americanism a meaningful concept. As some women stated:

1. I myself have some questions just about the whole Pan-Africanist movement. I certainly feel that the struggle for liberation is not peculiar to this country but involves Black people all over the world and particularly in Africa. However I question Stokely's position because I wonder do we attain liberation at the expense of somebody else's land? I think his whole position on Pan-Africanism becomes a little

# Pan-Africanism: What's That? 257

    shaky mainly because of that point and that's a point at which I have a great deal of trouble. I think it's beautiful that we identify with Africa as a mother land but it's not our land and I have heard this from many Africans who are also confused by Stokely's position because whether we like it or not we are in and of this country.

2. I don't think we should return to Africa. That's just another symbol. We don't see anything else here so we look at Africa because it's Black. They've got their problems too. We'd be jumping from the frying pan into the fire. I don't think that would solve the problem. We need to create something of our own. I think we can identify with the Africans because they're Black and we're Black and I think that's fine, beautiful but I don't think we should join forces with Africa or try to be a part of them as such. I think Black folks here in this country or countries all over the world need to establish a place of their own regardless of where they are.

3. As you may know the White mercenaries have taken over most of Africa so it's more an American country than this one is almost. I have some real problems with whether or not we can look to Africa. There are individuals in Africa to whom you can look for support, who have a small following. When Stokely came and said that we would have to free Africa and take Africa over, I don't know what the hell that means, because the nations there are fighting among themselves. Pan-Africanism doesn't mean anything to me at this moment, not a thing.

4. Why go to Africa? What are we going to Africa for? This is my home here. I was born here. My forefathers fought for this land. People say go back to Africa and I often sit and think: well, what am I going back to Africa for? I wasn't in Africa. My parents so many generations back came from there and I'm very proud of this and I respect Africa as

this but they were brought here as slaves and they worked for Mr. Charlie and they never got any money for it so I feel like I got to stay here and fight and make restitution for them in a sense. I've never seen Africa. I read about it and respect it very much because I think beautiful people are there because they are Black. But I also know there are some Black folks here and I was born here and since I was born here I ain't hardly letting nobody run me back to Africa. I'm ready to stay here and fight. This is my land just as much as Mr. Charlie's. Anybody who wants to go back to Africa let him go because I'm not a contrary person.
5. Our immediate problem is here in the United States. Our situation is too sad. We don't have time. I'm concerned about our Black brothers around the world but we must take care of the home front first.

Then there was that category of women who either had committed themselves to a Pan-African perspective or who believed that the idea had possibilities but would need much work and dedication before it could become a reality. Interestingly, perhaps, some women who admitted a commitment to Pan-Africanism also tended to manifest a continued trust of Stokely Carmichael. After he left the United States Stokely spent some time in Guinea studying under deposed President Kwame Nkrumah of Ghana. Nkrumah not only has been a persistent proponent of the Pan-African concept but he has interpreted the Black Power concept as deeply connected with the Pan-African movement. Unlike most of the women interviewed who tended to see Black power as a phenomenon contained within and applicable only to the United States, Nkrumah posits Black power as an international, ideological force. As he has written:

> What is Black Power? I see it in the United States as part of the vanguard of world revolution against capitalism, imperialism and neocolonialism which have en-

slaved, exploited and oppressed peoples everywhere, and against which the masses of the world are now revolting. Black Power is part of the world rebellion of the oppressed against the oppressor, of the exploited against the exploiter. It operates throughout the African continent, in North and South America, the Caribbean, wherever Africans and the people of African descent live. It is linked with the Pan-African struggle for unity on the African continent, and with all those who strive to establish a socialist society.
(*Kwame Nkrumah, The Spectre of Black Power, London: Panaf Books Limited, 1968, 1969, pp. 10–11*)

Since he appears to be a disciple of Nkrumah, Stokely now, no doubt, places Black Power in the same juxtaposition to Pan-Africanism as does Nkrumah. Furthermore Carmichael sees the necessity of Blacks carving out a land base in Africa, a land base which could be secured quite easily were Kwame Nkrumah restored to power in Ghana. Hence the first step in the implementation of the Pan-African philosophy is for Black Americans to unite with Africans and West Indians to place Nkrumah back in his 'rightful' position as President of Ghana. (See Stokely Carmichael, "Pan-Africanism—Land and Power," *The Black Scholar*, Vol. 1, No. 1, November 1969, pp. 36–43). Yet while some women in the study understand this position or implicitly trust Stokely's comprehension of it, others now reject Carmichael as a traitor and as one who has abandoned the struggle. As one woman put it: "Let's get off of Stokely because I have a bitter thing on him." The point to be emphasized is that there seems to be some correlation between a continued trust and belief in Stokely Carmichael as a Black leader and an adoption of a Pan-African perspective.

Other women who revealed a commitment to Pan-Africanism seemed to be disenchanted with life in the United States, or viewed America as a colonial territory from which or in which Black Americans would have to achieve liberation. Still others saw the possibility of Africa standing to Black Americans as Israel does to Jewish people in the United States. But those most committed to Pan-Africanism were deeply involved with and at work in organizations (such as the Center for Black Education) with a clearly Pan-African orientation.

Some representative comments follow from those women evidencing a commitment to Pan-Africanism or at least accepting the potential of such an idea:

1. It's the only hope for Black people around the world—Asians, Africans, South Americans, Americans so-called Negroes. People are going to have to come together and put down that small dog eat dog minority that crawled out of caves from Europe, and put the world back on even keel. Or the world will be left with nothing but that small minority that creeped out of the caves of Europe because they will extinguish these people.
2. Most of my African friends, my friends from Nigeria or from Ghana, they along with me appreciate Stokely's ideas in terms of Pan-Africanism, many of them do, the great majority. It was always told to them that we don't like them. A friend of mine is from Sierra Leone and I was telling her that I have relatives in Sierra Leone and she was very flattered. She was coming from a thing you don't like us so why should we like you? I said I thought it was the other way around. I think if we all got together . . . .
3. What SOBU (Student Organization of Black Unity) —like their ultimate sight is the Pan-African ideology, which would really establish Black people in the United States in a sense as a colony to Africa. When we begin to see ourselves as that, that would be very helpful. If we realize that our alliance is with Africa, that our strength, that our home, that our wealth is really with Africa and actually the destruction of anything that is hindering our development, I think we will be well on our way.
4. I think there are people, African nationalists, who

recognize the necessity of a pan-africanist movement and these are usually people moving behind the scenes who aren't proclaiming it—not yet any way.

5. Well that's sort of similar to the whole thing that Stokely talked about, and DuBois originally talked about. I think it's a very important concept because the Black people have been cut off from their roots, from their heritage, from where they came from. And it's important for Black people to feel that they are not the only ones struggling for liberation, to understand that their ancestors, their brothers and sisters are fighting also in their countries to free themselves. I think it's important to have that link between the two struggles. They in fact aid each other.

6. I can tell you what it isn't first. It's not a word to be thrown around loosely and not to be understood like the word civil rights or community rights. It differs from all of them in that Pan-Africanism is just what it says: all African. That means that every Black person on the face of the earth is an African whether he be in the Caribbean, South America, the United States or the African continent. He is descended from Africa and he should not consider himself a western being or an American or South American. He should consider himself an African because that's what he is, an African. We have only been de-Africanized by the European colonizer. In order for us to become free we have to realize who we are, what we're about. The movement of Pan-Africanism—the freedom of any people—lies in a land base. Obviously our land base should be Africa and so that's where all African people should be concentrating their efforts—to free Africa. We will not be free in the United States. We will not be free in the West Indies. We will not be free in South America, or

no place on the globe until Africa is free. That's basically—very basically—what Pan-Africanism is all about. It's not about music. It's not about songs. It's about work.

7. I don't know how it's going to be done. Africa is not only like a Europe of different languages and customs but it's a country where the tradition is not to unify. Forget the White man there, just within the different cultures. So when you talk about Pan-Africanism you are maybe asking for the impossible but the idea is tremendous.

8. I think the greatest thing about the Pan-Africanist movement is that it involves, it gives us a power base in terms of some kind of unification of Black people all across the world. We affirm the fact that Black people are indeed in the majority. There is a connection among Black people—primarily the fact that we are all oppressed by a very small minority of White people whether they be Europeans or Anglo-Saxons. But still I'm terribly hung up about the fact that with the exception of the Afro-Americans, most of the other countries and peoples in the Pan-African movement at least have a land base and most of them have a language base. I question whether then we would be welcomed to attach ourselves to land that does not belong to us. I'm not sure we're ready to even engage. I think about the FRELIMO movement and what's going on in Mozambique. Recently I had an occasion to attend a meeting with two representatives from the FRELIMO movement who were actually describing the FRELIMO movement, their active participation in armed revolution for the liberation of their country and I had an occasion to hear brothers, supposedly intelligent, militant brothers tell these two brothers from Mozambique that they were not ready and that they were not going to win the revolution. So I really

# Pan-Africanism: What's That? 263

question at this point whether we have the discipline and the kind of clear motivation that would even allow us to participate in any kind of movement. So much of it is by virtue of being in this damned country. We even participate in the whole egotism of being in this country in some very strange and subtle ways in terms of saying our position is correct. That we would have the audacity to say to people who not only have a language, a country, but who are actively—they are not playing, they are not engaged in rhetoric, they're carrying rifles and machine guns every day —that they are not ready and that they will not win the revolution is very discouraging. Personally I'm just a little frightened that it's something that we once again have latched onto without the kind of in-depth study and the kind of in-depth discipline necessary really to internalize it and make it work.

9.  It depends on what kind of pan-africanism. I agree that your roots are in Africa. That's where your heritage is. That's where your ancestors are. I've been to Africa, to Ghana, to the West Coast. I was based in Ghana but we went to Togo, Dahomey, Nigeria, and the Ivory Coast. I listened to Stokely and his pan-african thing. I would have hoped that, as simple as he put it, that that could work but I doubt it. I wish it could. I don't really know that much about pan-africanism. If Africa could be for Black people around the world like Israel is for the Jews, I think that's cool. Something like that could work.
10. Maybe we could build in Ghana a nation similar to what the Jews have in Israel. That sounds o.k. to me. It makes a lot of sense.

Although negritude represents one historical manifestation of Pan-Africanism in operation, few women were able to discuss the term. Moreover, even though the concept has been translated into a need for identity and pride in Blackness among Black Americans, few women recognized it in that context. Most often when the question was raised the response would be: "What the hell is negritude?" or "What is that?" or "What do you mean by negritude?" One southern college student saw negritude as maybe just another derogatory term for Negro. As she said:

> I know one time we had a chapel program and a White man came and he was talking and he pronounced the word Negro as negritude and a student got up and asked him why did he pronounce (it that way) and he said it was just his pronunciation of the word. I don't know if it's a sly way of saying nigger or not.

Still others refused to accept the term because it had been popularized by Leopold Senghor of Senegal. The quarrel with Senghor was that he had married a White Frenchwoman thereby seeming to negate all the beautiful things he had written or spoken about negritude. As two women said:

> 1. When I found out that Senghor was married to a French woman I feel that he is very shaky in terms of even postulating a concept of negritude. When I was in Paris this summer I saw how the French regarded their Black colonials and it is just disgusting. So I just don't even deal with it.
> 2. I don't have any positive views because I associate it with Leopold Senghor whose ideas I really haven't read. But the fact that he has a White wife turns me off. So I don't even talk too much about it. I don't like his talking too much about negritude.

But there were a very few women who did discuss the term with some real understanding of its historical underpinnings and its current use in the Black struggle.

> 1. I see negritude as an outgrowth of the New Negro Movement of the twenties. It worked in the thirties for those Africans who were in Europe getting

educated and it was an initial step of Black consciousness and as one grows if negritude becomes like form then it gets too small for the concept. But if you interpret negritude broadly where it's just like digging on Black then it could encompass anything from Mau Mau on.

2. People say negritude encompasses a reaffirmation of Blackness to the extent of annihilating White influence. I believe originally it wasn't that. It's just that in the face of so much negative response to Blackness people were saying Black is beautiful. Now in the sixties it has taken on a new thrust, not only to affirm Blackness but to devalue Whiteness to the point that it's not totally relevant to Black people.

That most women were not able to relate to the term negritude was neither surprising nor upsetting. Numerous Africans—even those belonging to the intelligentsia—have rejected it and decry its use.

Most recently, perhaps, Stanislas Adotevi of Dahomey has insisted upon the need to bury the term negritude and adopt in its stead the concept of Melanism which he sees as being more atune to and reflective of the current worldwide Black struggle. As he writes:

> Negritude was born dead; it was going to die and it died. A message, however, remains. Apart from the ineffectiveness of its negation, apart from the labyrinth of mystification, negritude was a rejection of humiliation.
>
> I would put forth the doctrine of melanism. . . . The melanism which I would propose to you is open to all Nubia, i.e. Africa. It is not a new racialism but an identification. It is an affirmation of the plain fact that to be a Negro today is still to live through the violent depredations of the slave trade.

> Melanism is the acceptance of a state of war, but with arms other than prayers and Negro spirituals. Said Machiavelli, "It is an act of humanity to take up arms in the defense of a people for whom arms are the only resource."
> (p. 32, Stanislas Adotevi, "The Strategy of Culture," *The Black Scholar*, Vol. 1, No. 1, November 1969, pp. 27–35)

And, after all, negritude (and even Melanism too) may be too much of an intellectual concept. One need not coin a mysterious term to explain a new identity and consciousness if a more familiar term will do just as well. In other words, had Black women been asked to explain the word "together" no doubt they could have done that with ease and their responses would have been reflective of whatever current use remains of negritude—i.e., the affirmation of Blackness.

If Pan-Africanism is to become a reality Black Americans must have some working knowledge of Africa and the Caribbean. As a measure of interest in or awareness of Africa and the Caribbean we asked the women of our study to indicate which African country and which Caribbean territory they admired most. Moreover, because of the orientation of Tanzania to African socialism, we asked the women to discuss how they felt about Julius Nyerere and his work in Tanzania. Finally, because the South African situation of apartheid is so notorious and often compared to segregation in the United States we were eager to find out not only the degree of knowledge about South Africa but also just what Black American women thought about that non-liberated area of Africa.

Many women were unable to cite an African or Caribbean country which they admired. In this respect the greatest number of "no replies" came in terms of the Caribbean. A few women stated that they had either associated with some West Indians or had West Indian relatives. For example:

> 1. I don't have any favorite Caribbean country but I've associated with a lot of Trinidadians and Bazians.

I don't know too much about their culture or anything like that.
2. I've never been there. My grandparents were from the West Indies but I can't say I have a favorite. My mother and my grandmother were from St. Vincent. My father was born in Trinidad and grew up in Grenada. I have no preferences.

While a few others expressed a desire to know more about the Caribbean, several also revealed that they had been turned off by many of the islands because of their lack of devotion to things Black.

1. I've never been to the Caribbean. I really haven't read too much about it. I have wanted to island hop this summer but I'm not going to be able to do that. I wanted to go to three different cultures like the Virgin Islands, Puerto Rico, and Santa Domingo to get a flavor of how they differ, to just get a feel for them.
2. As far as atmosphere I like them but you find they're being taken over by Whites so greatly that they are losing the distinction that they had—especially say the Virgin Islands.
3. I don't really know much about it. I wanted to go to the University of the West Indies. I was thinking about going there in history. Then Dr. (X) came back and told us that the students he met didn't even know that Garvey's wife was living down the street from them. I said wow. I can't deal with these people. But the Caribbean people plus the Africans, they're more intellectual than students here are. If they're going to go to school they take it more seriously.
4. The least would be Bahamas. I went to Nassau and I was so completely turned off by New York, the Westchester County, maybe Brooklyn syndrome that I saw. That's the only one I've been to. I

stayed only three days because of my disillusionment.
5. I really don't know that much about the Caribbean countries. My only direct experience has been in Jamaica which was very discouraging because at the time I was there they were very threatened by any kind of Black militancy both persons coming into the country and even literature.

Of those very few women who did select a Caribbean country one chose Cuba and the others Haiti. The choice of Haiti was quite surprising given the attention in 1970 to the Black Power movement in Trinidad and given the general American portrayal of Haiti as an extremely depressed area presided over by a wicked dictator, President for life Dr. Francois Duvalier, until his death in April 1971. Even the movie of Graham Greene's *The Comedians* which emphasized the alleged evils of a *tonton macoutte* and "voodo–dominated" island, did not seem to stop Black women from seeing something positive in Haiti either from a historical perspective or because White powers seemed to leave the island to itself. Some typical responses were:

1. I suppose Haiti. It's a Black nation. I've met a lot of interesting people from Haiti and I've heard it's a very beautiful place.
2. Haiti because of the revolution. There were some wise men. They surely moved.
3. Haiti because it's all Black. I don't pay much attention to the propaganda. In fact I feel when Whites are calling it a totalitarian government the guy must be doing something right.
4. I admire Haiti. I've never been there. I've been to Jamaica and liked what I saw there. I admire Haiti because of its early history of revolution and throwing off the yoke of the oppressor and even its recent kinds of activities and the fact that many people from the Caribbean and Haiti specifically are

5. Haiti basically because I believe it is such a mystery. Nobody messes with it. The reasons why nobody messes with it I'd be very interested in finding out. Papa Doc may be very very bad and all that but the interesting thing is that the European only has negative things to say about it. It makes me very interested. Nothing positive comes out of there ever, not ever and what little any European or westerner has seen has never been positive. And the only positive things I've heard of that have come out of there are not from coloreds, NeoNewgroes but Black people and Pan-Africanists. Now they feel as though it's very hip. And going on that I would say uh-huh.
6. I don't know if I have any Caribbean countries to admire. Haiti? The days of Toussaint L'Ouverture, the historical thing. I don't really know anything about the Caribbean in the present day.
7. You are not going to understand why I say this and the admiration may not remain for the coming months—but Haiti maybe. Only because it's the only Black ruled country and you know it the minute you step off even if he's doing it poorly.

With respect to Africa a few women, refusing to select any African country, cited negative opinions about Africans and the state of African development. As two women said:

1. I'm not particularly enchanted by Africa. From what I've read they're not particularly enthused about our back to Africa philosophy or whatever you might want to call it. In fact I've dated an African and I feel like Africans don't necessarily respect us. In fact they think we are cowards, can't much blame them. What will make us think that

Africa is more in tune with what's happening to us?

2. I have my own opinion about African development at this point. I think the best is mediocre in terms of what it should be and I know it's heresy for some people to hear and I'm prejudiced by it. If there was more wealth in the hands of Black people in Africa half the problems would be solved. If they could at the same time adopt the kind of cutthroat approach that the European used against them, they'd be all right but, and this is true of all Black people, and this is why no one can tell us Africa is not our home, even if Africa does not want us—we always adopt the nobler parts of any culture that we are in and forget the baser things that put you on top in terms of the survival contest.

When asked which African country they admired most, those who did respond tended either to state a general admiration for all of Africa or to mention several different countries including Somalia, Guinea-Bissao, Biafra, Ghana, Kenya, Tanzania, Guinea, Algeria, South Africa and Rhodesia (Zimbabwe). Two comments were typical of the "I admire all of Africa" responses:

1. My sympathies are with all of the African countries. I do feel that the African and Asian countries are going to have the greatest impact on the world along with the South American countries. I feel we are going into a period of decline of European and North American control.
2. Well, I don't know too much about Africa. They're always talking about sending me to Africa but I imagine if I got there they'd kill me (laugh). Anyway I don't know too much about Africa. It's just that I admire the people there because they have more of a battle to fight than we do in our way.

# Pan-Africanism: What's That? 271

The choice of country admired seemed to result from personal contact with Africans, the influence of the newsmedia, and study in college classes or general reading about Africa. For example, when asked to explain her selection of Somalia one woman said: "I just married a man from Somalia, East Africa four months ago. I have to say Somalia." One of the most surprising replies to the African country admired question came from a 23 year old woman living in the midwest who had had one and a half years of college. She selected Guinea-Bissao. Although Guinea-Bissao is one of the territories waging war for liberation from Portugal, very few people ever mention it—talking if at all, in terms of the battle in Angola and Mozambique, the other two African lands still under Portuguese domination. Moreover those few who do mention the territory tend to employ the phrase Portuguese Guinea instead of the name the freedom fighters have adopted— Guinea-Bissao. In revealing how deeply she was into the Guinea-Bissao question the young woman stated:

> It's a little country and the people are struggling against imperialism and they're doing so well. They're so wise about it. They're not attacking large cities. There's one large city within Bissao that they just don't bother. They walk around it because if they did (bother it) then all those countries would start to send in troops from the UN to restore order and all this but they occupy as much of the country as they care to and they rule the countryside, the hills and they're quietly organizing people. I've seen about four or five movies on that country. I just admire the spunk. It's like the people in North Vietnam. They've been fighting a very very long time and they're not independent but when they do get independent it will be on their own terms.

Biafra popped up several times. The Biafran response came most often from the South where telecasts of the Biafran plight seemed to have affected many. These women tended to develop an empathy and sympathy for the Biafran struggle and admired the

Biafran efforts to withstand defeat and their courage in trying to overcome the disastrous effect of war upon their population and land. One westerner even related that one of her relatives fought in the Biafran war on the side of Biafrans and eventually had to be smuggled out of the country. Support of Biafra generally was phrased in the following terms:

1. I admire Biafra because people over there are starving and here in the United States as a whole we have food that we just throw away and just to sit down and think that there are little kids over there, infants that are dying every day because of the lack of nutrition.
2. I sort of like Biafra because of the damn enduring they take. I don't think any other country done went through as much as they have.
3. That's the place where all them hungry people were dying or starving. They had progressed better. They did a good job for themselves.

Ghana was selected by several women who not only expressed a like for the Ghanaian people but who also reacted positively to Kwame Nkrumah's role in the development of the country.

1. I used to admire Nigeria because of all this idealistic stuff they used to pull on me when I was in high school—the democratic thing, the little America in Africa. But I sort of admire Ghana and the people I've met from Ghana. I don't know anything about it politically, just from my contact with African students.
2. I like Ghana because I read the thing Nkrumah wrote and I dig what they are trying to do over there.
3. I dug on what Kwame Nkrumah had to say.
4. I still think that Ghana is very progressive. I think people are slowly coming to the realization of what

# Pan-Africanism: What's That?

> Nkrumah really did for them. For instance if you go there they say look at my beautiful country and then they start pointing to all the things that Nkrumah did. They sacrificed a lot for it, yes, but in the end they're proud of it.
> 
> 5. I think Ghana because I was very much impressed with Nkrumah even though to most people he has negative connotations in Africa, and I suppose in America. But I just liked what Nkrumah tried to do. I think when anyone gets too much power—I don't know—it seems to be something in the human psyche that just can't take it. I think this is what happened to Nkrumah. He was not only a good leader but the people loved him and trusted him and he was either impressed by or affected by some White control, and more or less led him in the opposite direction of his people, led to his downfall and possibly a short downfall of Ghana. But I do admire him and what they have accomplished.

Kenya's Mau Mau movement and the whole Kenyan struggle for liberation seem to have influenced several women to choose Kenya as their most admired African country.

> 1. Kenya and Kenyatta should serve as a model for what he did and what he is doing is very significant —driving the English and Indians out of the country. That's a start.
> 2. Kenya I guess because of the people and their courage and their undaunted spirit, their resiliency, forward looking, pushy kind of thing.
> 3. I was kind of turned on by Kenya because of the kind of very open, violent kind of way they achieved their independence. Kenyatta has always been a fascinating man to me because of his charismatic kind of hold that he commands in Kenya.
> 4. Kenya. I know something about it. My Swahili

teacher was from Kenya and she told us a lot of things that had gone down in Kenya and how the British government had tried to take over and said that Kenya wasn't ready to manage its own affairs. And they now have their own thing going. They're really trying to build up a beautiful country.

A large number of women mentioning an admired African country chose Tanzania, even before they had been asked to discuss their attitudes toward Julius Nyerere and Tanzania. Many discussed the Tanzanian situation in enthusiastic terms and seemed to view it as a possible model for other African countries.

1. Lately I've been hearing a lot about Tanzania. It sounds exciting. There was a show on tv about a month ago where they compared what's happening in Kenya with what's happening in Tanzania. Tanzania is really more socialist and it is opposed to European and western influence. They're trying to build their country themselves.
2. There's an article I just finished reading about Tanzania. I feel that any man who is struggling to give his country self control is a person of worth. I know there is a great deal of controversy about him as to whether he's going about it in the right way but I think under the circumstances he's done a good job.
3. That's a very very poor country and that's interesting. He has used his people as a resource and his country is based on a socialistic form. He is a very strong leader and yet he comes from a very small tribe. That's going to be an interesting country to watch.
4. I think I am most interested in what Nyerere is doing in Tanzania. As I recall what he was doing —for instance developing this whole concept of African socialism, trying to make it our own as much as possible without the imperialist forms of

power still having a hand in the affairs of the country.

5. A lady from the university came to the freedom school and she was talking to us (about Tanzania). The thing that got me is that they have already politicized people in universities on a large scale. When the university first started the kids thought they were coming there and getting white collar jobs and pushing the buttons and everything. When Nyerere came in, Nyerere said we're going to go out and have farm projects, blew their minds —closed the school for a year and a half, almost two years. They came back after that period of time ready to do those farm projects, ready to go out and work with the people on nutrition and different things. This is a very basic step.

6. Tanzania because reading Nyerere's views on education and also his views on industrialism and the way people have supported him and his views I think it has a chance of surviving most as an African nation. He has thwarted off all of the attempts of the United States and a lot of other western countries to come in and just set up a lot of industries which they have done in other "undeveloped" nominally independent countries and this will immediately bring in other things—prostitution, differentiation of different people in the society. He wants to maintain the tribal system but at the same time give people the advantages of education. His education for self-reliance where he's saying people won't just go to school and come out and live in one little section of the country where all the educated people live but they'll go back where they originally grew up and begin to bring up all of the people there because the country doesn't have enough money to give everybody an education. I think it has really the most chance of surviving and maintaining an African thing of sharing

and of one person extending himself over to his people.

7. I like Tanzania best right now. It's the one I have had the most exposure to and that is principally through a program that was on Black Journal when they talked to Julius Nyerere and he explained the philosophy of the country, what it is they are trying to do. I'm very definitely looking in terms of those kinds of philosophical positions. He expressed them. Tanzania is engaged in African socialism. Even though there is some capitalism in the country they're moving away from it now and they want people to come to the country—especially Black Africans—with the attitude of contributing to the good of the people rather than trying to make some dollars for self which I strongly believe in.

8. Tanzania because of the Arusha Declaration.

9. Tanzania because of what we have heard and what we have read about Nyerere; what we have seen about the country leads us to believe there is something—well new ways of trying things with our people and probably socialism as it's being practiced there. I'd like to see what it is, what it's about.

10. Tanzania. I think it's on the road.

11. I am a great admirer of Tanzania and Nyerere. I'm very frightened because I think he's one of the most powerful, brilliant men in the world next to Mao because if it works. . . . For the past three or four years I've been very afraid for the brother because it does seem as though it's working and it's a very sound, valid kind of thing from what I see. What really impressed me was him closing down the universities and telling the students to go home when they began to remove themselves from the people.

# Pan-Africanism: What's That?

One or two replies favored Ethiopia, Sudan, Zambia, Nigeria, Guinea, Algeria, Liberia, South Africa, and Rhodesia (Zimbabwe). Those selecting these areas made the following comments:

1. Ethiopia because for one thing their spears and arrows beat Italy when Italy tried to conquer Ethiopia. Last summer I met some Ethiopians and a lot of African students that went to parties together with West Indian people and American people. I like what Ethiopia stands for. I went to the cultural shows they had, the whole line of history and what they're trying to do to get western countries out of Ethiopia.
2. Sudan because of the culture and the people. Another favorite is Egypt.
3. I admire in East Africa Brother Julius Nyerere and Zambia's Kenneth Kaunda.
4. I'd like to go to Nigeria.
5. Nigeria. Stokely said that Nigeria offered to let them use them as a base in which to gain control of Ghana. I don't know how true that is. Nigeria is a very progressive country that has potential almost for anything. It's like a modern New York. It's just fantastic.
6. Personally I think I would love to go back to Africa and then I say wait a minute old lady—do some research and study. I would like to go to the West coast because that's where most of us came from. I would like to go up to the mountains. There's a tribe on the borders of Guinea, Sierra Leone, and Liberia—the Kissi tribe. I saw that and I said oh boy those are my cousins. But of course I'm nuts. But I'd like to go.
7. I guess Algeria because they did get their independence.
8. I probably admire Guinea and Tanzania. They're socialist, progressive states. Their governments seem to be going in the right direction in terms

of trying to become independent of imperialist forces, economically especially.
9. I guess Liberia only because I have some relatives there. As far as moving along and progressing since their independence they've done a remarkable job and to see this happen you know it can happen and it gives you a good feeling.
10. I know more about what happens in South Africa, Johannesburg and places like that. I think maybe I would tend to admire that. I guess I'll say that. Rhodesia in a way. I'm familiar with it. Therefore I can empathize and therefore feel strongly about it. Also I know people from Rhodesia, know them fairly well and I just know what they did, not everybody else. And I admire those people. They were very dedicated and committed people.

As we anticipated, most women had at least a nodding acquaintance with the South African situation. A few women, however, had no idea about South Africa. As one southern woman said when asked about her views on South Africa: "Would that be Africa as a whole?" Almost apologetically, in response to the more general question: "What do you think about world affairs?" the same woman said:

> I believe the world as a whole is in a perplexed situation because they try to keep everything they can from the Black people. In this way they can say we are ignorant to a fact; that we don't know anything that's going on. If you want to know anything about the Black society or Black people in general you have to find it on your own because there's nothing published here that's worthwhile.

Knowledge and attitudes about the South African situation ranged from enough of a superficial awareness of conditions to deplore them (true for most women studied), to enough of a fairly detailed analysis of conditions in South Africa to believe that armed struggle was necessary. A few who reflected the latter sentiments felt that the struggle was not going well either in Zimbabwe or South Africa. As some women said:

1. I don't know that much about South Africa except it's a horrible situation. It's worse than Mississippi. I think—is it true that the population is, like the Blacks are way over half? What puzzles me is how they can remain in the situation they are in. They have them so tied up, wrapped up. Like I was talking to this minister who was over there and he said they carry numbers like the government suggested we have. They call them identification numbers. Anyone who's caught even talking about a revolution, that's their lives. So I really don't know of any solution for them because who has the money? Who has the guns? The Whites!

2. I know they operate under completely racist doctrine where the Black man is subjugated in his own country similar to that under slavery. He doesn't have any rights. The governments operate under this system and there is very little that he can do about it.

3. There's really not much difference than what's going on over here. I think to sum it up it's just a struggle for the people.

4. I don't understand how it could have continued for so long. Other countries in the world are supposedly against it and I know the people there must really be bitter and I can't see why violence hasn't really broken loose totally. From the little bit I've read and heard the White people are in the minority and they control the Black people, like you have to have passes to go to certain places and it's almost like a big concentration camp. I don't see how it can continue to exist for so long.

5. I think it's horrible. I would say that it was worse than the situation here in the United States, but Africans don't think so. They think ours is most inhumane. The thing that seemed to me most terrible was about the families, how they didn't allow the families to live together—only a certain length of time because they didn't want family ties and they thought that if too many people got together they could do too much. And there's some kind of code for the Blacks—that they don't allow families to be too close, only for a certain length of time that they can stay together.
6. It's a bad scene over there. You got all these White people. I don't care if they were born in South Africa. They're not supposed to be there. They rule the government and the apartheid system. They have to get a pass to come into the city. The father comes into work and he goes back out and the woman—the African culture is being destroyed. I think a revolution is needed, guns—that type of revolution. It's a whole lot of Africans there and a few Whites ruling. But the few Whites have the weapons. One thousand men could charge a guy with a machine gun and those thousand men could lose.
7. I'm very much concerned about South Africa, concerned about the overt racism that still exists there and the numbers of Black people still that are—not just oppressed—they are really enslaved there, and the fact that this country, our country and other countries still permit it and feed into it arms, funds, etc. I'm impressed with those Zimbabweans I know and their efforts of trying to do something, organize, get relatives out, and trying to educate those of us out here as to really what the situation is.
8. It seems to be a fairly well developed country. They're building a lot. I think the United Nations

should come out and take control of that government. South Africa is just a pathetic situation.
9. I was talking to my brother about this just recently and he said that he wishes that those Black people there would just in some way turn the country over and get those White people out of there. It can be done. I'm sure there're people down there working on the way it should be done.
10. I met with some people from South Africa at the World Youth Festival in 1968 and I met a number of the liberation fighters who were there. We talked for a long time. I think if any place in Africa is made a main focus in terms of liberation, it's got to be South Africa. It's just the most horrible situation possible. They've got a majority of Black people there who are ruled by this racist pig. On the other side of it is that the brothers and sisters are fighting. They're fighting for their freedom. They are conducting an armed struggle and they're going to win. There's just no two ways about it.
11. That's where Stokely's wife is from. I have some definite views about that country. Run it off the face of the earth with all those White people and their little land—all of them wiped out and give the country back to the Black Africans. They have a system out there that I understand to be worse than slavery even by American standards. That's saying a lot. I read one report in Newsweek that in South Africa Japanese have what is known as honorary White citizenship whenever they go in that country. Have you ever heard of being an honorary White? Honorary White? That's sickening. And their apartheid system is one of the worst things I've heard of in my life. Even this country deplores it—not that it means so much that this country deplores it but the fact that it deplores it means that it must be a million times worse than they think it is.

12. I think the White South African settler only has a matter of time. It's only a matter of time before they will not be able to hold the land. I think the threat itself will come from within. It will probably start from within although it's been going on for a good deal of time and also being crushed constantly, but I think along with the independent African nations who will have to take a stand when actual war breaks out. I think it will be a conglomeration of Black Africa. Given 60 years the resources of this country will be depleted. So to keep this country and the west in general at the level which it is accustomed to living, the only alternative would be to gain total power over the land, total use of the land itself. And with the independent nations in East Africa and all over Africa cropping up as they are, I think there's going to be a conflict; there's going to be a great deal of conflict.
13. I've been very disappointed with the struggle in Rhodesia.
14. Several years ago when I had many friends involved in whatever is going to happen in South Africa in terms of Black refugees going back and reclaiming their country I was privy to see how the internal friction between the Blacks kind of alleviates confronting the Whites and it all has to do with methodology just like here. Until the Black man there gets himself together there can be no thought of it no matter how sophisticated, and some of the ideas are very sophisticated in terms of taking over White South Africa; no matter how sophisticated that is there is treachery from within and I say the same thing for us here.

Fearing, perhaps, that Black Americans or the American government would be tempted to join the South African struggle, one woman ventured to say:

# Pan-Africanism: What's That? 283

> Personally I read about it and think about it as just another Mississippi or Alabama. But I feel like we should not send our little resources over there. I think the United States should not be involved in any economic situations over there. I feel like especially Black artists should stay out of there. I read not too long ago Otis Redding is over there autographing somebody's leg —in Jet magazine—and it's really silly. It's so many other places he could go or he could send for a couple of Black South Africans to come over here and hear him if it's that important that his message or his song get to so many places.

Pan-Africanism can be an extremely potent concept or it can just become a visionary, illusory idea. Africans, West Indians, and Afro-Americans united in spirit and endeavor would no doubt represent a new, emerging power with which others would have to contend. Yet to reach that stage some rudimentary knowledge about the Caribbean and Africa would have to be conveyed to Black Americans. As it stands now, even with a rising degree of Black consciousness and budding Afro-American studies programs, Black Americans seem to have little working knowledge of the African continent let alone the West Indies. Furthermore, if Pan-Africanism is to become a potent and viable force, more Black women will have to be convinced that looking inward solely to the Black American situation is ultimately costly and will make the struggle in the United States that much more protracted. In other words, if Pan-Africanism is to become a viable concept, the advantages of working within a Pan-African framework will have to be explained to those who are now so skeptical of its potential that they prefer to "battle" or T.C.B. (Take Care of Business) in one country— the U.S.A.

# CHAPTER VI

# Something's Got to be Done— But What?

*One of the most perplexing questions* confronting contemporary Blacks is how to combat the continuing bigotry and discrimination which is still embedded in American society. Should one retain the integrative strategy of the past as urged by the NAACP, SNCC, SCLC, and CORE? Or, should one stress the resolution of the Black identity crisis in order to evolve a high degree of Black consciousness? Or, should one associate with separatist movements? Or, should one engage in sporadic acts of violence? Or, should one commence a deliberate attempt to alter radically or even destroy completely the present American system?

We posed a variety of questions to the Black women of our survey in order to determine how they might resolve the most pressing issue of coping or dealing with the continuing bigotry which seems to permeate American society. Most of all, we attempted to probe deeply into the thoughts of the women in order to avoid superficial responses to a very complex issue. The responses were most enlightening and reflected the extent to which these "together" women have been alienated by "the system." Moreover, their conversations support their firm belief in the proposition that something's got to be done.

Our approach to this chapter manifests the varying strategies which Black people have adopted, or may utilize in the future, as a means of eradicating the terrible burden of discrimination. We focus first upon the integrative push, second on the resolution of the Black identity crisis, third on separatist movements, fourth upon sporadic acts of violence, and finally upon "system alteration" or "system destruction."

*The Euphoria of Integration:
White and Black Together*

With the decision in the case of *Brown v. Board of Education* (1954) came an intensive drive to make certain that the doctrine of integration permeated the American social and political systems. The drive toward integration perhaps had its greatest singular impact in the field of education. Liberals, and even some moderates in American society determined to heed the U.S. Supreme Court's admonition in the Brown case: "We conclude that in the field of public education the doctrine of "separate but equal" has no place. Separate educational facilities are inherently unequal." (*Brown v. Board of Education*, 347 U.S. 483 (1954)). Caught up in the integration push were many of the women surveyed. These women sometimes spoke openly—and even bitterly—about their integrative experiences in predominantly White schools and communities. In many instances it is clear that these experiences may have "radicalized" many respondents, or at least "turned them off" as far as the "system" is concerned.

To gain a deeper insight into the effect of integration upon Black women, we have selected four case studies. One involves a young woman whose public elementary and secondary schooling was integrative and who elected to attend a Black college. Another case study concerns a young woman whose public elementary and secondary school education all took place in Black institutions and whose college training also was in a Black school with the exception of one summer spent in a northern predominantly White university of allegedly high quality. The third subject was exposed to a mixture with respect to her schooling—with a stint in some all Black public schools as well as a stay in some integrated public schools, followed by a brief stay in a White northern college. The final case study is that of a woman whose elementary education took place in a southern Black school, whose secondary schooling occurred at a northern White private institution, and whose major college experience unfolded in a Black college after a brief stay in a "prestigious" northern White college. In the interests of anonymity we have renamed our subjects respectively: Cleophola, Hyacinthe, Nelesi, and Oananua.

#### CLEOPHOLA

Cleophola came from a small nuclear family consisting of a father who was a careerist in the armed forces, a mother who might easily be described as a "social climber," and two children including Cleophola. Cleophola's parents, not unlike many other Blacks, apparently concluded that only an integrated education could guarantee the proper development of their children. As a result, they established residence in a White community and sent their children off to "White" schools beginning with the nursery years. Cleophola recounted for us, in a deeply resentful manner, events which befell her, her sibling and her cousin as they sought to cope with life in a White community. Little White boys would throw rocks and dirt at the family car while calling the occupants "Blackie." In the classroom her cousin was called, among other things, "milky way." Nor did Cleophola and her sibling escape such name calling. No doubt it was the memory of being "stabbed" with pencils and assaulted by missile erasers in grammar school which led Cleophola in her later years to abandon non-violence as "a silly tactic." The vicious effect of Cleophola's integrative experiences was quite apparent in her story about a Black doll whom we shall call "Annie."

> I remember incidents where I felt sad because I was Black. One interesting thing that might inspire some sociologist—we had a little doll named Annie. All three of us (sibling, cousin, and Cleophola) played together. We all lived together in one big house. This little doll

> was Black. I was about six. The other two were younger. We put Annie through so much hell. We would bash Annie into the wall everyday and call her all kinds of names and submit her to all kinds of tortures. And we would kind of honor all our little White dolls. Maybe this was a kind of a displacement of our feelings toward ourselves upon this poor wretched doll.

The reaction to "Annie" clearly revealed the kind of self-hatred which those integrative experiences had engendered in Cleophola, her sibling and her cousin.

Cleophola could only describe her residence in a White community as "very unhealthy." She came away from her childhood integrative experiences convinced that instilling respect, pride and identity were much more important than learning ABC's or other knowledge in a "good" school (more often than not equated with a White school by many Black parents). As Cleophola stated:

> I think that to a child learning to love others, learning to respect, and most important of all being respected is a million times more important than learning that the dog is black or the cat's name is Spot. Learning this essential identity of self, essential identity of self pride and self respect is so completely more important than learning ABC's at six. The child can learn ABC's at any time. I think Black people have suffered from the horrible delusion—they're beginning to come out of it now —that there was something inherently wrong with their all Black schools and their all Black town, and an all Black barbershop—like somehow if you go in an all Black grocery store things aren't going to be as good as they are in an all White grocery store. Therefore, man because it's White it's right, because it's White it's better. They (Cleophola's parents) wanted to do what they thought was best for us. But in doing this we were hurt because what they thought was right was so horribly wrong. So they took us to these schools and put us in these "good" White schools. We learned our ABC's and

are very articulate because of this. At the same time what I went through from four to twelve did me so much harm and I was in such pain.

Apparently at a later point in time Cleophola's father was given an overseas assignment. While abroad with her family Cleophola refused to salute the American flag, let alone say the words of the flag salute or even stand while others recited the pledge of allegiance. In explaining why she refused to recognize the American flag Cleophola cited her shame at being an American and her intense dislike of the way Americans were treating the people in the country where her father was stationed. Perhaps her own experiences in White communities had some impact on her decision.

Interestingly, however, although Cleophola decided to enroll in a Black college, she arrived with an essentially "colonial" or White mentality. For her fellow students her wig served as evidence of a lack of Black awareness. Soon she came under the influence of three male students from different parts of the country as well as a strong and well known male professor. Largely as a result of these associations she "threw off" her "colonial" mentality and took on the garb of Black consciousness. As Cleophola related:

> I went into (X's) class my first day of my first semester at (Y) and I had on a wig. The three brothers were rapping to me: "Take off that wig." As the semester proceeded, I took off the wig and got my natural together. Along with these three brothers and (X) who in spite of my wig helped me, told me, encouraged me in a lot of ways—he was the main person (X). The first time I got my natural I realized that I was beautiful. People would stop me on the street and say you're pretty. I felt honest with myself. I felt liberated.

#### HYACINTHE

Unlike Cleophola, Hyacinthe lived through a childhood which was deeply embedded in a Black experience. Born in the South to a mother who worked as a domestic and had an eleventh grade education, and a father who was an unskilled laborer who had completed the eighth grade, Hyacinthe was one of several children. Hyacinthe and her family simply accepted the local patterns of a southern milieu which meant, among other things, attendance at all Black schools. Yet there were changes introduced as Hyacinthe grew older—changes which too were accepted as part of a local custom. Nevertheless these changes did not lead Hyacinthe's parents to seek out integrative experiences for her and their other children. In fact integration represented an alien concept for Hyacinthe's family. As Hyacinthe recalled:

> I come from a hometown of about 3,000 people. I come from the South where the lines are pretty much well drawn and people don't question so much lifestyle and the expected and all of this. I was like graduated from high school during the demonstrations but—and all of this had taken place so you didn't ride in the back of the bus. You could like sit down to have a hot dog and the honky next to you would leave. We never really questioned: "Man, why can't we go to the White high school?" It was just generally known that you just didn't, although I would ask my father why we had to sit in the back of the bus; but he gave me an answer like "you can see just as much from back here." I took it for the truth and it was just like that. So my parents never talked in terms of integration.

It seemed natural that Hyacinthe elected to attend an all Black college. There she initially resisted attempts to invest her with a Black consciousness. To her college came students from all corners of the United States including East and West. Two Black males in particular made a concerted effort to talk Hyacinthe into a new Black awareness but she closed her mind at first, largely because of her religious background which dictated that one love all others. As Hyacinthe stated:

> They first thought of introducing me to the Black thing and I was turned off. This was in complete contradiction to all the things I knew because my parents were

> religious people and they had always told me that the Lord is going to make a way and you got to be better than that folk and really don't get up tight with some of the stuff that's going on because our lives—you got to look toward heaven and the whole bit. So when they talked in terms of the honky, hate the honky and kill, and all this stuff I said: Man, where you coming from? People are people. You got to love each other and the whole bit.

In the summer of her junior year in college Hyacinthe was offered an opportunity to travel north to spend the summer in a White academic institution of extremely high caliber. For Hyacinthe the summer of her junior year proved to be a highly enlightening episode. In the midst of this integrative interlude she "got tuned in and related to other Blacks." This was true probably because she viewed her summer program as quite "paternalistic" in that a White private foundation granted funds to a White private institution to recruit Black students from Black southern institutions to spend a summer "beefing up" the knowledge which they allegedly were being spoonfed in the South. Looking back on this experience Hyacinthe concluded:

> It turned me definitely off. I said "I don't want this."

On the contrary, the northern experience seemed to have turned Hyacinthe on as she and other students on the program decided to form a coalition of Black schools. About this time also Hyacinthe had begun to read Malcolm X and soon became impressed by his charisma and organizational power, even though at that stage of Hyacinthe's development Malcolm X was already dead. Hyacinthe managed to convey the gist of her northern summer as well as those aspects of it which left her suspicious of some White intentions. As she said:

> I was taking one history course which was called civil reconstruction. A White dude was teaching it. I think he was a nut. As a matter of fact I'm sure he was. And I was taking a course called Modes of Political Dissent

which was kind of traditional. I always got the feeling in sitting in class that the professor was writing a book about us because the lesson plan that we got when we came into the class was pretty traditionally structured because we would study Martin Luther and the Protestant revolution, reformation rather, and we studied about Marx, never relating it to this country of course, and various things like that. But the thing about it is the instructor would try to guide the discussion into the Black thing. As a matter of fact he invited us to his house one night for a rap session and gave us some wine to drink and we went to the thing because we figured— at the time some of us were too naive to know what was going on; plus coming from where we'd been we took it as a sort of compliment that this man was listening to us. And on a Black campus, during that particular time, the teachers didn't do a hell of a lot of listening to students. It was like, at this time, we thought this was really a friend and all of this kind of stuff. He was a fairly decent teacher. As a matter of fact I would call him good especially on communism and the whole bit. But still in all, I definitely felt that we were being used and I'm looking for a book to come out pretty soon. So my summer awakened a heck of a lot of things.

Hyacinthe was unable to continue her studies after graduation from college because she had no money and thus had to work to support herself. Had she been able to enter graduate school she would not have deviated from her pattern of registering in all Black institutions for her choice for graduate study was a Black university. Despite her northern summer educational interlude, then, Hyacinthe remained unconvinced of the virtues of integrated education.

### NELESI

Nelesi grew up in an eastern section of the United States in a home divided by the "absence" of her father. Her elementary edu-

# Something's Got to be Done—But What?

cation took place first in an all Black school, then in an integrated school following the decision in *Brown v. Board of Education.* Neither situation seemed to please Nelesi and she faulted both in these terms:

> My elementary school started in a Black school. It wasn't anything happening there that stands out in my mind except the teacher spanked me once for flying an airplane in class. But I remember when they desegregated the schools. They switched when I was going into the fourth grade and I went to a White school down the street. I noticed that we never mingled. The White kids stayed on one side of the class and the Black kids on the other. The White teachers seemed to favor the White kids and didn't take too much interest in the Black kids. Negro teachers were very White minded and students who were dark complected or had characteristics of the masses of the Black people say like if they didn't speak grammatically correct or made a whole lot of noise in class and stuff like this the teacher would try to give him a hard time. I was sort of in between these people. The nice Negroes who came from the good homes and got good grades and were very polite advanced in school. Somehow it seemed I just sort of shuffled through.

By the time Nelesi reached junior high school she was back in an all Black environment since Whites, fearing integration, had fled the area. Once again Nelesi became frustrated in her efforts to expand her knowledge:

> In junior high school I started getting a thirst for knowledge and it wasn't there. I couldn't get any knowledge. For two grades in elementary school I was in an integrated situation but then it went right back into an all Black thing because the White people left and I was right back into the all Black school thing. The teachers were very hard on Black students. These were Negro

teachers. I only remember one White teacher. The teachers were very hard on Black students for disciplinary reasons. They would take more time disciplining students than teaching.

With the commencement of her high school years Nelesi returned to an integrated setting—this time in a school recognized for its alleged high academic caliber. Viewed initially as a "discipline problem" Nelesi struggled to find herself and to gain some knowledge from her daily trips to the school. Perhaps the intensification of the SNCC and CORE movements "saved" Nelesi as she found an academic outlet in Black history and a frustration release in activities in behalf of SNCC and CORE. The story is told most vividly by Nelesi herself:

At the time when I was growing up in high school you had all the civil rights things and being conscious of this I became involved in the beginning of SNCC here and I then began to see why I never really fitted in in school. For a while I began to think there was something wrong with me because my teachers would write up these things saying I was rebellious and insolent and this and that and the other. They were always saying I needed to be heavily disciplined and I was very quiet until they would do their thing. So I was thinking "wow, there's really something wrong with me." But when I got into the civil rights thing I said "wow!" Then when I got into high school I got some more White teachers. The high school I went to was half Jewish and half Black. This was supposed to have been one of the best schools here and the kids wrote all over their hands. They wrote on their slips and shirts and all those things. They cheated their way through school. They never studied. Yet this was reported to be one of the best schools here. I went there thinking I would finally learn something 'cause I had been in all these Black schools where they just sent me through like on a conveyor belt. I saw these students doing this and I could see that the Black students were deliberately being—their spirit was deliberately being messed over and they were deliberately being pitted one against the other and not encouraged to do anything except socialize. Here they had a track system: general education (basic), academic and honors. The teachers wanted to put me in the basic. That's where they put all the Black students. It didn't matter if you were intelligent, they just put them all in there. I told my mother I didn't want to go in there because I had some friends in academic. So she wrote this thing and said "well, no, put my child in academic." They did it and it was good because in the basic they teach you typing, basic math, basic English and that's it. You don't learn nothing. I would take classes with students in different tracks and I could see they were just as intelligent as the academic or honors students; some of them more intelligent but they were just made into vegetables. Being involved in SNCC, when we finally got into the democracy classes I finally got to the end of high school and the teacher was talking about how this is a great country and everybody is a citizen. Everybody's rights are respected and there is no problems. If you want to make any changes in the democratic process all you have to do is vote and get your congressman in. I said "no indeed, you understand, in so and so county in Alabama there are so many thousands of Black people lynched, thousands of Black people trying to vote, and thousands of Black people living in houses that are just incredible." The teachers got together and decided not to call on me in any of the classes because of this. I was raising so much havoc. I would be stimulating the other students who were half dead from the way the teachers had been going. They said "no good" and tried to isolate me. I was sort of isolated any way because I really didn't fit into what was happening. So I became more rebellious. I think they put me out (graduated me) of high school because I was determined to fail. That was the attitude of students: to get by. If you got a C or D, that's cool, just get the grade and get out of here. It wasn't to learn anything. So I took that attitude. Most of my peer group—brothers and sisters—were making C's and D's so I didn't want to make no B. I had to make my C and D. The last grade in high school I said "I'm just going to stay back" and I really got rebellious. I had a little white hat that I used to wear that looked ridiculous. I looked like a farmer and I wore those dark glasses in the eleventh grade. In the twelfth grade just about 50 students were wearing dark glasses. So they had a thing on their hands. When they would give the exams for graduation I would put all kinds of ridiculous answers on these papers just to test these people. I was testing them throughout because a lot of these teachers were from Vassar, Smith and Radcliffe. The contrast between the teachers was the Black teachers were concerned with having us sit in the seats and walk down the aisle on the right side and going through the right door, responding to all the little bells. The White teachers were trying to use us as guinea pigs. They were very liberal and you could see them testing out all these things they had learned at Vassar, Smith and Radcliffe. I would be testing them to the hilt and they just let me do my thing. As I say they just put me out (graduated me) because there was no way I could have passed with the answers I put on three of my majors. I never saw the results of the tests. I deliberately tried to fail but yet they graduated me. Of course my heightening consciousness—a lot of times we'd be on the picket line for CORE and I had my picture in the paper a couple of times. All the teachers saw this. The White teachers didn't quite know what to do.

After high school Nelesi journeyed far North to attend a White college. She lasted there three months and described her days in that environment as "like being a fly in buttermilk." Only fifteen Black students were enrolled in the college and, according to Nelesi, all the Black men had White girl friends. After trying another

# Something's Got to be Done—But What?

White institution for two years—this time one to the South of the college she originally entered—Nelesi returned home. But her two years in the White institution located in a large urban center transformed Nelesi's thinking to a significant degree. She became deeply involved in cultural nationalism and was influenced seriously by her association with a jazz group and a leading Black poet. Not only did she engage in cultural activities but also emerged even more highly politicized as a result of her participation in anti-war activities. One anti-war activity in particular stood out in Nelesi's thoughts. She had joined a Black contingent of some 4000 people during a parade against continued American involvement or entanglement in Vietnam. Her contingent was attacked by policemen when the group decided to move out of a congested area despite orders by the police to hold their position. The police were mounted on horses and carried clubs and other weapons while Nelesi held in her hand only a poster of Malcolm X. Nelesi drew a very clear picture of the scene:

> They had clubs, chains, sticks, and carryings on. You just can't keep going out in the street like this completely defenseless. I didn't even know how to fight if I had to. I could see that King's thing of just sending people out in the street like that was for the birds.

Upon her return home Nelesi not only became a Muslim but also more deeply immersed in Black cultural activities as well as a liberation school.

For Nelesi, then, both her exposure to all Black schools as well as to integrated schools helped shape her Black consciousness. But it seems clear that her integrative experiences served to channel her more quickly into a Black awareness.

OANANUA

Perhaps Oananua might best be described as a rather precocious child and youngster whose family background provided a warm, secure atmosphere for her growth and development. Since her father was a successful professional man, Oananua's mother assumed the role of housewife and mother on a full time basis. The family traveled quite frequently, moving from state to state, but eventually settled in the South on a rather permanent basis. There Oananua and her family found themselves in the midst of the Black struggle. As many southern communities adopted the boycott as a tactic for terminating odious and arbitrary discrimination, so too Oananua's community found itself resorting to an economic boycott. Oananua described how caught up she was in the flow of history at that time:

> I remember the mass meetings we used to have getting the boycott together and we were just kids at the time. But we had a feeling that this was a tremendous effort that we were all undertaking together and it made us proud.

In describing her impressions about segregation in southern communities and the impact it had upon her, Oananua recalled:

> Black people and White people lived separately you know. There was no such thing as going to school with White folks and you were aware of learning not to have to go to the bathroom at inopportune times 'cause there was no place to go to the bathroom. And you know, you remember packing just tons of food to take on trips 'cause we couldn't stop anywhere. Our parents made us feel this was an adventure, this was fun. I'm sure for them it wasn't fun. When we had to go to the bathroom there was no place that we could go, or when we were thirsty and wanted something to drink there was no place to get something to drink. But you know we never felt terribly persecuted at that time because of them. I'm sure they did. They just didn't transfer (it).

When Oananua and her siblings reached high school age, their parents decided to send them off to prep school. No doubt Oana-

## Something's Got to be Done—But What?

nua's parents felt compelled to seek private educational institutions for their children because the local Black high school, built for 900 students, somehow stuffed 3000 students within its walls. Oananua sent off applications to some half dozen northern private schools and eventually elected to go to the cheapest—perhaps because she knew the financial strain imposed upon her father by having all the children educated at private high schools. Forest Head (fictitious) proved to be a rather unique institution in that the emphasis was placed not only upon a high degree of intellectual development but also upon the necessity of avoiding attitudes of superiority which might result from treating the students as privileged subjects whose only role in life was to think. Consequently Oananua found herself enmeshed in a very rigorous and disciplined schedule at Forest Head. Each of her days began at 6 A.M. and each included some form of domestic work—cooking and cleaning, for example.

It was not long before Oananua began to feel the spectre of discrimination cross her path. During her first year at Forest Head —perhaps to overcome a sense of social isolation—she decided to date a White teenager. Needless to say, Oananua represented the sole Black student in her school. Her decision to date a White youngster apparently set off a spate of meetings as anxious faculty members (and probably former graduates too) worried about the "image" of the school if this liaison between Oananua and her companion were aired publicly. Oananua vividly recalls the strong reaction engendered in faculty members by her social contact with the White teenager:

> When I was a freshman, I was going out with this little White boy. I was going out with him about two months. Now mind you, when I say go out we could only go out once a week on Saturday night. It was very structured. Each class had a social chairman. You know when you're acting social chairman you plan the activities and sign up with who you are going with. You know that type of little funny stuff. But anyway when I started going out with this fellow, appropriate faculty members undertook to have a discussion with me about

the fact that I was going out with this White cat. And he got beat up by some of the fellows in the class for going out with me. But that lasted for about two months. After that I think during the whole time I was at Forest Head I went out maybe three times. 'Cause I said, you know that experience, I said 'later.' You know, I don't need them.

At the end of her sophomore year Oananua expressed a desire to room with two other young ladies. Previously she had roomed alone but as the months passed she established a rather close friendship with an oriental student and with a White girl. Although there were no rooms on campus for three girls, the 'triumvirate' determined to make a special appeal once they discovered a room large enough to hold three persons. Oananua was called aside and informed that the need to protect the "image" of Forest Head outweighed any need to ease her loneliness. As Oananua recalled:

Well, that was quite a shock because I was getting very good grades and I was doing all this other fool ignorant shit and I realized then just what the situation was. I guess I'd really never wanted to face up to it before and really (at home) I never had to because the Black folks were really just very united and you weren't just out there by yourself. You really weren't on your own. And I realized then what a lonely thing it is, it can be, to be Black. There was nothing I could do but it taught me a lesson. I mean it shaped my whole attitude. And so you know, like I didn't call the chick any names and I didn't say 'well, I'm going home.' I worked hard and I just said 'later' to all these folks. I'm here to get what I can out of this place.

Ironically in her senior year, Oananua rose to a position which by the rules of the school required her to have a roommate. As she related:

> So my senior year I did have a roommate. I had this White girl for a roommate. And the reason I had to have a roommate my senior year was that I was a 'cop.' You know each floor, each dorm had a 'cop' and you're responsible for doing all this stuff. And all 'cops' have to have roommates because if you're not there then your roommate has to do the things that you have to do. So I had to have a roommate that year. By then I didn't want one, but I did have one.

When Oananua began to think about college her mother urged her to choose DuBois (fictitious), a Black institution. The reason advanced by Oananua's mother was that in college one forms friendships which are destined to last for a lifetime and that Oananua should be able to select other Black women for her associates. But Oananua ignored her mother's exhortations feeling that she could not obtain a good education in a Black college, and further that her college friendships would not be her lifetime friendships. So Oananua enrolled in the prestigious Oak Hills College (fictitious), a White institution in the North. Soon she discovered many resemblances between Forest Head and Oak Hills. The most obvious resided in the low enrollment of Blacks. This time, however, there were other Black females registered in Oak Hills, albeit less than a dozen. Although Oananua formed a close association with the other Black women at Oak Hills, she abandoned her studies there and decided to follow up her mother's idea and attend DuBois for just one semester. As Oananua said:

> We were all very friendly and I got to be very tight with—there were three Black girls in my class and I mean we just stuck together all the time really. There was a definite gap between the Black girls and the White girls at school and we were all friends. We associated with each other but it was just different. The four of us used to get together frequently—away from them. And I just couldn't stand it. I thought, if I stay here for four years I'll come out and people'll say For-

> est Head, Oak Hills—WOW! You know, so forth and so on. But you know I figured by then I'd be a dried up frustrated prune. So I left after my first semester. And you know my advisor and everybody said "This is wonderful. We like for our students to do this—go off and work for a semester and blah, blah, blah" and I had every intention of going back.

Her adjustment at DuBois proved to be quite difficult. After all Oananua had become accustomed to a fairly rigid discipline and the pressures of performing at an extremely high academic level. She described her initial experience as follows:

> I was miserable. Each and every day was more traumatic than the day before because I hadn't been used to being around fellows for one. I hadn't been used to being around Black kids my own age in great numbers, number two, and I just thought everybody was jiving around playing cards, dancing—they weren't studying. The teachers would come to class late. And I just couldn't understand it 'cause I was used to working very very hard.

As the summer of her freshman year began to draw to a close Oananua was confronted with a serious decision: should she return to Oak Hills or continue at DuBois? Said Oananua: "I had the choice of going back to Oak Hills or DuBois and I decided the reason why I was so unhappy at DuBois was I was just that maladjusted." She was not disappointed in her decision: "So, I decided to go back (to DuBois) and I did and I had a ball. I had a BALL. I really did. It was the rightest decision I ever made in my life."

Soon Oananua approached graduation. As she did, she found herself being wooed by yet another prestigious institution—this time for graduate study. And once again Oananua confronted the prospect of entering the predominantly White world. She revealed the steps leading up to her decision to reject the offer of graduate study at the White elite institution:

> Well, I was gonna go to grad school. Someone recommended my name to X and they were spastic because they did not have any Black applicants. So they came down to DuBois to beg me to apply 'cause they didn't have a prayer getting anybody else you know. And it was after the final day for applications and scholarships and so forth and so on. So I said 'now I'll apply.' So I applied. They flew me up there for an interview. There were about ten principals of the school to interview me and they told me that if I was accepted I would be the only Black person in the school and I would be the only girl. So I could just see me with 199 White men and for two years working very very hard in a field I wasn't really sure I was committed to. I studied all summer so I could go there. The day before I was due to arrive I sent them a telegram saying I wasn't coming and that was the end of that. I really didn't want to go and I felt relieved when I didn't.

In retrospect, Oananua seemed almost thankful that she had transferred from Oak Hills to DuBois. For her DuBois represented a means not only of discovering what it meant to be Black but also of inculcating a Black consciousness:

> The change was so great, it's incredible. It's really incredible because I learned what it really was to be Black, to learn to be proud of the achievements of Black people, to learn to look at things without judging them by White standards. You know, it was really a fantastic experience. It really was. And, I think too, I really began to take more interest in domestic politics and urban trends which I don't think I would have done so much had I gone to Oak Hills. I don't think I would have learned to appreciate the predicament that we as a people are in. There I really felt Black but not isolated Black like I had been like a zoo specimen like at Oak Hills and Forest Head. But here I was

> able to be more myself because people weren't always looking at you and saying, Oh, this is (what) Negroes are like. And I was able to be myself.

For Oananua, then, while the seeds of her Black consciousness may have been planted at Forest Head and Oak Hills, they did not sprout or bloom fully until she withdrew from an integrated setting and placed herself once again into an all Black world.

All four women—Cleophola, Hyacinthe, Nelesi and Oananua—at some point in their lives were thrown into an integrated situation. Although the duration of their integrative experiences varied from a summer to several years, each woman felt the impact and even burden of being thrust into a predominantly White atmosphere.

Like Cleophola, Hyacinthe, Nelesi and Oananua most of the other women studied had been forced to ponder the direction of Black people under the rubric of integration. One woman with a relatively vast experience in the civil rights movement revealed how her thoughts, shaped by historical events, moved her off the path of integration:

> Maybe I thought at one time that integration would work. I'm sure I did. As we moved in the South talking about voter registration we started out being an integrated group of people. And as I looked at John Lewis, Stokely Carmichael, Marion Barry, Lester McKinney and folk like this who were offering some Black leadership, they found themselves out in the field working, knocking on doors while the Whites were in the office, giving them directions—telling them where they should go. So they would have to then compile the information out there, bring it in and turn it over to somebody at the desk. I always found that the person at the desk was White. He was the one that kept the records. And what's most important is the record keeper, not the one who makes it but the one who keeps and compiles it. After we gained the right to sit at the lunch counter we found that we could not afford it, so it was not inte-

gration. Prices remained the same. Attitudes were not changed. Hash was still slung at you and you had to pay that enormous amount of money that you did not have. Now did that work? No, it didn't work. It was only when we went into the field of separation that Blacks decided how they were going to dress. I think the way we're going now, and I see us going backward a bit, is perhaps the best way. It's like your mother had three children, you had company and something was broken: her one good stem glass which she treasured because she couldn't have any more. And what did she do? She said, 'all right all the company go home.' What is she getting ready for? She didn't call it that but she was getting ready for a family council where we could sit down and iron this thing out and map out the punishment if it's going to be any. She separated the family from the friends and you had this good talk. That's what separation was. And that was good. Whites made it look like something else. And some Negroes who didn't know what it was about made it look like something else—segregation in reverse they called it. To me that's not what it was. Integration helped but it did not do the job. It made us really look at if we're going to be equal we can't go this way either because we're still not equals so we'd better go and get rid of all the Whites for a while until we sit down and assess where we are and then go back out there.

Yet it is clear from the study that not all women have abandoned the integrationist thrust, especially at the educational level. Some typical comments reflected the view that facilities in all Black schools simply were inadequate, and that integrated schools offered a better chance for a more meaningful education.

> 1. I'm in favor of it because if the schools are integrated you know the White schools have better facilities and they have a better curriculum in them for students than in the Black schools. If the Blacks

go to the White schools and the Whites to the Black schools there's going to be a good curriculum in both of them. I really do believe in school desegregation.

2. I see the fight for integrated schools as a thing now that immediately has to be waged in order to give children a better education—and White children because White children aren't being educated either as long as they are separated.

3. In our community it's too bad you can't take a survey of the area to see where our children have to go to school. We've had people here from Washington, D.C. and they thought that part of our schools were sheds where you kept tools and things. So we said 'no, that's where our children go to school' It's a disgrace.

4. I think that schools should be desegregated only because it's my belief that boards of education are not going to put money into all Black schools or not enough money to achieve quality education. I'm concerned about a quality education. I think the only way you're going to achieve it is to put the Black kids with the White kids. And then they're going to put the best textbooks in. And they're not going to have broken windows in the school and inadequate heating systems.

5. I had a very good case in point. A friend of mine moved, took her child out of one of the inner city schools and put him into another school that was predominantly White and he failed. So the only way I feel to get an equal education and to bring them up to the educational standards of White children is to integrate. Integration is the only solution. They speak of separate and equal but there is no such animal.

One of the more provocative aspects of the study was to observe how parents 'worried' over the type of schooling to which their

Something's Got to be Done—But What?

children were exposed and the variety of solutions adopted in the search for a meaningful and sound education. For example, one woman reported that she had placed her child in a special school where there are no restrictions as to curriculum, reading or writing. Parents are also obligated to attend the school. In addition, children are encouraged to travel all over the world. One of the woman's friends, for example, allowed her child to spend six months in Cuba as a learning experience—all an accepted part of the curriculum.

Disenchantment with the results of public school desegregation can be gleaned from the comments of many women. Generally these women felt that desegregation could best be described as a myth or farce, and further that enrollment in an integrated school more often than not has a negative psychological impact upon Black students since they leave the school feeling much more inferior than when they arrived. Others expressed no desire to be with Whites. Still others complained about the unfair treatment which Blacks receive in integrated schools.

1. Integration, school integration has never worked. It's another one of them myths. We may have five or six people in a White school. You may have White students in a Black school but by the very nature of the neighborhood Black people live in a concentrated area because of the whole housing discrimination thing so the schools are segregated. I think that Black children ought to go to predominantly Black schools with predominantly Black instructors, if not all Black instructors with a total Black administration—which is what you rarely see —with parents actively involved in the decision-making, money-making level. I think that White people ought to go to White schools in White areas with predominantly White instructors, predominantly White administration and with the parents and the students and everyone in the community involved in the money-spending level, policy making, decision making level in education and not

leaving the education of their children to somebody else.
2. I can't dig school desegregation. I think at this point children need to come from Black teachers. They need Blackness to identify with. They need someone who knows their problems, who knows the community, and who have a love for Black children—little, nappy-headed or whatever you want to call it. They don't need White teachers at this point. I think in the elementary and high school especially you need to come from Black teachers.
3. It (integration) ain't got nothing to do with nothing. I don't care where we put our children. They're not teaching them anything about *them*. They're not teaching them anything about their community. They're being taught how to get away from it and leave the rest of the brothers and sisters there and to act like you are White. So they're missing the whole question—quality education. It's an insult to think of busing children out of their community talking about giving them adequate schooling because no one can explain to me why adequate education could not be in that community school and relate to the school, the problems, the people and the heritage of that community because before they can move on to deal effectively with any other culture they have got to be aware of self and you don't expect for them to go into a White community and have them to change their situation because it's perfect. Their educational system is perfect for them. We must have our own.
4. I think school desegregation was good in the sixties. I mean 1960, 1965. There was something there then. I think with the whole idea of awareness, desegregation, school desegregation doesn't offer as much to Black people as we originally thought it would. The only thing I can see with desegregation is the opportunity for Black teachers to move about,

possibly the opportunity for Black youngsters. But what I would appreciate is the uplifting or the upbuilding of our Black schools and our Black neighborhoods, of making our Black schools what we would like to make them. Now Black people have ideas. There are no more follow the leaders. They no longer want just the sterile, staunch type education you get with integration or desegregation. They want to add more color or meaning, more depth to the education and you can only do that when you are in control. There is no control when you send your youngsters across town. There is no control when your youngster is the only child in a White class. Nowadays when Black awareness is important and when Black awareness helps in building the mind and the body, I don't believe a Black child profits from sitting in a White classroom and being the specimen or the experiment. I think it hurts the child more because the child is growing and learning and they are pure. And when they have to be an example at such an early age you don't find them profiting or benefiting from it. So desegregation I think is a lost cause. I think it's dated. I think what we need now is—I wouldn't call for equal but separate—but I would call for what we have, use it and build it up.

The concept "community control" has become quite popular in some Black areas. More often than not it represents a euphemism for Black control over all institutions in the Black community including schools, police, health services, welfare offices, and others. We purposely asked the women of our survey how they would react if confronted with a choice of integration or community control. Some of the responses were interesting in light of earlier attitudes which surfaced on the school desegregation issue. A few women who favored school desegregation opted for community control as the preferable social reconstruction pattern. In fact, most women surveyed who made a choice between integration and community control (and many did not) selected community control. Apparently they did so with the belief that Blacks need to build self-sufficient communities.

> 1. I think right now you need community control. That might sound a little contradictory in terms of what I said about integration of schools. I think on some things you have to have integration in order to get money. I don't think these governments are going to release money to all Black groups, not without considerable hassle and considerable time gone by.
> 2. I think everything should be more community oriented. I think there should be within the community a community development so that the community is made as self-sufficient as possible. There should be community centers within the school that are open all night, community instructors from the community, community aides. Teachers should live within the community in which they are teaching. The community base would give the community more power.
> 3. Community control movements are mostly always good and result in a lot of positive things. It helps a lot getting Black people aware that they're more than themselves, that they have a whole people to rely on. And those things usually work out to be very beautiful.
> 4. I support community control most strongly in reference to education. I'm not familiar with other aspects of community control, economic or social but I do support community control in education. When I speak of community control what I speak of is the community or the people that are attending the school their parents controlling what they are taught, controlling the kinds of books they learn from, controlling the fact that if I'm in an all Black neighborhood and my child attends an

>    all Black school then he should be able to learn Black history, Black social life. They should be able to perform Black. They should be able to act Black. That is what I view as community control where the people are in direct control over education.
> 5. I'm not for integration. I think it's a very empty kind of thing because it's not a total integration of self and people relating to each other. It's always some kind of fucked up neurotic thing. I think it's much healthier for Black people to integrate with each other until they become really holy and groovy. I think community control is instrumental in doing that if for no other reason than that it sets up really good communication links so that we can get to each other and know what's happening when we have to move.

In examining some of the responses carefully, though, one is struck by the fact that few women spoke in terms of control over the entire community—preferring instead to limit their remarks mainly to the school situation. This may indicate, as at least one woman's comments reflected, a skepticism about the locus of power under community control: would Black people in fact control the institutions of the community or would the reins of power still reside within the grasp of large corporations, or universities, or White governments? This skepticism clearly manifested itself in the responses of those who rejected community control as a viable concept—rejected it at least until the moment when Black people realistically could become the power in the community and until Blacks actually acquired the skill of nation–or community–building. As some women said:

> 1. I prefer integration because even though you have community control the funds for the schools and the hiring of teachers, and the equipment for the school—everything—the decision is made somewhere else. Even though you have Black people

paying taxes in this community, who's going to control? The people who have the say so are somewhere else. And it's still going to make a difference in this school over here controlled by this Black community. I prefer busing, integration.
2. I think it's good if the community really knows what it is doing and how to go about doing it. A lot of times I've seen it happen where they advocate community control but no one knows how to go about setting up a structure. A lot of people say we don't need organization; that's the White man's thing and whatever they're working on flops. If you just had a little bit of organization it might have worked. I think in the community they should have people who know how to go about setting up the structure so it can be workable.
3. They got some community control of schools but the schools still are in bad shape as they ever was because those people are not together about what they want and until Black folks get together we just going to be floundering around in the stream, not really knowing how important the whole thing is.

A few women were unable to make a clear choice when given the alternative of community control or integration since they thought that each concept might serve a useful function in different settings.

1. I think they both have their role. I can see that if you have a large community of Black people with few Whites, sure they ought to run it. But where you've got a mixed community then we've got to look at the thing in a different light. So I don't think we ought to dichotomize and say one here and one there. I think it's a matter of community assessment of what is best for this situation.

# Something's Got to be Done—But What?

2. This is interesting, community control versus integration. I have a kind of mixed view in that I see integration taking place at certain kinds of levels but I didn't see integration as lacking control. I see integration as mixing people at certain kinds of levels—jobs, education, etc. But I still see their being able to control that community but not getting lost in the crowd because you're integrated. I see Black people not having all to live in the same physical community but being able to live throughout a community but still being able to exert control on that community. I see an open kind of thing going on instead of saying that we probably all need to live in the same area. That's not integration but segregation and you should be able to control that community. But I worry about it because it's also isolation and you're more subject to being hit by arrows when you're clearly set aside. So I have those kinds of things running around together. I don't want us to get lost anywhere in the social groupings, but I want us to be set up in a way that we can survive and get that much more and have some community control.

Probing more deeply into Black women's attitudes towards integrative endeavors we sought to discover their feelings towards some groups and individuals who had sparked the integrationist thrust during the decades of the forties, fifties, and sixties. Two images of Roy Wilkins, leader of the NAACP, emerged from the study. One, held to a lesser degree, is that of a man who has done his share in the history of the Black struggle but who now must recognize the need for new leadership.

1. I think he has done a lot to improve race relations but it's gotten to the point now where it takes a little bit more than he is willing to put out, in the sense of him being too moderate. We need a more

forceful force to bring about changes. I think he's a little too mild but he was very effective in his day.
2. I'm not going to put Roy Wilkins all the way down because I think that Black people tend to be unfair to Roy Wilkins and people of his type. I think his day is passed and he doesn't understand Blackness especially as it exists today.
3. He's a nice old man. I think he's done his part. I think he needs to step aside and let someone a little more progressive move into his role.
4. I'm at a phase right now where I don't see a condemnation of anybody Black. I don't think we can afford it. I think we dissipate energies that way. I think that is the most detrimental thing to our race when we condemn somebody else for being a Tom, condemning somebody else for not being Black enough. Roy Wilkins played an important role in history. He did what he could do with his own beliefs. He might be obsolete but that's history and it'll take care of itself.

The other is a more derogatory image of one who has betrayed the Black community.

1. There's a nigger for you. He's just no good for me. These are the kinds of people they want in the White House; these niggers, my house niggers and that's him. He's a perfect house nigger and nothing more. It might be something less now. I'm not going to tell you the words but he's less.
2. I'm sure you don't want profanity. I think he's, as Eldridge Cleaver would say, a mother fucker. He's one of the Black people who represent a problem and I really think he should be dealt with. He is a traitor.
3. I think Wilkins is probably the biggest Tom in this country. I think that his ideology is leading Black

people back into slavery and right into the same system and it'll never free Black people.

In a similar vein Bayard Rustin, often described as a strategist for the civil rights movement, was given credit by some women for his contributions to the movement while others criticized him harshly and severely.

1. He's just another Tom, just another flunky the administration needed to hang up and dangle before the American public.
2. He's outlived his time. I'm not saying the man ought to go somewhere and die but he's talking about when he was coming up times were this, times were that. Things are good now. I don't know nothing about when he was coming up but I know about when I was coming up and I still ain't got and won't. I don't think he should be running that. He's become a reactionary in his old age.
3. I don't go for him at all. He's one of those brainwashed Negroes. He's certainly not Black.
4. He's a labor man. He did a good deal for labor. He served his time well. I think that now, however, Black people in labor have to take a different direction. He's getting up in age now. He served his time but I think the thrust now is for Black people to be much more militant about unionism.

Parenthetically it should be noted that some of the younger women in the study were not familiar either with Roy Wilkins or Bayard Rustin—especially the latter. For example, one woman struggled with Rustin's identification as follows:

Let's see. Who is he? He's older and I think he was a pioneer in some of the civil rights stuff. Isn't he an NAACP lawyer? Wasn't he the one who won the desegregation decisions—or was that the man who's the Supreme Court judge?

Not only did most women reject the continued leadership of Roy Wilkins but also the legal tactic which the NAACP and its companion NAACP Legal Defense and Educational Fund have relied upon so heavily during the past decades. While a few women praised the role of the United States Supreme Court in bringing about changes beneficial to the Black community, most cast a cynical eye toward the entire judicial system. Most severely criticized were the local and lower courts which, in the eyes of our respondents, constantly sapped the Black community of its strength by imprisoning its Black male population and in general dispensing injustice. The comments of some women even revealed personal encounters with the repressiveness of the judicial process.

1. I think the courts have become an oppressive tool in the society. At times they've played an aggressive role. The Supreme Court under Warren was fairly progressive in terms of desegregation, challenging congress. They overturned a lot of those reactionary laws. But now with the Nixon appointments the Supreme Court is going to become the worst oppressive tool there is. They already have made rules and all kind of antilabor law and things like that. The regular court system is just the most horrible thing you have ever seen. I was in court the other day. I was arrested at City Hall protesting the murder of X and we disrupted the city council meeting. They refused to hear anything. There were about 200 of us and they refused to listen to anything we had to say. Four of us were arrested. I went to court and Blacks and Browns were the only people that go to court. The room was just filled with them—all kinds of charges. It's just like mass production. They shove you in and shove you out. It's really terrible. They had these stupid public defenders who aren't interested in you, your case or anything else. They just interested in getting that monthly salary from the state. It's just horrible.

2. I have been in some of the courts just to look around to see how the court procedures are. It all depends on how the judge might feel that morning on how he's going to decide who he's going to convict that day. I've seen attorneys actually selling Black people down the river. They're not really working that hard.
3. They definitely oppress Black people because the courts are prejudiced toward Blacks. It just seems to me that courts deal with Blacks in a whole different way than they do with Whites. Blacks fear courts because they feel they won't be dealt with fairly and I don't feel the courts do deal with Blacks fairly. Usually they get longer sentences and higher bails. Most of the time their trials are held up. They spend more time in prison waiting for a trial than Whites do. Most Negroes I've talked to who have been to jail have been beaten. They still are beaten. Even policemen if they don't like your attitude they will beat you in the streets.
4. I don't think they're helping. They're actually oppressing. They take the stand of the White people always and against the Black people. Look at the Hoffman thing with those guys in Chicago: gagging Bobby Seale up, treating him like a common dog. No, I take that back. A White man would never treat his dog so bad. But they treated him worse than they would treat an animal by gagging him. They had that thing on too tight from what I could hear. The maximum penalty they could have given Huey Newton? Two to fifteen. He got that two to fifteen. The maximum sentence they could have given to Clay? Five years and all that fine that broke his back. They gave him the maximum. Black folks have always got the maximum. White folks have always got the minimum. No Whites have ever gone to jail for raping Black women.

5. The courts don't ever help Black people. All they do is assuage guilt occasionally. Courts and Black people like have nothing to do with each other. I spend a large part of my day in juvenile courts and criminal courts downtown and I watch the judge look. Like if they are White and their hair is cut maybe they get off and if they're Black no matter how their hair is fixed they'll probably get the book thrown at them. I don't believe in the legal system. I think it's all a farce.
6. Courts are made up of men as everything else in this world. And men on the court regardless of their charge to be completely objective, carry some of their subjectivity into their decision. Those men can be harmful as well as effective and we've seen evidence of that. I'm sure you're familiar with a book that's recently been published in which one of the judges here . . . has been charged with rendering decisions that generally are discriminatory against Black people. I had experienced some of this myself. Perhaps you are aware that a couple of years ago the X engaged in a boycott of downtown businesses and we were very effective. Consequently the businessmen here brought a court case against thirteen members of X of which I was one. And we sat in that court and our lawyers refuted every charge that was brought against us very effectively. And if you listened to that court hearing not any person in his rational mind could have seen how the judge ruled against us. But he did.

So then the local and lower courts are viewed as particularly oppressive instruments as far as Black people are concerned. In addition, while some credit is given the Warren court for helping to stem the tide of discrimination in some phases of American society, it is obvious that most women are not looking toward the Supreme Court either for their salvation or for the implementation of an integrationist policy.

Of the three organizations most active in the civil rights move-

Something's Got to be Done—But What?          319

ment of the sixties with its integrationist flavor—CORE, SNCC, SCLC—we chose to concentrate upon SCLC because of the charismatic appeal which Martin Luther King held for so many Black people throughout the country. Our aim was to discover not only views held about the validity of King's approach to the Black struggle but also the viability of an SCLC in the decade of the seventies. A quiet admiration for the leadership and person of Martin Luther King was the most consistent attitude expressed about this central figure in the battle of the fifties and sixties. As one woman said:

> I admired him. A lot of people say he was the modern day Moses. I wasn't living in Moses' time. From what I've read I would say he was a modern day Moses. I respected him because he believed in non-violence and he practiced what he preached from what I could see. On the whole I admired Dr. King even though I think sometimes I might have become violent.

Yet to the extent that SCLC and King represented an embodiment of the integrationist—and even non-violent—philosophy, many of the Black women now view those philosophies as incorrect paths which ought to be avoided—or at least tread most carefully—during the seventies. As one woman pointed out:

> Dr. King's philosophy in his day was good. That started a long time ago, during the time of the desire for integration. At that time Black people weren't going to get up and fight. They weren't going to get up and walk up and down the street with guns 'cause very few of them are going to do that now really. But in that day and age it was that new thing. But if you recall, toward the very last days of Martin Luther King he expressed a feeling of a discontentment more or less towards this non-violent action because he made a statement to the effect that we've tried non-violence and I warn you White people that if you don't get together something bad is going to happen. My people are going to break

loose or something. And sure enough that's what happened.

In terms of Black women's current perceptions of SCLC it is abundantly clear that most respondents view the organization as having been rendered impotent by the assassination of Martin Luther King. For them the assassination seemed to terminate hopes for a peaceful-integrationist solution to the plight of Blacks in America. To the degree that SCLC is attempting to project the same philosophy reflected during the life of Martin Luther King they are, in the eyes of our respondents, following a hollow and bankrupt route. In fact, the only bright light which some women detected in the SCLC today is the Breadbasket operation launched by the Rev. Jesse Jackson. Some typical comments follow:

1. They're trying. I think the loss of King was a blow to them that they really haven't recovered from because he made the organization and all of the efforts that have followed since his death have really been failures in terms of their standards. They're integrationists.
2. I think SCLC more or less died after King's death or died with him because I think the appeal of the organization was manifested in King.
3. SCLC has always been pretty together in my mind up to the time that King died. I think what happened when he died was kind of like a realization among Black people that we couldn't love the master any more. It was a total understanding that that was over. Abernathy seems a little dull to me.
4. I think it's falling apart now that King isn't there. You don't read or hear as much about it as you used to. It's just like King could draw crowds of millions of people. Like he had that big march on Washington. But I don't think Abernathy could do it. Like Abernathy came here with a team of mules and he didn't have a block long, he didn't have people a block long following him. But I think if King had

of come honey, they would have declared it a holiday.
5. With the exception of Operation Breadbasket and Jesse Jackson's thing in Chicago I hear very little about it. It's my feeling that it's just kind of fading away.

Interestingly only one or two women praised the efforts of Rev. Abernathy and these women lived in the South where the impact of SCLC probably has not diminished as rapidly as it has in more northern areas. As one woman summed up her praise for Abernathy:

> I think they are doing a tremendous job being led by Dr. Abernathy. I really do think so. We're able to have more people voting and being trained how to mark their ballots and also being trained to be able to read and write.

Needless to say, a handful of people cannot perpetuate the integrationist-nonviolent philosophy of SCLC. The reduced fervor for SCLC in Black communities across most of the United States may underscore the lukewarm sentiment for a general permeation of integrationist thought in society and the futility of peaceful marching, picketing, and sit-ins.

### *The Search for a Black Identity*

With the assassination of Martin Luther King came a new assertiveness of Blacks throughout the country. Angered by yet another murder of yet another valuable Black man, the message traveled rapidly and painfully for some that Black people would no longer tolerate and submit quietly to the cloak of White oppression. Many Blacks, for example Stokely Carmichael, began to see that the first step for Blacks had to be the inculcation of a Black consciousness. This could be accomplished only through the resolution of a Black identity crisis which affected virtually every member of the Black community and which in many instances may have been instilled as a result of exposure to "harmful" integrative experiences.

One of the mechanisms for developing a heightened Black consciousness turned out to be the educational process. Black students began to demand curricula changes which would not only take into consideration the heritage of Black Americans but also lessen the gap between Black students and Black communities. Moreover Black professionals, sociologists, social workers, psychologists, political scientists, historians, etc. launched an assualt on the pristine quality of many predominantly White associations which continued to be insensitive to Black interests.

Soon controversy began to rage over Black studies programs as they were more often than not challenged by the traditional educational system as revolutionary or anti–intellectual. Yet Black students insisted on the psychological and educational need for Black Studies. In light of the controversy and dissension over Black Studies programs we endeavored to determine just how the "together" Black woman viewed the direction and value of Afro-American Studies, especially as related to the resolution of a Black identity crisis.

Most women were enthusiastic about Black Studies programs, seeing them as a means of inculcating a deeper Black awareness by re-examining the lives and contributions of Black people in history. Moreover they looked upon Black Studies as a way of lessening the influence of White culture or Anglo-Saxon civilization upon the mental processes of Black students, and in the long run avoiding the production of carbon copies of White Anglo-Saxon Protestants. As some women said:

1. I dig it. It's something very much overdue. Blacks need to learn about their heritage and their culture and get their Black thing together. I think Black Studies is doing that for Black people.
2. Again I must say that I am in total agreement with that if for nothing else than to shock White people. I think for so long we have—I grew up thinking blond hair and blue eyes was beautiful and it took me until I guess high school to realize that it wasn't.

Black Studies gives a sort of pride, a sort of warmth and connection with Black people in the community.

3. I think in pushing for things such as Black Studies if they are important to Black people as a race—most of them being brought up the way they are with only the basic history of White people—because we really don't know where we're from. And if you don't know where you're from and your background, you can't very well determine where you're going. We know a lot about the White race and their history so we must find our place in history—way back so we can decide where we're going, where we're headed.

4. I think it's long overdue because I still remember Little Black Sambo from grammar school and it still leaves a bad taste in my mouth. Children were brainwashed to think we were all Little Black Sambos. I have learned so much about my people since and I think there's a lot more to be done.

5. That's long overdue too because I know that when I was going to elementary school, even there the only time we got any Black Studies at all was during Negro History Week, you know one week out of the whole year and then we learned about the same people: Booker T. Washington, George Washington Carver, Frederick Douglass, Sojourner Truth. I'm not putting these people down of course but you didn't hear too much about Nat Turner and Marcus Garvey—you know people who were really trying to do something really effective. The people that we heard about were people who made contributions that White people thought were important and didn't mind Black people knowing. It wasn't until really just a few years ago that I learned that it was a Black man who came up with the blood plasma and he died in the South as a result of not being able to be treated, to get a blood transfusion in a White hospital. These are things that you just don't

learn automatically. You got to search these things out and find the book that all these facts are in and different things like that. Things like the rolling pin, the traffic light, the pencil sharpener, the shoe lace—things that were invented by Black people that I just recently learned about. It's very important that there is a push for Black Studies not only on the college campuses and the high schools but the elementary schools, especially the elementary schools—more so there than even in the high schools.

There was, however, a small group of women within our study who decried Black Studies programs, feeling either that they did not go far enough in developing meaningful Black programs, or that Black students had left themselves open to abuse and use by White "radical" students.

1. In the beginning the strategy was great: you don't have class if we don't have a Black Studies Department but then the White radicals moved in with the Black students. The Black students ended up being used. This has stifled a lot of movement on the campus, being used by the White radicals.
2. I find that in the Black history courses they offer you, you find more Whites in them than you do Blacks. Also it's so peculiar now that we can come up with all these books and all these famous people. Where they been hiding that? Where were the books at before? I believe a lot of the stuff is being written to pacify us. I think we should learn more about the economy, what we can do to build ourselves up and get ahead rather than read about the past.
3. It's primarily a waste of time, academically a waste of time because I see like in twelve years there won't be a need for a Black Studies program because I think students will come and they will know it already. They'll get it from their own curiosity. Black

# Something's Got to be Done—But What? 325

> Studies are usually involved in the social sciences, history or literature and I think if you really want to know about those things and what Black people have done, there's time enough in life, in the space of a day for you to do that on your own. I think there needs to be a technical threat in the Black community. We can't pose a threat until we can make a bomb. There are only ten Black mathematicians right now. This is an atrocity. You need to spend some of those social science hours getting some skills. The social sciences are not going to liberate us. They might highlight the problem but I haven't seen a poem liberate anybody yet.

As Black Studies programs flowered many Black students insisted upon adding a community action component. That is, Black Studies for them should not be seen as the act of sitting in a classroom taking notes on the life of Benjamin Banneker, or sitting in the dormitory reading the autobiography of Malcolm X. Rather the program was viewed as a combination of gathering knowledge and engaging in some action project in the community, whether it be tutoring elementary and secondary school children or chasing drug pushers from the community, or simply establishing an empathy and rapport with the Black community which would set the stage for the later acceptance of Black college graduates in their efforts to assist the local community. Many of the women surveyed had some exposure to the community action concept because of their involvement in campus Black Studies programs. Most felt that community action represented an essential ingredient of any Black Studies Program or any Black student's life.

> 1. I think it's a good idea. Just thinking about some of the students we have down this summer (in a community action program), they are just about as bad as White folks. They don't know nothing about the poor folks. A lot of things they are experiencing this summer they never experienced before so I think

    they are doing a lot for the Black community this summer. I think they are doing an awful lot and I think they are learning an awful lot. With this they might go back home and do the same thing or something on that basis.
2. I think it is essential to the education of the modern college student . . . Black college student that he's involved in what's going on in the community; he is involved in the affairs of the nation at large. Whatever area he goes in it has to be relevant and this is one way of making it relevant. It is also one way of redefining our Black institutions. Involvement in the community—allowing them semesters off for participation in voter registration and all this kind of thing is a very good way of making the college functional within the community. Physically speaking, the way the Black colleges are located they're generally right in the middle of a Black community. They're right in the middle and they form a nucleus for the total operation of the community. I think it makes the education much more significant, much more relevant.
3. There was an issue that had developed this past year and it was unique in that for once students had made an alliance with the workers. That was new for a lot of Black people. If those types of things continue it will be good just to unite the entire Black community—students, professors, undergraduates, graduates, workers. If that can be done it will be a good thing.

Yet some respondents deplored the fact that greater numbers of Black students had not found their way into the surrounding Black communities but continued to move directionless on the campus, exhibiting a sense of frustration due to a lack of meaningful involvement but still not recognizing the curative powers of community action.

1. I think basically that Black students just are not committed for long range goals. Your freshman year, "all right I'll be in this community program but the second semester I'm going to do this." They just don't get involved and don't work the thing straight through. They need more than just a short range thing. (The people in the community) need long range programs.
2. See that was the major problem with the whole fight just around Black Studies because it didn't affect the community completely enough. Black students tended to be separated from the fights and struggles in the community where the fight for open admissions, opening the doors for Black people to come into school does have more effect. I think it's absolutely mandatory for students not to just spend their time on campus. They have to live in the community, have to work there. They have to be able to relate to the community 'cause otherwise it just becomes to their benefit, not to the benefit of Black people.
3. It was '68 when I was a freshman that the students took over the administration building. Many students were just frustrated because of the fact that there wasn't any student consciousness. I mean students weren't conscious of exactly what they were getting as a so-called education at the school along with so many other things like different people on the Board of Trustees who were very shaky. At that time the big thing was relating to the community which is an old, very much used phrase but in fact it wasn't happening and the students were becoming more aware of that because of the simple fact that there were more students there than ever at that time from ghetto areas if you want to call them that, or just from areas where Black people are deprived more so than other Black people in the country.

They couldn't believe these Black people were walking around in a daze, like zombies, not really realizing that just around the corner there were people like themselves. The students weren't even thinking about how they could raise say the literacy of these people, their people in effect, or any kind of program, things like that.

Not only were Black students bent on asserting themselves and exhibiting their "new" Black consciousness, but Black professionals too began to group into identifiable Black caucuses. Some Black professionals even decided to splinter off to form their own associations, for example Black social workers, and the African Heritage Studies Association which had waged a long struggle against the insensitivities of some members of the predominantly White African Studies Association. While a few women saw the value of remaining in national professional organizations, the sentiment of a large proportion of our sample was: Why spend time taking over predominantly White associations when the best solution for Blacks is to form their own conferences and organizations which would allow them to concentrate exclusively upon matters of deep concern to Blacks.

1. That African Heritage Studies Association which is Black historians (sic) which broke off from the history conference—I think it was in Montreal, the last one—they just had a beautiful conference in D.C. Everything was geared toward what we need to do. Like if we had been with the White folks maybe we would have had one person here dealing with that, one person somewhere else. I think we definitely need our own professional organizations.
2. They can take over conferences if they want. People who are integrationists, that's an activity for them. I think they should start their own (conferences and organizations). If they are integrationist inclined and they take over these things and begin to find

that there was nothing that they took over and they got to start one any way....
3. The Black social workers in its embryonic stage took over the national conference of social workers for one session. I mean they literally took the stage and talked and rapped and then we walked out saying it was irrelevant. I think it should be done but I don't think a great deal of energy should be put in that. Just like with this particular thing the Black social workers' organization was formed to try to do things within the Black community with Black social workers rather than continue the effort to badger the national conference of social workers.
4. I think it's a poor strategy. I don't see why you go to those conferences. If you feel the conference is irrelevant and if you feel the organization isn't going to do anything to address itself then I don't think you should go. It seems to me why go to a big hotel owned by White people and a conference financed by White people and then stand up and curse them, telling how bad they are and then leave. I don't see that you have built anything. I would see getting Black scholars to have their own conference and define some things that are purely Black and don't worry about what the White people say. Let them develop their theories.

Although we have chosen briefly to explore how Blacks within the educational and professional arena have sought to grapple with the need to resolve their identity crisis by shaping a new Black consciousness, needless to say these are not the only arenas where the colonial mentality can be discarded. A whole range of institutions and activities have been developed to cope with the identity problem. Several of these will be mentioned before the study concludes. Suffice it to say at this point that Black people, moving from sometimes intensive involvement in integration, saw fit to pay attention to the problem of identity which had plagued the

Black populace so persistently throughout their history in America. And one of the most convenient ways of devoting time to the problem of identity rested in reshaping educational institutions and professional associations.

## The Separatist Thrust

Excitement spilled over in the fifties when, in the midst of the drive for integration, a voice for separatism of Blacks emerged on the national scene. Soon Black Muslims or members of the Nation of Islam found themselves being scorned as the advocates of hate, violence and "odious" separatism because, among other things, they constantly referred to the "White blue–eyed devils" of American society. Many Blacks, trained to accept integration as the legitimate doctrine of the country, frankly were embarrassed by the rhetoric of Elijah Muhammed, Malcolm X and other Muslim ministers. They could not understand nor accept a group which vigorously attacked their belief in Christianity and their association with members of the White American culture.

Yet, rather than fading away as a result of verbal assaults from White and Black alike, the Muslims began to grow and strengthen themselves into a very noticeable community characterized by a discipline which emphasized sound moral habits, politeness, and hard work.

In an effort to determine how deeply wed to the idea of separatism might be the women of our survey we asked their opinion on two of the leading separatist organizations today: The Nation of Islam and the RNA (Republic of New Africa).

With respect to the Black Muslims many women were willing to admit to a generally positive attitude toward the Nation of Islam but also to an unwillingness to become an active member of the group. Expressed often was a general respect and admiration for the Muslims because of their togetherness:

> 1. I really admire them. I wouldn't want to be a Muslim because I don't believe in their philosophy and I don't believe I have to eat that certain kind of eat-

ing and I don't believe I have to dress that differently. But I admire them for what they are doing, how they stick together and pool their monies together and their talents together. And this is a good way for the rest of us to do too. But I don't think we could get together like that. I admire them. I think they're great but I wouldn't want to be one. I don't believe in their faith.

2. To me the Muslims try and they do their work. But they got their shit together.
3. Well I have a great deal of—I couldn't say awe but a respect. I think the Muslims are one Black movement that I know has managed to stay together for as long as it's been together. And I'm not sure I understand yet how it is. I think the idea is that they build their ideas totally around the philosophy of Elijah Muhammed. They have their separate schools and separate farms and it's really something.
4. I think a lot of Black people respect them but aren't willing to give up their little vices.
5. Well I'm not into another dogma but their ideas. Like they just bought an airplane here that transports food supplies. And they got land and food and they are stockpiling and doing very definite things. It's a kind of militancy that's really beautiful if you can get past the Allah stuff but not into another God anyway. The thing that you see there is a real kind of Black togetherness and people really work. It would be really bad though to ever put them down because there are a lot of brothers and sisters who in learning the basic fundamentals of living that they teach are managing to survive because of it and even though they need the God crutch. The Muslims I think are really excellent. As I mentioned before I've really flirted with the idea of joining them except I don't want to have anything limit my mind.
6. I think the Muslims are the best thing that's happening to Black people. There's no Black Muslims

you ever see that's unemployed. They're always meticulously clean forever and they're very polite. They have that kind of perseverance. They stand out there every day through rain and snow and sell that paper. They have their own schools. They're a nation within a nation.

Then, too, a few women stressed the value of the Muslim economic program:

1. I'm for them. I feel Black people should own their own businesses and develop in the direction to better themselves and training programs to train people to do other jobs than just skilled non-skilled labor.
2. I don't too much understand the Muslims. I think some of their programs are good. I think down in X county they have a program where they are raising a lot of crops. I think that's great. I think Blacks really need to do their own thing rather than depending on White folks all the time. So I really think that's a great program they have going.
3. They've done miraculous things. In fact they are quietly approaching the capitalistic method in their own way and of course nobody is letting them do it either. The land that they acquired in the South, everything has happened to it so they have announced that they have to sell it. The land in upper Michigan for the cattle and all; I think they have reached a truce at this point but the townspeople and the Muslims are always at odds. So they are a living example of how we gain capitalism in a quiet manner. There is not going to be anyone else around to support us but ourselves.

Yet, an awful lot of criticism was directed toward the Muslims. Many accused the group of being too inbred and isolated. That is, they were charged with not reaching out to the non-Muslim Black community and not attacking directly the ills of the White structure with more than verbal vehemence.

1. I have a lot of respect for the Muslims. I don't appreciate their isolation. Neither do I appreciate their orientation toward one individual. I think, if anything, that will hamper their progress especially being in a nation such as America where they are surrounded by White folk. I think their lack of dealing with White folk, their lack of dealing with present times will hamper them to progress. I think their refusal to deal with politics which is the psychic of America. I think America thrives on money and politics. And for an organization to stand fast and refuse to deal with those things I think that will cause it to regress. Now economically the Muslims are doing as far as their farms are concerned, their bakeries but that is limited people-to-people type industry. I think if they are going to succeed we're going to have to venture out into that cutthroating type economic type situation—large industries, Xerox, General Motors, Ford, various companies like that which I don't think the Muslims are either willing to deal with or want to deal with.
2. I think it's beautiful any time Black people are united for any effort but I cannot see where there have been any gains made. For instance, what have the Muslims contributed to the people that are not Muslims? They take care of their own.
3. When I was little I used to think so, the Black Muslims they're here and they're guarding us and all these things. But now it seems like—even the fruit of Islam that's supposed to be their arm, their security arm, you know it's there to protect Muslims. You don't or I don't feel like the benefits they've built up for Muslims is extended over to Blacks. It's extended only in so much as you can come in and buy but anybody can come in and buy things like from their shops. You have to join in order to be able to get the benefits. It doesn't really allow for a national movement of Black people.

Other women found the Muslim discipline and behavioral code unacceptable:

1. I don't believe in all this stuff about not eating swine and all these things they believe in. I think they have saved a lot of souls so to speak. They're nice clean–cut people.
2. I just like kind of being an individual and to me when you're in something like the Black Muslims, you do what the Black Muslims do, say what the Black Muslims say, wear what the Black Muslims wear and I'd rather do my own thing. That's what keeps me out of a lot of these organizations, or whatever you want to call them. I call them a bunch of shit but that's what keeps me out of them.
3. I feel in their belief they are to the extreme. They have this hang up of certain foods you can't eat, certain things you can't do. Most of them were raised on that and they are just as healthy on the same food and if—you know, the way it's going now, every time you pick up something, something is wrong with it. There's nothing left that you can really eat, or nothing that you can really do.

Still others faulted the leadership of Elijah Muhammed, viewing him as much less than a devoted spiritual leader and much more as an exploiter of Black people.

1. I'm not going to say anything about the Muslims. The only thing, I mean they got a good program too but the thing I can't agree with is everybody looking up to Elijah Muhammed. I mean he's a man like everybody else. He's subject to human error. You can put your trust in somebody but not to the point that you worship them like a god. Because of his fallacies he can make mistakes.
2. Well, they seem to be having the most success and I just have some problems with having a man dictate

like Elijah Muhammed dictates and some of the things he says sound sort of stupid to me. I'd have problems following that. Muslim philosophy, real Muslim philosophy makes a lot of sense but as the Black Muslims practice it I don't like it.
3. I think that they train their men and women better than any other religion to really believe in that doctrine. Their father has a place, the children have a place. The father is honored in that house. And also the values they have—a man doesn't smoke, doesn't drink. They talk about a man respecting his wife, not committing adultery, being clean and wholesome and that sort of thing. And on the other hand they learn karate, self-defense and all that kind of thing. I don't believe in all their doctrine. I can't buy all that stuff because to me that dude is out to get all he can out of them folks. I think he's sponging off people.

Others attacked the economic orientation and output of the Muslim community. Some found them too capitalistic, others discovered that their services were inadequate and even inferior, and a few women saw a contradiction in insisting upon separation but then asking "The Man" for land.

1. I think the Muslims are perhaps the most capitalist-oriented Black organization. I think they have the best newspaper in the country with the exception of the pictures of Elijah Muhammed's program. I think the Muslim program is incorrect. I'm opposed to an all Black nation and I'm opposed to a Black nation especially that depends on Black capitalism. This seems to me to be just exchanging a White exploiter for a Black exploiter. There's no struggle. They don't involve themselves in concrete struggle and activity. They're still buying stores and things like that. It doesn't benefit all Black people.
2. I think the Muslims are a community to be admired

for their collective work and responsibility and also for their ability to make money. I have serious questions about the distribution of wealth just within the Muslim community. I have had people offered pretty phenomenal salaries. I know of two instances related to me where people were offered pretty phenomenal salaries to go work for the Muslims without necessarily becoming a member of the faith. I tend to believe that the Honorable Elijah Muhammed controls all that with all the financial advisors he's had and I don't know how positive that is. One problem we've had here is that the Shabbaz and Pyramid Industries are nothing really to write home about. I had them do some shades for my home and I had hell getting them to get the materials sewn right and the shades are now sitting in my closet. Their food store here is not the best. Most of the good vegetables, meat, fish and so on are distributed among the members of the mosque and that leaves the lower quality food for the community to buy. Another thing that happens is that they haven't been able to get the skill to put together the kinds of industries that Muslims nation-wide are known for.

3. I do think they are middle class in a sense—like one of their goals is to separate and I want to know for myself how can you separate from an imperialist power like the United States? How can you go to the White man and ask the man for land? He's never going to give it to you. You know, power is not given, power is taken. The United States knows that in their revolution as well that you do not give power, you take power. And this is what revolution is all about—land. The controlling factor is to control the land and you don't go to your enemy and ask him for land. And this is one of the goals of the movement, to separate—but who are they going to for the land? The White man. And they are

> moving now to be more of a non-violent type organization and I think history has passed the Muslims on by too.

Finally, some women hesitated to endorse the Nation of Islam enthusiastically because of the treatment and ouster of Malcolm X. As one respondent said:

> In a way I dig the Muslims because I feel that they've got an organization they're developing to take care of their own. But ever since Malcolm X I have not felt the same about the Muslims. And I find a lot of Blacks agree with me.

The Republic of New Africa was not as familiar to the women of our study as were the Muslims. For example, when asked what she thought of the Republic of New Africa, one woman replied: "Is that some place Elijah Muhammed wants to take the Muslims?" Other respondents confessed only a vague and superficial knowledge of the RNA.

The Republic of New Africa has been described by its leaders as "a black nation, to which all black people in America who wish to, can swear allegiance." (RNA pamphlet—Now We Have a Nation. The Republic of New Africa). Founded in 1968 the RNA has experienced a series of internal crises revolving around its leadership. Most involved in the power struggle were Robert Williams who spent time in exile in China and Tanzania, and two brothers—Richard Henry (Brother Imari) and Milton Henry (Brother Gaidi). Despite these internal crises the RNA has emphasized, quite consistently, the need for Black people to concentrate on obtaining land. "Where is our land?" queries the RNA. For them:

> Our land is in two areas. First, scattered across America, our land is sections of the Northern cities where our people now live and have lived, in some, for two hundred years. Second, lying in a great black belt across the South, our land is the counties of the South where

we have lived and worked the land and clung to it for 300 years despite the most brutal oppression the world has known. All of this land is illegally held in captivity as a colony, by the United States government.
(*RNA pamphlet*)

Three means of obtaining "our land" are suggested by the RNA: "Black determination," "international law," and "by arms if necessary."

It was this stress on land, especially obtaining land in the South, which vexed most of our respondents. Repeatedly they pointed to the futility and danger of Black isolation in a concentrated southern area where they could be "off'd" so easily. Moreover many women decried the wisdom of migrating to agricultural areas deficient in resources and having very little if any industrial capacity or capability. Some typical comments were:

1. I think that's nonsense. It would be hard to run a society right next door to an imperialist country. It would be more oppressing. Down South it's mostly farm. It's not industrial.
2. I believe what Stokely says. The land in the South is old and tired and if they give it to you it's just for that reason—that you can't do anything with it because they drained it. So far as I'm concerned I wouldn't move to takeover, as for—I don't think you can take the five specific states. If they put the people in those five states all they got to do is put a ring around it and drop a bomb on it or something else like that so it's not practical.
3. As far as I can see they don't realize that they're not going to be allowed to exist in this country. I don't see any way they're ever going to be allowed to and they will have to realize that this thing has got to be destroyed if they're going to survive like we want to survive, not just survive but if we're going to be. It wouldn't work. It's not realistic. As far as I'm concerned they haven't really analyzed

the situation thoroughly. It's an incorrect analysis of what's going on.
4. That bothers me—Black people in a concentrated area. That thought just doesn't stick with me. Americans have a tendency to go bomb crazy with something they don't like. I think that would be like eating into the man's hands. I think that's what he wants. That's why I would not be surprised if we got our five states. He'd give us the whole South.
5. I don't think it is very realistic. For one thing what part of the U.S. do we want? I can't dig that because when I speak in terms of a Black nation in the U.S. I want to speak in terms of New York and Pennsylvania and parts of the Mid–West like Chicago and that area or else the west coast and that area because the thing that is necessary for a nation is natural resources, industrial power and some kind of military might. And when you speak of the Southwest and the South you are speaking about undeveloped country. If you think a Black nation is going to be able to strive and survive on an agricultural system, in this industrial age, we're fools.
6. I don't go for that We all get down in those five states and the man doesn't have to drop anything. All he's got to do is poison the water lines. Too easy to eliminate. That's one thing about it. They can't drop a thing here, can't tamper with anything here without hitting X, Y, Z, and all the surrounding areas. We're in pockets all over this nation and they don't like it because we are in the major cities.

In August 1971 some RNA members who had moved to Mississippi and were endeavoring to purchase land became involved in a confrontation with Jackson, Mississippi police. The police had gone to RNA Jackson headquarters with warrants for the arrest of four persons on various charges apparently unrelated to RNA efforts to purchase land from a Black Mississippi farmer. During the confrontation one Jackson police officer was killed, and a Jackson patrolman as well as an FBI agent were wounded. Subsequently seven RNA members were accused of murder. This incident may highlight the concern of many respondents for the safety of Blacks who desire to isolate themselves on southern territory.

A few women, however, recognized the symbolic and propaganda value of the RNA. That is, while they tended to dismiss the idea of acquiring a land base in specific southern states as highly impractical, still they saw its organizational potential in terms of pulling Blacks closer together and articulating their struggle within the chambers of international organizations such as the United Nations. As one woman said:

> The Republic of New Africa is a good idea in terms of focusing Black people's minds on nationalism—maybe and then it's unrealistic. The government of the United States is not going to give anybody five states and if they gave you five southern states then crackers would kill you if you came down there and what would you do with them if they gave them to you? But it's moving to something; it's organizing people toward a goal, the goal of a nation. And I think that the most tremendous thing that could come out of it would be a plebiscite at the UN which they may be able to pull to get it on an international scale, if they ever get to the UN floor. It's good just in terms of heightening the awareness of people, getting them involved in a function and getting them over into it so that they begin to find out how things really work.

If the separatist thrust for Black people is to be led by the Muslims or the RNA, it is clear from our study, at least, that Black women will not become active participants but rather will content themselves with the role of interested observer. It would be misleading to assert, however, that rejection of Muslim or RNA leadership spells abandonment of a separatist thrust. Perhaps the most accurate statement which can be made about the women in our study is that while many expressed separatist leanings (especially in terms of giving up on integration and stressing instead community control) few were willing to label themselves 'hard core' separatists.

### Defensive (and Offensive?) Violence

Aside from integration, the resolution of an identity crisis through a search for a 'new' Black consciousness, and separation as curatives for societal bigotry, Blacks have at different points in their history chosen to rely on sporadic acts of violence.* In the decade of the sixties and on into the seventies reliance on violence as a necessary tactic became more prevalent in Black communities as many witnessed the futility and few returns of a peaceful, non-violent approach. Then, too, Blacks in increasing numbers became convinced that the White power structure had planned carefully for their elimination from the general society—either by slaughter or by herding them into detention or concentration camps. Belief in the possibility of widespread Black detention surfaced as one of the underlying currents of our study. Several women emphasized that if the American government had been bold enough to round up quickly and meticulously all Japanese living in America during World War II and promptly place them under detention, then the same fate could befall Black people. Some women even pointed out that the 'rounding up' and 'herding off' process might not even be necessary since Black residential patterns, especially in urban areas, already are conducive to on the spot detention since Black residential areas in many ways could be described as reservations whose access and resources could be controlled quite easily. Two women perhaps best sum up the concerns of our respondents for an arbitrary future detention:

> 1. The idea of a Black concentration camp is not far fetched. As a matter of fact the idea of a Black

---

* See for example, Robert Brisbane, *The Black Vanguard*, Valley Forge: Judson Press, 1970.

concentration camp, when people hear it they reject the idea because they envision concentration camps like they were in Germany, like they come and get truckloads of people and ship them away. That's not the way it is going to happen. The White man could do it—he very well could have put that up his sleeve anyway; but when you look at all the reconstruction that's going on in the city, take for example they're building highways, main highways, expressways and things like that right around Black areas. They're clearing out parts of the Black areas and sending highways through them. After they get this thing together you will stay in your home. Your home can be your concentration camp. You may wake up one day and walk out your front door thinking you're going to work and you might be greeted by a pig with a gun in his hand saying, 'Where the hell do you think you're going nigger? You're staying here.' And the next thing you know what's happened is that all these main highways they've put in could all be vamping off the Black areas. And see, they could cut off all the means of communication. You couldn't contact anybody in Jersey, D.C., Philly, any place like that. All they'd have to do is just circle the area, box you in with guns and what not. That's your concentration camp. Your home will be your concentration camp. We have to realize that these things are possible and there's not a damn thing wrong with having a gun, not one thing.

2. I'm doing a paper on it. I have a whole lot of material on concentration camps USA. I'm not through reading it all but I think this stuff has to be rewritten, put into very very understandable language instead of the long process and all this kind of stuff. Especially this one: the King Alfred decision, the King Alfred plan, I think it's called. And it has to be distributed to people so that they know about

> it. I'm making copies of the stuff now. I show it to
> people and they don't believe it. I say something
> about it and they don't believe it. Detention camps
> are just that next step. We will do it by social op-
> pression. We will do it by political oppression. We
> will do it by economic oppression and if all that
> fails we will stick a gun up your nose and put you
> behind a wire fence and gas you if necessary. I am
> going to rule. There's a precedent set. They did it
> to Japanese people during World War II and they
> didn't put not one German, not one Italian, not
> one Pole, nor one Russian into a detention camp
> but they put a yellow race of people. Took their
> land away from them, their homes, their land out
> in San Francisco. Put them in detention camps.
> When the war was over put them out, back on the
> street, didn't give them their land back.

This fear of, or belief in, the possibility of detention may lead to support for groups which adhere to a philosophy of defensive and even offensive violence. Moreover it may direct some to engage in sporadic riots or rebellions as a means of conveying the message that Black people are not to be "messed with."

Ever since several Panthers marched boldly into the State Capitol at Sacramento, California on May 2, 1967, with rifles in hand, to protest the passage of legislation designed to control the use of guns, Black people from many quarters of society have looked toward the Black Panther Party as the leading force in a defensive and sometimes offensive spearhead against White oppression. Underscoring this Panther Party emphasis on defensive violence was one young woman in our study who belonged to the Panther Party:

> We want to put revolution and political power in the
> hands of the people, which means arming the people
> with the ideological and arming the people with the
> tools of liberation. It could be guerrilla warfare, urban
> guerrilla warfare, but what I'm trying to say is it will

> be like self-defense 'cause like the pigs here are going crazy now. For every Black person who's arming himself house to house, block to block, community to community, it will be like you know, people will be ready. I say get allied with another country. That's me speaking.

One of the goals of our study was to determine the extent to which Black women supported not only the idea of a Black Panther Party but also the tactics and methodology employed in actuality by the Black Panther Party. Again and again we encountered enthusiasm and admiration for the posture and program of the Panthers. Many women applauded the Panthers for their threat to the White power structure. They viewed the Panthers as involved in the defense of the community, not just through the use of violence if necessary but also by implementing programs designed to ameliorate hard social ills, such as hunger or drug abuse. But most appreciated by the women in our study was the Panther determination to assert themselves in the armed defense of their communities should this step be deemed necessary. One woman spoke poignantly of her understanding of the Panther philosophy which, for her, had to be couched against a history and background of southern White violence against Black people. As she revealed:

> I think they have a good point. You see I live down here. We've seen violence perpetrated against Black people. I've had people follow me home and block my driveway—White people—where I couldn't get up to my house. I had to come out and stay at this center for a night because of that, because there are White people who were against what I was doing and what I stood for. I tried to call the sheriff and couldn't get an answer. I know darn well that office was open but they wouldn't answer. I called the police at night and they said, "We can't come out until tomorrow night." I could have been killed. So, we've seen these things. Perhaps if I had been a man I probably would have been in-

volved in a shoot-out but I never would have carried a weapon. As I told you I believe in my God. I never carried a weapon. By my not reacting I just may have saved my life. But I've seen violence. I've seen my son pursued by police for doing nothing. Every corner he turned they seeing if he made even one little traffic violation so they could arrest him. One of my sons was arrested and beat in the mouth because some White woman said he said something to her. She was lying but when it comes down here this is what they're going to say. We've seen these things happen and we know why they happen. They happen because when certain elements of the White people don't like what you're doing they'll do anything to hurt. Now I feel that a lot of kids who have seen that—I can see where my own son might be it. They say, "What the hell, I'm not going to take this stuff. They come at me, I'm going back at them." And so I see the background of the Panthers. And I always feel like this: Why is it—we know the Klan down here has an arsenal stacked full of guns and we know the police know it and they don't do a thing about it. Now why do they get so excited when the Black man does that? This is the type of thing I think about when I think about the Panthers. They know the Citizens Council has got their arsenals. And they know where they are because all of them belong to it. They don't get excited about that. That's o.k. But let a Black man get a gun and everybody gets up in the air. So I think the reasoning behind what they are saying about the Black Panthers is just completely illogical.

Other women, too, reflected their general agreement with the Panther approach.

> 1. If it wasn't for the Panther's presence I don't think I could feel whole as a Black woman. All of my 31 years has been spent hoping to see that Black

man who could stand and speak for me and for my family and believe me the first 31 years were very hard and very sick. I think the Panthers represent a very beautiful example for young Black manhood. I think they are one of the most misinterpreted groups basically because people do not read. They do not know what the Panthers stand for. They have listened to the slander and so forth that has been given. Once you understand the platform, anyone that disagrees with them is very sick. Who can best protect the community better than the young cats who are in it? We will see that no outside force like pigs as they call them will come in here, go through somebody's house without legal warrants and beat up people and take them through changes and disrupt households and so forth in the name of the law.

2. I will say that they've had a stigma that has been hung to them but I feel that they're the ones that's in the bottle and they don't know how to be heard. If it takes a war to make them be heard then that's what they're going to do. The Panthers have courage enough to do—stand up and fight for what they want. I mean not just fight. They got courage enough to die for it. They have all of my push. People like the Panthers will move to the top eventually. They won't get rid of them, not by killing one or two. More people are going to grow more militant.

3. I admire and respect the Panthers very much. I've seen quite a few of them lay their lives on the line and it wouldn't be the case of following somebody who's going to turn around and run you over. I love their breakfast program. The brotherhood that they preach—they seem to be living it. Even if they are not, they appear to be sincere in their efforts.

4. The Panthers are the people that try to help the

Black people and the White people are all scared of the Black Panthers.

5. I think the Panthers are very hip. I think the Panthers obviously have the potential of being something very very great and tremendous and they are an obvious threat to the White power structure because if they weren't they wouldn't be killed, they wouldn't be mistreated and they wouldn't be political prisoners as they are now either. I really think that people misinterpret the Panthers very much and much of it has to do with the news media—the propaganda that goes on through the White power structure because they want it to be misinterpreted because it is a dangerous organization for them.

6. The Panthers I think are the most threatening to the structure of this society because they are talking about coalitions; they're talking about radical change. And they aren't talking about it on racist lines and this country can't deal with that.

7. Well, I like them because for one reason I like the things that Eldridge Cleaver stands for and Bobby Seale.

8. Men must be men and this is why I can admire the Panthers. At no time in history have Black men stood as tall as they are trying to stand now. I think Black women should do everything in their power to encourage this. I think we ought to take a back seat.

9. The reason they are after the Panthers is that it's the first group that has organized a party that has international overtones. These people are bodily afraid of the Black Panthers and what they have done inadvertently is develop more and more support for them. According to J. Edgar Hoover they set up all night planning how many pigs they were going to rip off tomorrow. This isn't their bag. They are not stupid people. They are not

high school drop-outs. These are college kids that have gone through the man's system. This is one thing that frustrates whitey. They have gone through his system and they're supposed to be totally brainwashed. As Nathan Hare said, universities are nothing but brainwashing institutions anyway and you've got to be awfully Black to go in them and come out Black. But these kids have gone in there and gotten their education and come out very Black and determined that they are going to liberate Black people by any means necessary. And I love them. I really do.

10. I dig them. I dig them. I really dig them. I remember the time when I first started hearing about them. I'd flinch every time I heard the name. And that comes from the communication gap from where I was. The Black Panthers were strictly hush hush where I was. But after I got here where you really feel it, everywhere you go you can really feel them. I'm not afraid of them. I respect them for standing on their own. They know what they want to do and they're going to do it. There's a guy who works with me. He's taking night courses and he's doing a paper on Eldridge Cleaver. And everytime I read it I just start smiling. Just something inside me seems like it glows. The guy, he's had troubles. He's had his troubles but he's still got that something about him. That's the kind of guy you look up to.

Yet not every single comment praised the Panthers and their approach (though admittedly the majority did). Two Panther Party tendencies clearly bothered some women. First came the visibility, verbosity, and openness of the Panthers. That is, some of our respondents were vexed by what they considered an unnecessary sacrifice of life stemming from rhetoric and public forum pronouncements of intentions to assault openly some aspect of White oppression. As several women pointed out:

# Something's Got to be Done—But What?

1. They talk too much. I think that the time for debate did a lot by speaking out—Black is beautiful, and this and that. But as far as their strategies are concerned and what they're going to do, like they talk too much and they tell things. And like this is how the man has gotten to cutting down their whole thing. Like they were beautifully organized but somebody is letting a leak into the whole thing and the man has cut it down—Cleaver, Seale, everything. I just think they are too loosely at the mouth.
2. I think the Black Panthers should have learned a lesson in that to a degree I feel that they should be more underground than they are because being open it's a good example but they are throwing away too many good lives for so little gain. I think it's bad for young Black guys who know what they want to just be killed like that.
3. The only thing that I feel is bad about the Panthers is their visibility. I feel like if they had been underground or if they would go underground they wouldn't be wiped out so much. I mean their leadership is depleting. The man knows where they are and they up there just talking and carrying on. I just read a book, the Godfather. It's about the Mafia, the way they operate. I wish the Panthers could operate like that. I have a lot of respect for the Panthers. I just wish they would operate in a way so they couldn't get wiped out.
4. Every time you look up somebody is being killed or they're fighting or they're standing and screaming on television about this, that and the other, and not really doing anything.
5. One thing I found wrong with them is that if I'm going to shoot in the White House I'm not going to advertise it the day before on the TV because they're going to be ready for me. I think they got big mouths. They advertise what they're going to do. Like I'm going to get you. If you say that,

> they're probably going to wait for you. And I think that the police department and all the national guard, whatever, are eliminating them one by one. Where there's the least little charge it's trumped up into a big thing. Like they shot and killed all those Black Panthers self defenseless in their apartment.

Obviously some of our respondents would feel much relieved if the Panthers were to go underground. In fact, one former member of the Black Panther Party seemed to have left just for this reason as she observed the infiltration of the Party by law enforcement agents. As she said:

> I think probably the Panthers are very worked over in terms of the government. I think that probably they have a great deal of infiltrators. Personally I think the Panther Party is dying and I'm very sorry that it is. I think it has changed its direction a great deal as a result of its leaders being vamped on. The emphases were changed out of necessity—having no leaders and having to deal with the courts and the police to such a greater extent. The emphases are now on survival I think, just surviving as a group.

Second, some women bitterly denounced the Black-White coalition which the Panthers had established. These women could not comprehend any kind of coalition with "the enemy" and tended not to distinguish between White conservatives, moderates, liberals or radicals. For them all Whites must be viewed as belonging to the enemy camp. As they asserted:

> 1. I don't agree with their ideology of sleeping with White women, of sleeping with the devil and still be able to fight them.
> 2. The reason why I say the party I don't think will continue to be very relevant is that they are now very much into this mingling with Whites and I

don't dig this personally because of the nature of self-survival and I can't dig me no White talking about offing his mother or his sister or his wife or any of the other.

3. They are becoming a bunch of integrationists. As of late I haven't had a positive attitude toward the Panthers. Any time you let White people enter the organization, they almost always begin to infiltrate and control major areas of your organization. You become dependent on them and the program loses its uniqueness and its appeal to Black people.

4. The Panthers I really dug in the beginning because they really seemed like they were right honest. When I first came to (Y) and went down to the Black Panther office—like I was going to join and register and see what was happening and talk to the people and everything. It had a kind of life about it and it was really vital. Things were really happening that I could see that I could deal with, that kids were really learning about: like how it was oppressive and not being tricked into thinking that it held anything for them as far as it wasn't going to make them wealthy or give them something even though they didn't have school. But now, there was the Panther office in (X) that has been "vamped on," as they say, by the police. As a result all of the people were asked to come to the Panther office and I went down there. And most of the people down there were White. We drove up there and I said, this can't be the place. This is not what I came for. All these White people talked to us, and we just walked back, got in the car and went home because I'm not out there to protect any White people.

5. I will never be a Panther for the simple reason I don't like their strategy. I don't like the people that are Panthers, the White people. It's too many of

them and I don't trust them. That's the only reason I would not be a Panther. There are White Panthers in the thing and that blew my mind.

6. Let me tell you about the Panthers and one thing they did to us at school. When these people from Kent were killed they sent this White Panther down to school to talk to us. Half the school walked out when the kids from Kent were killed. They could have shot the whole university. It wasn't no big thing; let the brothers and sisters alone. But next week when the kids from Jackson were killed we called up the Panthers' headquarters. You know what they said? 'We are busy.' They didn't even send their little White boys out that week.

It was interesting to note that some of those who condemned the Panthers most strongly for their association with Whites were teenagers or recent high school graduates. Clearly, then, some Black women have strong reservations about any liaison with Whites. For them the Black struggle must be pristine and if blood is to be shed all of it must be Black.

In addition to viewing how steadfastly the women of our study adhered to an organization which espoused defensive and sometimes offensive violence, we wanted to obtain their reaction to the sporadic acts of violence which erupted in urban centers in the sixties and which sometimes are referred to as riots or rebellions.

Many women saw the riots as having their greatest impact upon the White community especially in terms of being a teaching and informing mechanism, that is, translating to the White community, through a process of destructive action, their frustrations and inability to tolerate any longer the 'dregs of misery' imposed by a racist, oppressive society. As some women related:

1. I was in the middle of it. It was a big fire. Oo I loved every minute of it. Oo I just loved it. I loved it because of the fact, not that I thought it was right, then again on the other hand I don't know if it was wrong. I heard people say, 'Sure is a shame.'

# Something's Got to be Done—But What?

I didn't think it was a shame because it made me feel good. We have been oppressed so long. White folks have done anything they wanted to us so what the hell difference did it make for us to burn down some cotton-picking stores. I thought it was beautiful because them White folks has been on the streets for years taking my money, my mother's money, especially my mother's money because she was too ignorant to do anything else. Black folks were ignorant. He gave her all this credit, all the credit she wanted—charged her an arm and a leg and she spends the rest of her life paying for that bunch of junk that we tore down before she even got it in the house and he talk about he been in the neighborhood for all them years and he was the friend of the Black folks. He ain't no friend. He ain't given us nothing. Burn him down. I didn't care. I thought it was good. I said burn baby burn. Burn them all down. That's the way I felt, get all you can and burn them down.

2. I feel this was the first time the damn White man stood back and said, 'These damn niggers mean business.' He heard them. He didn't hear them when they sat down at the table and be nice. Say 'White man, I'm going to be nice to you and tell you like it is.' He didn't hear that. You had to burn that ass a little bit before they could feel it and hear it.

3. The attention that the riots have gotten has given a great deal of publicity nationally and internationally to the movement that the Black people are carrying on in the United States. The White people have tried to camouflage this thing so many times and they're always saying look at America. Look at how beautiful and free we are over here and look what we have. We are a rich and prosperous nation. We have disproven the propaganda that the United States has been spreading by showing other countries that all is not well in the United

States. There are so many favorable points for the riots. I would have to say yes they have done a great deal of essential good for Black people and the Black movement.
4. It is only, and I must reiterate and emphasize, it is only when property is damaged that White people realize how sad a condition Black folks are in.
5. If you will recall, out in (Y) the night of April 4 I believe when Dr. Martin Luther King was assassinated, a riot broke out. For the first time in history Black people had a leader snatched from them and they began to realize what it meant to have to face this mean world by themselves with no one to guide them or no one to lead them and say stop, let's go this way. Stop, let's not be violent. In doing this the Black man gave the White man a chance to see that we are not afraid any more.

Still other women felt the riots had the greatest value in a heightened awareness among Blacks. That is, for example, Blacks in the South could see that Midwestern Black people, or those in the East and West suffered the same frustrations as did they.

1. I was 15 when Watts occurred. I thought it was crazy for Black people to be burning down their homes in their own communities but I can understand it now. It had a psychological effect. If you had hopes coming from the South, and had been told it's the promised land and then you find that it's not, that's a terrible feeling.
2. They helped us get somewhere. They helped to awaken people. A lot of people were asleep. It helped awaken them to the realities of our situation.
3. They gave the rest of the Black people around the world (a chance) to look and see what other Black people are doing. We found that people in the North feel just like I do down here in the South.

# Something's Got to be Done—But What? 355

At least we got that much in common. We could see that. You start wondering what else you have in common.

4. I think they had meaning in that the common Black man in the street who probably feels very helpless at times was given an outlet to see that he is not helpless, that he can create a lot of havoc if he breaks loose.
5. I think it did stimulate a lot of thinking in the Black community and it seems to me that the whole Black cry—Black is beautiful thing—started with that.
6. It certainly heightened the awareness among Blacks of the generalized maintenance of such a bad system around the country because many times I felt as a Black, certainly when I lived in (X)—1) I wasn't aware of how many fellow Blacks there were and 2) certainly not aware of the extent of their problems in the society. This was many years ago when I was younger. I think this was very necessary in terms of dealing with it and being aware of the nature and size of the problem.

For some women the period of the riots even marked the beginning of an active involvement in the concerns of poor Black people. For example one woman, a former welfare recipient who had worked her way off the roles, related how the TV and in particular the reactions of Stokely Carmichael via the TV media, had aroused in her an awareness not only of the extent of Black people's problems but a firm conviction that something could be done about them. Revealing her initial total ignorance and isolation from a conceptualization of Black people's plight the woman said: "Stokely Carmichael was on TV talking about a struggle and I really didn't know anything about a struggle because I hadn't read anything. I was raising my children." The riots apparently had such an impact on her that this woman concluded that she could affect events even though society would normally reject her, a little educated, former welfare client, from any kind of leadership role. As she pointed out:

I was in the house all the time and watching the TV and I said, "Well, I'm going to get out here and do something." That was in December of 1966 and I've been out here doing ever since. They showed me where I could do something. And I was thinking, "Well, with no education I don't think I can do too much." I started talking one day and I've been talking ever since, and I've just been going and going until there's no end.

In terms of concrete benefits to the Black community, while some women cited long-term improvements which had been made, others cynically saw only short-term pacification efforts, or no gains at all as a result of the riots and rebellions. Some felt that Black people missed an opportunity to capitalize on their sporadic violence because of "ego tripping" which made one's person loom much larger than the total community in making claims on the power structure. Some typical comments were:

1. Since the riots, (things) have improved a whole lot. It was plenty of people that didn't have jobs before. They really have jobs but they pay good one week and the next week they're off two or three days. But at least it did make a start.
2. In Watts I know there were some results. Like they actually did put in money to put some businesses up. Like natural combs came out of that and natural hair products and stuff that got started so that people could have like a righteous Black business and all that. In Newark it resulted in getting a Black mayor I think; a couple of weeks ago he got voted in. That was really the result of having all the attention focused on it and having the community together.
3. It did produce some results. You got a lot of money poured into the Black community. A lot of projects started would never have started I don't believe if this hadn't taken place. It's getting now where peo-

ple are getting back to being content. They quelled the fires in the ghetto and the only time they look at it is during the summer waiting for something to break out.
4. The riot may have been effective in getting some response from the establishment but I feel at this point that unlessen they move in a different direction than they're going now, they're going back to just status quo. I think the riots brought about an awful lot of drastic change hurriedly in some areas but it's not remaining. It's tapering off.
5. As for having a real definite impact on change I question them. I don't see where we're any better off now than we were in '65. I've been to that Washington area about once a year since things happened. I don't see it (change). In Watts I've seen a few little things happening. One group is making toys. Now, they're doing a good work but the people affected is so small in number as against what needs to be done that you can't say the impact has been really felt. This is the way I feel. I just don't think that five years after we're any better off.
6. It pumped all kinds of money into Black areas. You could write a proposal on the back of a shopping bag and get all sorts of money for it. The mistake Black people made was that their egos were involved in their programs. Their programs and only their program was the right one and there was no effort made to get together and to use the money in a way that it would start refunding itself. So now three years have passed. The money has slowed up. The grants are not as large and not as frequent as they once were and there's no money there any more. There's no return on the resources. So people have remained dependent on the federal government to fund their programs.
7. I don't think they produced nothing. I don't see nothing. I never heard of nothing.

Quite a few respondents deplored the destruction heaped on the Black community by the riots and rebellions. For them the violence should have been directed primarily towards surrounding White business centers or residential areas where its impact would have been total. One young woman vividly recalls her initial joyous response to the riots as she walked among liberators of food, liquor and other supplies. Her sense of joy was followed by a feeling of depression upon seeing the harm which befell Blacks rather than Whites. In her words:

> I went through kind of two extremes. The first extreme, along with everbody else, was a kind of catharsis. I was sitting there knitting. Somebody called me and told me that King was killed. I was so angry. I remember my knitting needles just clacking I was so angry. I had to do something so I left the dorm and went out on the street and there was a lot of things going on. People were busting windows and things were being taken. There was a whole air of riotous, ecstatic chaos—I don't know if you could call it that but it seemed like that to me—kind of an air of surprise and happiness. The second day there was the same air. Only then they called in the troops and there was an air of togetherness like of an oppressed people—togetherness because of the oppressor. I remember one particular incident. A friend of mine and I were riding down an alley and this brother came by with a big barrel of pint bottles of scotch and was handing them out to everybody like Christmas presents. Everybody took one. Like, here sister. There was this old man giving out these things. The third day I was hungry and I went down to get a loaf of bread and there were so many children and so many old people and they had nothing to eat, nowhere to go. The more I walked the more I saw this and I suddenly realized that there were no stores anywhere near us. Traffic was jammed and the hospitals were packed and I became very anti-riot at this point. And I said, "What has happened? Why have we

done this to our own people? We've done nothing but hurt ourselves by rioting." I still feel that way. It accomplishes nothing because after the festivities die down, it's like being drugged and waking up with a hangover. You have to wake up to the reality that you destroyed what you had, even though it didn't belong to you. People will suffer and die because of you and what happened had to happen because there was so much tension. But once it happened we were left to pick up the pieces. I would have packed up a bunch of rioters and taken them downtown. If you really want to hurt White people, hit their stores, not ours even though ours are owned by them. Hit the chains, maybe hit the credit bureaus which have records of what Black people owe, and places like that—the managers that control the city. Burn their place of business down.

Still others lamented the decision to wreck Black rather than White communities:

1. I'm a little bit unhappy that it was just contained in their own communities. I'm sure that they did affect a lot of the White storeowners with their endless credit but it would have been more effective if they had spread out in the White communities and done the same thing.
2. I wish that it could have grown into a planned revolutionary movement rather than a spontaneous act of violence because I think in many ways we suffered and we got killed. I just wish we could have wiped out all the honkies and just got it together.
3. There was so much destruction in terms of our own. We didn't burn the White communities. We burned our own communities. And that was my displeasure or unhappiness with the riots. I'm all for going downtown and burning down some of those big White stores. That's just fine but I don't think you should burn it in your own neighborhood. There

> needs to be a revolution as such or a civil war in order to turn some people around. I think that's the only way it's going to be done. I don't think we ought to burn up our own homes.
> 4. The thing that annoyed me about them things was that we burned our own. The greatest one I think was in Watts. If I'm going to burn something I want that honky to be as poor as I am. If I'm going to burn I'm going to an all White neighborhood where they won't let me live and put a bomb up there. I ain't got nothing no way but why I got to burn it down? This was the thing that annoyed me the most. They burned within their own community. You think I'm going to burn my house or where I'm living? Hell, no, I'm going to go up there where that honky live sitting on his green behind, putting his foot behind cadillacs and rolls royce. I'm going to attack him 'cause he's got everything. Make him spend his money until he builds what I done tore down.

But the underlying consensus seemed to be that the riots were a necessary stage of the Black struggle, although a few women interpreted them as senseless acts with absolutely no pay off. Equally, many women agreed or implied that while the riots and rebellions of the sixties were a necessary tactic, they must now be considered passé. That is, riots and rebellions no longer can be seized upon as a positive thrust for Black people. As one woman summed up this sentiment:

> I see the whole struggle as a series of steps, or steps in reaching a goal. I think they (riots) were necessary. They played a necessary part in the whole struggle. I think they were effective at that time, in terms of waking up the White community, the nation as a whole and then giving Black people an idea of their own potential. I think they were good there. But I think in terms of steps that we still have to move on because now policemen, or the police force as a whole is more

sophisticated and that rebellions per se wouldn't be as effective as they were then. I think that now we would have to use something like guerrilla warfare. But I think that then they were effective.

In contrast to the deep dedication to the non-violent philosophy evident in the late fifties and early sixties, the message being conveyed by the "together" Black woman is: We like the Panthers because they have moved away from a passive resistance, turn-the-other-cheek philosophy and are prepared to defend their communities. Moreover these women accepted the necessity and validity of the sporadic acts of violence which hit oppressive sections of urban centers in Watts, Detroit, Washington, D.C. and other communities.

*Confronting "The System"*

If the "together" Black woman proved willing to embrace the Panther philosophy and to understand the need for sporadic violence, would she also reflect enough alienation with the American system to advocate radical changes in it or even its total destruction? Then, too, would she be willing to make a clear choice between non-violence and violence as a tactic for liberation?

If one is searching for a monolithic approach to system confrontation on the part of the "together" Black woman, indications from our survey are that the searcher will not be rewarded with a definite find. No monolithic approach to system confrontation emerges from our study of Black women. No consensus can be found, for instance, on the ability or willingness of the system to cope with demands for fundamental (or radical) structural and functional changes. Moreover no underlying agreement can be detected on the methodology which should be utilized during system confrontation. Yet patterns of thought on the issue of system confrontation do emerge clearly and do enable one to state categorically and unequivocally that "The System" does not enjoy the unquestioned loyalty of the "together" Black woman. On the contrary, she may be characterized, in terms of the system, as adhering to a range of positions including aloofness (plans to leave the country and go to

Africa for instance), ambivalence with the edge clearly toward the side of hate, or seething frustration which threatens to boil over into an unleashed fury aimed squarely at the system.

When asked how they regarded the system and whether they thought solutions to Black problems could be discovered within the framework of the system, three schools of thought emerged among our respondents. First came the view that fundamental changes in the system which can benefit Black people are possible. This proved to be a minority view.

1. There are just so many different systems in the world. I can't really express any type of true feeling that there is anywhere in this world a system where there is true happiness. I am willing to work in the present system. I am willing to work with it because I think it gives Black folk a leeway. In any system I think we can work in but if we do not succeed then I think all systems lead to some kind of revolution. I think there's always the possibility of working in the system and I think it can be done politically.
2. I would like to see just one Black man control say General Motors or be a Rockefeller and I bet there would be a multitude of change. We are going to have to get that kind of power. This is what will change the system because they are the ones who control the system—the Rockefellers, the Vanderbilts, the people who head General Motors.
3. I think you can destroy the system with the system. It's something like finding out that I have a charge at (Y) and I went in there the other day and I didn't have my plate. I had just forgotten it. I said, "Oh, I have a charge but I forgot the plate." So the lady wrote the thing up and she asked me for my address and my identification. She wrote it all down and I signed my name. She pulled it out and she bagged it and she gave it to me and it came to me. I didn't have to have a charge in this place. You

mean this thing is really so shaky that you can just walk in here and say I have a charge and that woman didn't look it up? I'm sure there's an amount of money at which they look things up but like the $30 level. You can go around and buy 10, 15 and 20 dollar things and clean up pretending you got a charge account. And I think the system works a lot like that. I think the system is not so intricately designed and not so sophisticated that it wouldn't tumble itself. I think there has to be change but you can destroy it with its own tools. That's the only way you're going to destroy it is with its own tools. You can't use a sledgehammer on it. If Black people in America attack the system from the outside they become aggressors. They become enemy agents in the country and they get killed. But if they attack the system from the inside and do it in their own subtle ways like they been doing all the time, but do it on a grand scale, then they are just Black people who believe in the democratic process as it really is written.

Then there was that school of thought which clung to the idea that maybe some changes in the system are possible but the probabilities for fundamental change are slim.

1. It's a problem I run up against especially at school. Like if the Black students have something they want to say to the administration which is totally White, almost all White, you go in and have a good discussion with them. But they still don't listen. Like the dean of women there. We had a discussion with her and it just did not hit the spot. It did not stop in her brain and allow her to think about it. She'd just skip on to something else as though she didn't even hear you, which she didn't. She wasn't paying any attention because she sort of turned herself off as to what we were saying and she continued in her

way as if you hadn't even said anything. Like some of the bills they pass for Black people in the last decades, Whites have turned to use for themselves. At the beginning they might have a plan of using it for the Blacks and getting more equality in the system but later on down the road they can find that they can use it for their advantage.

2. Well I believe it's becoming harder and harder to get any kinds of concessions out of the power structure, that it was much easier during the Kennedy and mainly the Johnson Administration to get concessions—the war on poverty which wasn't anything but on paper. I think you have to fight for it. I think you have to fight for every damn thing that you can. There is some possibility of some gain, even if it is that you have to fight for it.

3. Any time there's something that comes about in the system trying to change it, it just has, like Nixon said on TV the night before he went up the hill at 5 o'clock in the morning, he said the American system is made with so many buffers that whenever there's a little tension or a little upset it's made so that it buffers itself out, and it's either resolved or destroyed. I think it's becoming more and more absolute toward the thing of destroying anything that doesn't fit. Some small amounts can take place within the system but no significant change.

The third school of thought asserted that the system is diseased or hopeless and therefore must be destroyed.

1. I think the system is hopeless. I think that as much as a capitalist system we have to recognize that it is based on racism and that it's no accident that Blacks don't have the economic power of the Jew. We have to realize that the only thing we are for sure are Africans. We are not Americans to other Americans.

2. Our problem is that we have already prostituted the

system and the system now is helpless. It is weak, not because of its own doing but because of us and how we have acted upon it. When I say we I mean them. The system has already been perverted. It is diseased already.
3. It gets to the point where you don't feel you should continue—certainly not if you have children. You don't want them to grow up under the system. I have a son. I certainly wouldn't want him to grow up with such a bad feeling, with such a feeling of uselessness, as a human being and helplessness to do anything about it. I think it's reached a point where we should be prepared to take any steps necessary.
4. The only thing I can think is that it has to be over-all change. You talk about destroying the system but you have to destroy more than the system. You have to destroy the people, the work of capitalism. You can't just destroy the system. Well, you could destroy the system but if the people still believe in the capitalistic society they could build it back up. So we have to destroy the whole thing of capitalism and then work to build up something new.

When confronted with a choice between violence and non-violence as possible roads to a resolution of the " Black crisis," the overwhelming majority of women selected violence. These women have concluded that the psychological burden for Blacks under the system's thumb is too much to bear. Therefore, for them violence must be seized upon as the only legitimate weapon. In many ways the "together" Black woman's thinking on violence parallels Frantz Fanon's view of violence as a cathartic or cleansing agent. Said a woman who obviously felt the weight of years of oppression:

Sometimes I get so flusterated with the society, with just sitting here and thinking what needs to be done. Five years ago I didn't think the way I do now. I thought militant but I would stop before I would act militant. But I feel like if I walked up in front of a judge and this judge was unjustly doing me, I'd tell him where to go and that's how I feel. It's nothing he can do to me other than just do it because I'm already destroyed, I feel like. That's just the way I feel. (It would take just a little push for me to be) a very violent woman. It wouldn't take me very long to pick up a chair and tear something up. And I wouldn't care.

The comments of many women revealed that one single incident could become a spark for the surge of violence. To illustrate, one woman recalled her attempt to purchase a car for a new job:

I don't really want to be hit. It's a funny kind of thing. I know that the violence that is within me is really real and it comes out sometimes and I do violent things. When I first got the job I remember going downtown. I had to have a car and we didn't have a car. And I didn't have any money to buy one and I was going to rent one to do my job. The guy had talked to me over the phone and because of the way I talked he thought I was White, from the sound of my voice. So I said, "Look, I don't have credit or anything like that, or any charges, but what I can give you is $200 to buy the car and all these character references and stuff like that." And he said it would be cool. I walked in and he looked at my Afro and he said "No, we called up your job and they said you don't work there." I just got so hostile. It's the first time in my life that I was in a bloody fucking rage and I picked up his ashtray and threw it on the floor and cursed at him and was just angry. He said he was going to call the police. I said "call the fucking police." There it was. It was pretty unpeaceful. I didn't have any Ghandian non-violent thing to pick up on. I thought in my head, "What would Ghandi have done?" and I said, "No, this isn't India." What can you say? There's violence in us and it's going to be more of it until things are more straight. It's going to have to be different otherwise you keep being violent.

## Something's Got to be Done—But What?

While the general theme of the "together" Black woman's view of the ultimate resolution of the Black struggle is that violence is a *sine qua non*, degrees of dedication to violence surfaced. Some women could be categorized as reluctant proponents of violence. Generally they believed that Blacks should be prepared to employ violence, if necessary, for example, to avoid concentration camps.

1. (I would be prepared to use violence) under the condition that someone came in here and told me that I was going to a concentration camp at five. I remember the Panthers several months ago ran the headlines I guess of a '43 newspaper and in it it just said all people of Japanese descent report at 5 P.M. this afternoon to. . . . They had had no warning, no nothing. I'm probably preparing myself all the time because five years ago I never thought that I would be thinking what I'm thinking now.
2. I would prefer to see a revolution take place, if it could, without any violence but I don't think it will because the capitalist class which is now in power will fight to the last dying breath to maintain that power and they have already unleashed their pigs on the people. They're shooting people and killing people to prevent the kinds of protest that are taking place. Therefore we have no choice but to fight back. It's a matter of our very lives to fight back against them. If the power structure is willing to give up their power peacefully then that's the way we want to see it go but if they're not, then we're willing to fight them tooth and nail.
3. It's very strange too because I am one that do not believe in violence. It makes me sick to even think that I would have to take up a gun and shoot someone and this kind of thing. But I do realize that I must be prepared to stand for my survival, defense of my family and so forth.
4. I hate to say violence but then if that's the only solution, that's it. People have probably said this to

you a lot of times but America was built on violence, the American revolution, and America has always been in wars. She's always sticking her nose into things that do not concern her. But that's the only solution I think.

Others in the "reluctant proponent" classification insisted that even if violence is suicidal still Blacks might have to use it:

I think the violent means is what we need, unless we separate. Violence might be suicide but in some ways that might be better than what's happening now.

Still others pointed out that they might take some actions despite age but that if they themselves did not engage in violence there stood ready a Black age group (17–22) which would not hesitate to resort to violence.

1. Believe it or not militancy is going to move up because it's a lot of people that's standing quietly by who really admire the militant people but they won't go out there and participate with them but they'll go home and say I'm glad they did it. They're behind closed doors then. It's a lot of people. If you ask them their opinion about it, they'll say o.k. I don't agree with it but in the meantime they have to admire them because there are very few people that will stand up. You have to have some kind of courage to pick up a coke bottle and face a machine gun. This takes the courage of people that our parents and foreparents never had before and we have a group that do, that's a group between 17 and 22. It's uncontrollable. Believe it or not they don't care any more about dying for what they stand for than living. If they really believe in it they'll die for it and they're more together than all of the organizations that have gotten together.

2. I am ambivalent about violence. I think that basi-

cally I am a nonviolent person but if I am pushed I will become violent. We just had the passage of the D.C. crime bill this week and there are several provisions there that are completely repulsive to me, this no-knock. If anybody tries to get in that door, the closest heavy weapon that I have he's going to get across his head or in his groin if he's a man, even if it's nothing but my shoe. Whatever I have he's going to get it because nobody is going to come in that door unless I know he's announced and I can see who it is and I open the door voluntarily. But don't break down my door. I'm going to start putting a hammer and a butcher knife right there on that little table. That's right. Nobody's going to come in my door. But I wouldn't hurt a fly if that fly didn't bother me. . . . I'm not saying I'm a revolutionary. I guess at my age I'm a frustrated bystander. I wish I could be out there in the revolution but you know the old legs aren't what they used to be.

The other degree of dedication to violence could be described in terms of "strong and convinced proponents." Those in this category reflect very strong convictions that violence is the only possible route.

1. I'm like this: violence and non-violence both have their places, but it's no place for non-violence in the South. I would say that the only way you can be liberated is to take the step that you see fit, that is better for the situation you are in. And for me I can say it: I go all the way for violence.
2. There's nothing but violence and non-violence. And the White man believes strongly in violence. And he's up there and if we want him we're going to have to try violence to get him.
3. I think there has to be violence. There's no other way. If you don't demand or take it you don't get

it because if you ask, it just takes so long and there are always so many rules and rituals that you have to go by. Those rules and regulations are just going to keep you down so that you will never get ahead.
4. The Black people in America can't outvote the White American. We can't outbuy him. In the financial world we can't compete with him so we really are getting down to the only alternative that we have and in my mind it's going to be violence. That is the alternative for Black people in America. And I'm not talking about the kind of thing that we had with the riots. I think that ultimately there's going to be created within Black America the leadership that will have the intelligence and the savvy and everything else that is needed to organize Black people for violence. I see that violence taking the form of the same kind of thing that they've got in Vietnam and in these other places, what they had in Cuba, the guerrilla type activity, the occasional burnings, the bombings, the terrorism, because ultimately that's all we're left with and if we can't outbuy the White man we can't do anything else within the structure and the establishment to win this fight. We do have a very destructive power in this country. We can't build it and we can't change it, but we can destroy it.
5. When Congress comes back in January and they have the State of the Union message and all that, everybody who has power for decisions is where? Up on that hill for the state of the union address. From the diplomatic corps, from the House, from the Senate, the White House, the Pentagon. Everybody who's got power is there at one time. Well, if you're together you can take care of business then.

Only a handful of women remained devoted to the ideal of nonviolence. These did so mainly because of a belief that the social cost of violence simply is too high.

1. I don't believe that we're going to accomplish too much by violence because violence brings violence and that will mean that if I'm dead I can't accomplish anything. I think we can accomplish much more by non-violence, because all the leaders of the Panther movement have been killed in their sleep.
2. Non-violence would be the answer for me. I tell my people all the time that we shouldn't have violence and if we put our trust in the Lord and ask him to direct our leaders, we wouldn't have all this violence.
3. I think ultimately (violence must occur) but at this stage the people who are talking about violence, it's really foolish because it's almost like a suicidal syndrome because people who are running around talking about doing all these violent things and running —hit and run bombing and stuff—it's not going to change anything and it really pushes people more toward repression and accepting fascism, fascism from the right. Violence is something that almost has to be backed off verbally.

Even some of those who felt violence was inevitable pondered the social costs, and preferred to see the emergence of organized violence with a "responsible" leadership that would not lead the people to unnecessary slaughter nor abandon the group at the whiz of the first bullet past the ear.

1. I believe in organized violence, organized assertion, organized violence such as what Martin Luther King —the bus boycott. It was violent as hell and it was organized. But I don't like to waste myself or see individuals wasted by moving with disorganization or with few people.
2. Personally I'm willing to do anything to help the cause or to achieve our liberation. But on the same token I'm not going to die on the "humbled." There are so many revolutionaries who will lead you into the arena and by the same token will run over you

> getting out of the way and I do not want to die in that way. I will fight and die with you but I see so many proponents of the movement who will actually run over you getting out of the way.

One woman even warned that actual participation in violence should not become the sole preoccupation of "revolutionaries." For the danger of total attention to violence is that after the "revolution" Blacks might find themselves in the same boat since "someone" will be waiting in the wings with carefully laid plans for the reconstruction of society.

> And while you and I are fighting each other and trying to make the decision about how this new government is going to be set up, here is a man already over there who's been sleeping with us. He's got it all mapped out. You and I so busy fighting we did not have sense enough before the revolution came, while it was in its infancy, to sit down and write the government structure. He's going to kill some of those folks and then sit down and write it and this man over here who's been with us all the time, he already has his plans. (Question: Who do you see that man as being? Answer: Another White man.)

For many the resigned or strong acceptance of the necessity of violence may prove startling. The idea that a cross section of Black women may not only nod approvingly to the use of violence to eradicate oppression but also advocate it openly and strongly, may strike a discordant note in those accustomed to viewing women as the more passive, peaceful element of society. Nevertheless the "together" Black woman represents an element in society that is so frustrated and cynical about the prospects of "good deeds" from White society, that they now clearly accept the inevitability of violence if the lot of Black people is to be improved to any meaningful extent. Hence for them the system must be changed radically and if it resists radical change, then the only route left is complete destruction of "The System."

## CHAPTER VII

# Thanks to Martin, Malcolm, Stokely et al But the Rest Is Up to You and Me

*Throughout the study* one was struck by the deep legacy of Martin Luther King, Malcolm X, and Stokely Carmichael. Although they represented different philosophical strains in the Black struggle, each man's contribution was acknowledged—whether the quiet dignity and persistance in a non-violent form of direct action personified by Martin Luther King, or the psychological genius of Malcolm X and his ability to tap the very nerve centers of Blacks who bitterly had resigned themselves to an unwelcome fate, or the strident but brilliant oratory of Stokely Carmichael who aroused young Blacks to a heretofore unknown depth of pride in Blackness. Yet while honoring the legacy of these three, and others, the "together" Black women clearly resisted a temptation to live in the past by constantly singing the praises of heroes and martyrs. Rather, they not only recognized the necessity of avoiding an odious stagnation by moving on to the next stage of Black development but also indicated an unwillingness to remain on the sidelines as passive bystanders. The perplexing factor is the nature of the next stage of the Black struggle. Perhaps it can be said, truthfully, that many women who have hurdled successfully the identity stage of Black development are now in a state of limbo—not quite knowing in what direction to move. Doubt persists, despite an awareness of the ultimate necessity of force to eradicate the oppressive quality of Black existence, as to whether Blacks should now—without further ado—enter a more revolutionary phase of existence by participating in activities of a more violent nature, or accommodate themselves to a new Black consciousness and a verbal militancy until the time is ripe for a more organized assault on societal racism, or escape in a separatist-nationalist setting within the frontiers of the U.S.A., or hasten into exile in some area—preferably Africa—where a Black majority may be found.

Some women admit to a tension created by the successful completion of the identity hurdle or phase of Black development and frankly confess that they are uncertain where to go from there or how they might react should the pressure to make a definite choice become too great. As one westerner stated:

> I know that I like nice things and I like to be comfortable and that some day it might be necessary for me to make a choice of working in an institution, getting a nice salary and all that, as opposed to having to live up to all those convictions I just said I had. I know I have to make the choice. I don't know what I would do. I might just commit suicide rather than make the choice. I don't know.

Significantly, perhaps, only this one woman raised the possibility of suicide as the ultimate solution to the pressure and conflict created by a sound comprehension of the undesired position of Blacks in America, and the temptation to cop out by stressing an individualism which enables one to lose herself neatly in some corner or haven of American society. Several women were just unwilling to reveal how they had resolved the dilemma and what for them represented the next stage of Black development. But, one can glean from the many conversations that Black women, in addition to the ultimate violent solution to Black oppression, are reflecting upon those institutions or groups which might guide the next stage of Black development as well as the functions and actions which must be accomplished if that next stage is to be a successful one.

In terms of institutional and organizational development the "together" Black woman has questioned seriously whether the better known groups can become points of leadership. To traditional civil rights groups Muslims, RNA, to Black politicians, to Black capitalists, and to Pan-Africanists, the "together" Black woman casts that critical eye which in the final analysis forces her, at least in this stage of her thought, to stamp an "unfit to lead" label on each. This final rejection comes even though in some instances (the Muslims, for example) the Black woman is able to dissect some favorable programmatic pitch; and it emerges in other cases (regarding politicians) because she is unable to detect that depth of commitment or that political atmosphere which would permit careful and persistent attention to Black interests. To Panther type groups the "together" Black woman asserts "maybe," provided some strategies which grate on the nerve ends are discarded. To organizations which grope for a place in local community development she states another "maybe." That is, the potential value of local tenants organizations, or decentralized branches of the National Welfare Rights Organization, or workers' unions, for instance, is stressed. To illustrate: the need to organize more tenants organizations to withold rents from landlords owning dilapidated houses was one of the clearly perceived necessities which emerged from the study. So often, particularly in the South, Black women responded enthusiastically to the question of how they felt about tenants organizations which worked to force repairs in bad housing. Many spoke bitterly about the kind of housing Blacks were compelled to live in, and resentfully and thoughtfully about the resigned attitude assumed by many Black people forced into these conditions: "We got to live some place."

In terms of institutional development Black women are pondering the possibility of revitalizing the Black church. Repeatedly the church was cited as the one sound, ever-present institution of the Black community. While many women complained of the passive state into which Blacks could be lulled by a lot of preaching and praying, and further bemoaned the sterile posture of the Black church towards the Black struggle, invariably the church was seen as a potentially effective force in stages of Black development. As some women said:

1. They should play a leading role in the revolution. They can't just ignore it and say like take your trust in the Lord and stuff like that because that way they're losing the congregation. I think the church should be like I think someone said it was before—the foundation of the Black struggle, slavery all connected with the church. They took their misery there to discuss it or whatever. It's the first Black organization and it should keep that leading role. But it cannot do it by not discussing problems.
2. I think if there's any place to express views, if there is any place to give Black people a forum, to give Black people the freedom to express themselves, it will be the Black church. If there's any place that will give Black people leadership as to how they can improve themselves, how they can organize themselves, it will be the church. If there's any place that can save young people, and I don't mean from the standpoint of them giving their souls but putting them on some sort of constructive road and directing their energies, I think it must be the church. As far as the struggle is concerned I think if we had more people in the church who are interested in the progress and upbuilding of their race, I think our race would move on. I think I must have said that there are so many things that can help build our race. I think the church is one of the most important aspects of it.
3. The church could play a very good role but it hasn't. They could be in the forefront because the church is the largest organization that Black people have. If the church would play its role—for instance the church could start a welfare thing for the community on their own. The church is really capable

of supporting its people in the way the society has neglected to do but so far it has refused to.

4. The two most viable institutions you find in the Black community are the Black colleges and the Black churches. These are two institutions that should be strengthened as fast as possible. What both of them are going to have to take on in religion and education is a relevancy to Black needs, providing Black services and pooling Black resources. You are going to have to get some committed ministers in there who know how to channel the resources. They got a heck of a lot of financial resources that could be used for the community and not buying cadillacs and building big houses for the minister and be directed toward providing health facilities for the community instead of having missionary meetings and big dinners and teas and all of this other bullshit it goes through. And whenever they start doing this, and in some cases they are, it's going to be one of the institutions that's going to push the movement along.

5. I think that really the best service that the Black church could do is close its doors to church services as such—the ceremonious type of service—and really begin to use the church as something where people can come and organize: politically use the church for education, use the church for community development, use the church for all those type of things that the people in the community need like they can't usually get without going outside of their community. Organizational meetings—the church could use its thing as a sanctuary. It could use the thing as a tax exempt place and let day care centers come in.

While it is apparent that Black women are wondering about those groups and institutions which can become the central thrust of the next stage of Black development, undeniably no "pat" formulas have been offered. The most that can be said is that existing groups and institutions, held up to inspection, have been found lacking and incapable of performing effectively in the next stage of Black development.

In addition to reflecting upon institutional and organizational development, the "together" Black woman is meditating on the needs which must be met if the Black community is to become functional on the optimal level. "Skills for nation building" is one theme which emerged often during the course of many conversations. Some women worried that Blacks were being encouraged to gain, and indeed fed, too much theoretical, bookish knowledge which represented little value in Black development. In several cases the real "worriers" were women who had attained a relatively high level on the educational ladder. For example, one woman now pursuing a doctorate in one of the social sciences pondered the possibility of gaining a skill in nursing—presumably in the interest of making her contribution to "nation building" much more valuable. Beyond skills, the women surveyed emphasized the need for a closer interaction among all strata of Black society, especially between Blacks teaching and studying in colleges on the one hand, and on the other hand those living in adjacent communities. Much discussion has revolved lately around qualifications of Black people for specific jobs, especially in the educational field. Administrators have been reluctant to abandon the traditional criteria of BA, MA, PHD while angry young Black students have pressured for recognition of the value of Black people on other levels. One woman in her forties seemed to have embodied the ideal of Black students. Born and raised in the southern part of the United States, this woman moved to a marginal area in her late teens and started off as a domestic. Without higher education she became involved in setting up pre-schools and now has worked her way into a staff position as a resource person at one of the metropolitan colleges in the area. In that position she works on the development of new projects in the areas of nutrition (especially for poor mothers to give them ideas of a balanced meal), and designing clothing (especially the use of clothes deemed to be outmoded). Of particular interest to her is the development of community projects in which students could participate on a personal level. It is this type of closer interaction among different strata of Black society which Black women envision as essential to meaningful Black development. One other need projected constantly was that of self-sufficiency, that is ultimate independence and interdependency among Black people. In fact "self-sufficiency" has become the key word for one Black enterprise working closely with societal "drop-outs" and others. The idea behind the concept "self-sufficiency" is that Black people should reach such a level of development that they will not have to run to whites for resources and aid, but not such a level that Black individualism will be all pervasive. Hence, stress is placed both upon independence and interdependence.

Perhaps in their wisdom the women of our survey have resisted any crystal ball predictions of the next stage of Black development. Moreover, they have proffered no neat strategies for that stage. Yet one would be remiss not to recognize that rather than simply marking time and enjoying whatever crumbs or plumbs the wider society is prepared to hold out, the "together" Black woman is hastening to plot the next course for development. For as we said earlier, "the 'together' Black woman is typified by a high degree of consciousness (Black or social), commitment (especially to the Black struggle), involvement (in the Black struggle), selflessness (i.e., the primary goal in life is not a new car or a new home but a dedication to a larger community), fearlessness (i.e. a refusal to cower to the wishes of a wider, White society and a willingness to employ non-traditional or commonly unacceptable methods for change), conviction and confidence (i.e., a strong belief that commitment and involvement will produce change)."

For those who desire a more concrete identification of the "together" Black women, suffice it to say that they are beautiful sisters who cannot be pigeon-holed neatly into sterile categories. They may sport naturals or processed hair, the latest fashions or a pair of dungarees. They may be high school students or high level professionals. They may be ardent Pan-Africanists or deeply committed to "taking care of business" at home. Yet most important they are not passive creatures. Rather they have left the fringes of the crowd—those onlookers and cool observers of the scene—to join those who are participants in a deadly serious venture. And while they remember, with warmth and deep appreciation, the work and talents of Martin Luther King, Malcolm X, Stokely Carmichael and others, the "together" Black women themselves must be regarded as a reservoir, a reservoir which though active still awaits the spark for the next and perhaps most significant stage of Black development.

# Index

Abrahams, Peter, 250
Adotevi, Stanislas, 265–266
Advocacy of polygamous relationships, 112–121
African Civilization Society, 248
Alexander, Clifford, 166–168
Alleged failure of integrative strategy, 286–321

Billingsley, Andrew, 59
Black Africans and the American Negro, 254–256
Black men and black women, 55–79; on alleged black "matriarchal tradition," 57–62; on Moynihan Report, 55–57
Black men and white women, 79–88
Black opinions on the pill, 106–112; the pill seen as genocide, 107–108
Black Panther Party, 343–352
Black women on abortions, 103–106
Black women on children, 99–103

Black women and Haiti, 268–269
Black women and women's liberation, 32–55
Brooke, Edward, 138–145
*Brown v. Board of Education, 347 U.S. 483 (1954)*, 286
Burnam, Dorothy, 236
Busia, K. A., 189

Carmichael, Stokely, 201, 258–259, 321, 355–356
Cashin, John, 177, 184
Cayton, Horace, 59
Cesaire, Aime, 251
Che-Lumumba Club, 236–237
Chilembwe, John, 248
Chisholm, Shirley, 152–160, 176
Clay, William, 176
Cleaver, Eldridge, 80–81
Collins, George, 176
Congress of Racial Equality (CORE), 172–174, 285, 294–295
Conyers, John, 176

381

Cruse, Harold, 185

Damas, Leon, 251
Davis, Angela, 190–196, 226–243
Defensive (and offensive?) violence, 341–361
Delaney, Martin, 248
Dellums, Ron, 176
Diggs, Charles, 176
Drake, St. Clair, 59
Du Bois, W. E. B., 59, 187, 188, 249
Duvalier, Francois, 268–269

Equal Employment Opportunity Commission (EEOC), 166–168
Evers, Charles, 178
Example of Japanese-Americans cited, 342–343

Fanon, Frantz, 196–201, 222–226
Farmer, James, 168–174
Freedom New Party, 200
Friedan, Betty, 34

Garvey, Marcus, 252
Gibson, Kenneth, 183–184

Harper, John, 184
Hatcher, Richard, 177
Hawkins, Augustus, 176
Hawkins, Reginald, 184
Henry, Milton (Brother Gaidi), 337
Henry, Richard (Brother Imari), 337
Hernandez, Aileen, 34, 50–51
Herzog, Elizabeth, 59
Hurst, Charles, 177

Islam and the American Negro, 112–113, 330–341

Jackson, Jesse, 177, 215
Johnson, Charles, 59
Johnson, Wallace, 250
Jones, Leroi (Imamu Amiri Baraka), 201

Kaunda, Kenneth, 277
Kenyatta, Jomo, 273–274
King, Martin Luther, 318–321

Ladner, Joyce, 59
Lero, Etienne, 251
Lewis, Hylan, 59

Malcolm X, 112, 330, 337
Maran, Rene, 251
Marcuse, Herbert, 192–195
Marxism-Leninism, 185–186
Maulana Ron Karenga and polygamy, 118–121
Mazrui, Ali, 189, 249
Metcalfe, Ralph, 176
Militancy, 13–29
Mississippi Freedom Democratic Party, 200
Mitchell, Parren, 176
Muhammed, Elijah, 112, 330–331, 334–336
Murray, Pauli, 33–34

Nation of Islam, 112, 330, 337
National Association for the Advancement of Colored People (NAACP), 313–316
National Democratic Party of Alabama (NDPA), 184
National Organization of Women (NOW), 34
National Urban League, 59
Newton, Huey, 218, 317
Nix, Robert, Sr., 176
Nkrumah, Kwame, 186–190, 243, 248, 258, 272–273
North Carolina Committee For More Representative Political Participation (NCCFMRPP), 184
Nyasaland Uprising of 1915, 248
Nyerere, Julius, 190, 243, 274–276

Padmore, George, 185
Pan-Africanism, 245–283

# Index

Paterson, Basil, 177
Powell, Adam Clayton, 145–152

Rangel, Charles, 176
"Red Book" of Mao Tse-tung, 213, 219–222
Reflections on Nixon-Agnew administration, 123–138
Republic of New Africa (RNA), 330, 337–341
Robeson, Paul, 191, 230–231

Senghor, Leopold, 190, 251–252, 264
Southern Christian Leadership Conference (SCLC), 319–321
Stokes, Carl, 177
Stokes, Louis, 176
Student Nonviolent Co-ordinating Committee (SNCC), 285, 294–295
Sutton, Percy, 177

Sylvester-Williams, Henry, 249 (*See also* Pan-Africanism)

Togetherness, 13–29
Toure, Sekou, 190
Toussaint L'Ouverture, 269
Traditional marriage seen by blacks, 88–99

United Citizens Party, 184

Valentine, Charles, 59

Walker, Joe, 236
Wilkins, Roy, 313–316
Williams, Robert, 337
Winneba Ideological Institute, 190
Women's Equity Action League (WEAL), 49